Amish-Country COOKBOOK

Volume 1
SECOND EDITION

Edited by Bob & Sue Miller

Evangel Publishing House

Nappanee, Indiana 46550

Amish-Country Cookbook: Volume 1
Second Edition

Evangel Publishing House
P.O. Box 189
2000 Evangel Way
Nappanee, IN 46550-0189
Telephone (800) 253-9315
www.evangelpublishing.com

Cover design by Jim Ferm
Interior book design by Ramona Severn
Text illustrations by Ken Nissley

LCCN 2001094021
ISBN 1-928915-20-5

Printed in the United States of America
10 9 8 7 6 5 4 3 2 1

Publisher's Preface

BOB AND SUE MILLER grew up in a small Amish community in Sugarcreek, Ohio. Christian teaching and good home cooking were part of their upbringing, a heritage which continued when they established their own home.

In 1968, the Millers purchased property on U.S. 20 in Middlebury, Indiana. Back then it was a 24-hour truck stop named Everett's Highway Inn. But the Millers saw other possibilities. After renovation, the restaurant reopened on January 1, 1971 as Das Dutchman Essenhaus, a six-day-a-week Amish restaurant complete with Amish and Mennonite cooks and wait-staff.

The history of Das Dutchman Essenhaus is a story of growth — growth of a family as well as a business. When the Millers moved to Indiana, they had two small children. Today, their family includes five adult children with their spouses and seven grandchildren. The Essenhaus has grown from a staff of 24 to nearly 450 during the tourist season. What began as a small restaurant has expanded into one of Indiana's largest and finest restaurants with a baker, a country inn, numerous shops, and a wholesale food business.

Guests to the Essenhaus restaurant, flagship of the corporation, enjoy the barnlike structure supported by heavy oak beams, each hewn and hand-fitted by Amish craftsmen. The decor is replete with old wood stoves, horse collars, rustic farm tools, quilts, and antique furniture.

On a busy day, nearly six thousand people enjoy a family-style meal here. Many stop by the bakery before leaving to purchase homemade favorites like apple cinnamon bread, chocolate chip cookies, noodles, dressings, and red raspberry cream pie.

Over the years, the Essenhaus grounds and services have expanded to include charming village shops, Amish country tours, and buggy rides along the well-kept lawns and gardens. The facilities include a windmill, a children's playground, a petting zoo, a miniature golf course, and a covered bridge with scenic trails. Many more acres of the lake-dotted Essenhaus property have yet to be developed, except in the minds of the Millers.

Bob and Sue are dedicated to Jesus Christ and seek to operate the Essenhaus by Christian values. They believe that providing

iii

excellent service, good measure, and quality food to their guests reflects their conviction that God desires all of his creation to live in harmony.

After enjoying a memorable dining experience, many guests ask about the unique recipes prepared in the Essenhaus kitchens. The Millers have responded by compiling three cookbooks containing their own original recipes and others gathered from their employees, many never published before. **Amish-Country Cookbook: Volumes 1-3** will help you create the good taste of Das Dutchman Essenhaus right in your home.

Who Are The Amish?

THE AMISH are one of the most colorful and distinctive religious groups in North America. Who are these people that wear plain clothing and ride in buggies? What are they really like? Why do they embrace such distinctive practices?

It is difficult to describe THE Amish because there are more than a dozen different Amish groups—each with its own customs—across North America. The buggy tops of some groups are white, others are yellow, but most are black or grey. Some groups only permit open buggies. Farmers in some groups milk their cows by hand, but most do not. Some women bake their own bread, but many buy it in stores. Even within the same Amish affiliation, some local congregations may permit the use of power lawn mowers while others do not. Some adults till the soil while others work in factories, and still others operate their own businesses.

It is tempting to assume that the Amish are all alike, as if all 180,000 of them were pressed from the same cultural cookie cutter. However, social customs vary from one settlement to another, though most Amish communities do share some basic values and practices regardless of their affiliation.

Growth and Expansion

The Amish are growing. Many of their communities double about every twenty years. Today approximately 180,000 children and adults live in twenty-three different states. About two-thirds of them reside in Ohio (49,000), Pennsylvania (41,000), and Indiana (33,000). Smaller settlements can be found in twenty other states, mostly east of the Mississippi River. Following the big three, the next five most populous states are Wisconsin (10,000), Michigan (8,000), Missouri (6,000), New York (5,000), and Kentucky (5,000).

Amish growth is fueled by sizeable families and strong retention. Typical families have six to nine children and, in some of the groups, ten or more. The average Amish person has at least seventy-five first cousins, many of whom live within several miles. Large families, however, are not enough to make the Amish population grow. Young people must be persuaded to join the church as adults, and indeed most of them do. On average, 85 percent request baptism and join the church between the ages of sixteen and twenty-two.

Deciding about church membership is a crucial step for Amish youth. Those who join are expected to follow the rules of the church for the rest of their life. If they are baptized and later violate church standards (e.g., by driving a car or buying a television), they will be asked to confess their transgression publicly before the church. If they refuse, they will face excommunication and likely some form of shunning. Some youth join the church because it is the natural thing to do; others weigh the consequences carefully because joining entails a lifelong commitment.

On the local level, the Amish are organized into more than thirteen hundred local church districts in 250 geographical settlements. Large settlements such as those in Holmes County, Ohio; Lagrange, Indiana; or Lancaster, Pennsylvania have 100 or more church districts. New settlements, on the other hand, may have only one or two church districts.

About twenty-five to thirty-five families live in a church district. This basic social unit of Amish society serves as parish, precinct, shop, and club. The families meet every other Sunday for a three-hour worship service in their homes. Services rotate among the homes of a district throughout the course of a year. A bishop, deacon, and two ministers typically serve as unpaid leaders in addition to their regular occupations. They receive no theological training and serve for life. Religious, social, and family life revolve around face-to-face interaction in the local district which forms the heart of Amish life.

Religious Roots

Amish roots reach back to the Anabaptist movement that emerged in Switzerland, Germany, and the Netherlands during the Protestant Reformation of the sixteenth century. They were nicknamed "rebaptizers" or "Anabaptists" by their opponents because they baptized adults who already had been baptized as infants in the Catholic Church. The Anabaptists believed that baptism should be reserved for adults who confessed Jesus Christ as Lord and fully understood the consequences of their decision.

Early Anabaptists emphasized the authority of the Bible for daily living, the separation of church and state, and the importance of following the teachings of Jesus in everyday life. Heeding Jesus' call to love our enemies, many of them espoused pacifism and refused to wield the sword or even retaliate against their persecutors. Indeed, thousands of Anabaptists were killed for their religious beliefs. Government officials as well as Catholic and Protestant leaders hunted the despised Anabaptist "heretics," who were considered a threat to civic order. Those who were caught received the capital punishment of their day—burning at the stake. The bloody stories of Anabaptist martyrs who died for their faith are told in the *Martyrs Mirror*. This 1,100-page book is found in many Amish homes today. The severe persecution shaped strong convictions among many Anabaptists that the church should be separate from the evils of the world around it.

The *Amish* name comes from Jakob Ammann, a Swiss Anabaptist leader who converted to the Anabaptist faith more than one hundred and fifty years after its beginning. He introduced several practices, including shunning, that led to a division among the Swiss Anabaptists in 1693. Ammann's followers became known as Amish. Many other Anabaptists were eventually called Mennonites after Menno Simons, a prominent Dutch Anabaptist leader.

In addition to the Amish and Mennonites, Hutterite and Brethren groups also trace their roots to the early Anabaptists. With a few exceptions, most of the Amish came to the Americas in two waves, in 1730-70 and in 1817-60. The first migration settled in Pennsylvania and eventually moved to Ohio, Indiana, and other states. Many in the second wave went directly to Ohio, Illinois, Indiana, and Iowa.

Current Beliefs and Values

As members of the larger Christian faith, the Amish endorse basic Christian beliefs—the authority of the Bible, salvation through Jesus Christ, the church as the body of Christ, a belief in heaven and hell, and so forth. The Amish also subscribe to an Anabaptist confession written in 1632 in the Netherlands. The language of Amish spirituality emphasizes the importance of living in community, in contrast to the individualistic language of American Evangelicalism.

Beyond their basic Christian beliefs, the Amish accent some distinctive values that shape their identity. Here are a few:

Separation from the world is a key belief that undergirds many unusual Amish customs. Based on biblical admonitions such as "love not the world" (1 John 2:15) and "be ye not conformed to this world" (Rom. 12:2), the Amish teach that Christians should live apart from the larger society. Followers of Jesus, the Amish believe, should walk on the straight and narrow way of moral purity, not the broad way that glorifies violence, sex, entertainment, and pleasure.

Speaking a dialect known as Pennsylvania German or Pennsylvania Dutch helps to clarify the line of distinction between the Amish and the larger world. Separation from the world, however, does not mean a wall of social separation. Many Amish interact freely with their non-Amish neighbors.

Church authority is another important Amish emphasis. For the Amish, the church is a redemptive community whose authority spans their total way of life. Each member participates in a local congregation (called a "church district") with specific geographical boundaries formed by a road, a stream, or a township line. The regulations of the local church district govern many aspects of daily life including dress, the use of technology, entertainment, and education. Their entire way of life reflects their religious commitments. Religion is not practiced only in special segments of the week, as is often the case in modern society; religious values permeate the entire fabric of their life.

Obedience is a cardinal Amish virtue. Children are expected to obey their parents without question. Talking back or challenging a parent or teacher is not tolerated. Younger people are expected to respect and honor their elders. Married women follow the lead of their husbands in major decisions related to family and church. Younger ministers accept the guidance and wisdom of older ministers and bishops. Obedience to traditional customs and authority undergirds the harmony of Amish communities.

Unlike most of American culture, which celebrates individual rights and freedom, the Amish emphasize *humility*. Members are expected to deny personal and selfish interests for the sake of their community. They believe the welfare of the community supersedes the rights of the individual. The church discourages activities that highlight individual achievement or call undue attention to oneself because self glory may lead to pride, arrogance, and spiritual downfall. Unbridled individualism will surely lead to pride (the most dreaded Amish fear) and disturb the harmony and equality of community.

The rejection of individualism undergirds a number of Amish practices. Posing for photographs is forbidden. Using make-up and wearing jewelry, wedding rings, and wrist watches is strictly taboo. The plain clothing worn by the Amish underscores their separation from the world and also nurtures humility. Plain dress is a collective badge of group identity, but it also discourages individuals from buying fancy clothing and designer fashions, which would be extravagant.

Amish communities hold *traditional wisdom* in high regard. Elders are reluctant to change practices that have successfully served their community in the past. Amish folk are likely to try one of their grandmother's herbal remedies before running off to visit a doctor. They are reluctant to have their members study science or take up professional occupations, but they are willing to pick some of the fruits of modern progress. For example, they use the services of outside experts—veterinarians, dentists, doctors, lawyers, and accountants. At the same time, they are more likely to tap the wisdom of seasoned elders than to seek the advice of a consultant, therapist, or financial planner. Many customs are entrenched in long-standing traditions that are resistant to change.

A Basic Education

The Amish emphasize learning practical skills that will directly help them to make a living. Until the middle of the twentieth century, most Amish youth attended rural one-room public schools. The rise of large consolidated schools worried many Amish parents because they feared that big schools would expose Amish youth to alien ideas and friends that could lead them away from the church. In some communities, harsh confrontations erupted between Amish parents and government officials when parents refused to send their offspring to consolidated schools. Indeed, some parents were jailed in the 1950s and 1960s for keeping their children at home. In 1972, the United States Supreme Court favored the Amish with a ruling that permits their youth to end formal schooling after eighth grade.

Today, most Amish youth attend private, one-room schools where they are taught by Amish teachers and surrounded by Amish peers. In a few communities, Amish children attend small, rural public schools operated for the Amish. The vast majority, however, attend approximately twelve hundred private schools operated by Amish parents. One teacher is responsible to teach all eight grades. Classes are conducted in English. Science, sex education, and religion are not taught in Amish schools. Practical subjects like reading, writing, spelling, and basic math are emphasized.

School regulations and practices vary somewhat from state to state. Amish parents support their own schools as well as pay public school taxes. After completing eighth grade, young people learn technical and vocational skills by working in apprenticeships in the homes, shops, or farms of their parents or relatives. The practical skills gained through Amish education prepare young people for successful lives in Amish society.

The Puzzles of Amish Technology

Some Amish practices are puzzling at first glance. Why may they hire and ride in cars but not drive them? Why is electricity from a battery preferable to energy from a public utility line? And why would God smile on a tractor at the barn but not in the field?

The Amish use of technology varies greatly from settlement to settlement. Despite public misconceptions, the Amish do use modern technology. They are not antiques in a nineteenth-century museum. Some new forms of technology, such as gas barbeque grills and chain saws, are used without reservation. Other types of technology which they fear will hurt their community are rejected outright. Examples include television, radio, video players, cell phones, personal computers, and use of the Internet. Outsiders are often perplexed by how the Amish adapt technology in specials ways to serve their community.

For example, they believe that owning cars would pull their community apart. Horse and buggy transportation limits mobility and keeps the community close together. A symbol of individualism and independence, private automobiles would encourage mobility and eventually fragment the community. Nevertheless, as families spread to new settlements and as more Amish became involved in business, the use of motor vehicles became more attractive. So many groups struck a compromise. They permitted members to hire vehicles (with a driver) for special needs, but not to own and drive them. This practice of hiring "taxis" flourishes in settlements that are involved in business. More conservative groups frown on this compromise.

As public utility lines spread across the country in the first half of the twentieth century, the Amish feared that tapping electricity from the lines would tie them too directly to the outside world, make them dependent on it, and provide too easy access to unnecessary conveniences. Since they already had been using batteries, they decided simply to use 12-volt electricity from batteries for small tools and appliances. This compromise continues in many communities today. Many farms and businesses also have diesel engines to produce air and hydraulic pressure. This so-called "Amish Electricity" operates heavy equipment, pumps water, operates fans, and powers washing machines. Without 110-volt electrical current, Amish homes are remarkably quiet. They have no noisy microwaves, air conditioners, televisions, videos, and CD players.

Tractors are not used in fields because they would encourage large-scale farming, steal work from Amish youth, and possibly lead to the use of cars. However, tractors are often used at barns for high power needs—such as to blow silage, chop fodder, and pump liquid manure.

Telephones in homes are discouraged because they provide another direct connection to the outside world. Strangers could enter a home via a telephone call at any moment. Moreover, face-to-face visiting is the social glue that holds an Amish community togther. If one can talk on the phone, why visit? In many settlements, members may use public phones or one in the home of a neighbor, but not install one in their own home. In more progressive settlements, a "community telephone" for several families is permitted. In some cases, individual phones for business outside the home are permissible.

Thus, the Amish do use technology. They try to control it so that it supports rather than tears down their community. Some Amish practices that look silly from the outside are actually ingenious compromises that allow them to use technology, but with restraints, so that it serves the welfare of the community. They often make a distinction between using and owning technology. For example, it may be acceptable to use a public pay phone but not to install a phone in the home. These many compromises create the riddles that enable the Amish to tap the power of technology without sacrificing their community life and identity.

Amish Food and Cooking Practices

The Amish are known for their beautiful gardens and hearty tables. Some of their food traditions such as pie-baking trace back to their roots in Switzerland. Other food habits can be tracked to Germany as well as colonial America. Food practices vary considerably from settlement to settlement, but most Amish families have gardens and preserve large quantities of food—often by canning. Yet, not all food is home grown. Prepared foods such as instant pudding, snack foods, pizza, and soft drinks may be purchased at stores.

In some regions of the country, favorite Amish foods include shoofly pie—eaten as coffee cake with breakfast—snitz (dried apple) pie, applesauce, cornmeal mush, chicken pot pie, homemade noodles, and mashed potatoes smothered with gravy. Snitz pie is a staple at the fellowship meal following Sunday services in some regions. It is not unusual for a mother and her daughters to bake more than thirty pies for a fellowship meal. Noon meals during the week, often called "dinner," are the hearty meal of the day for farm workers.

Some Amish kitchens are equipped with fine cabinetry and have state-of-the-art stoves and refrigerators powered by bottled gas. In more conservative communities, cooking is done on wood stoves and ice is used for refrigeration. Generally speaking, the responsibilities for gardening, food preservation, and cooking fall to the women. Husbands sometimes help to prepare the garden for planting and help to harvest vegetables. Some men help to cook at large social gatherings like weddings or reunions, which may involve two large meals in a day. In recent years, some progressive families have begun hosting outside visitors in their homes for sumptuous Amish meals. This is often done to provide a sideline income as well as to extend a hand of hospitality to outsiders.

Occupations and the Future

Farming has long been the trademark of Amish life. This began to change in the last third of the twentieth century as farmland became more expensive and commercial agriculture became more competitive. Tourist markets and various business opportunities offered Amish people new ways of making a living. In some of the more rural areas, the bulk of Amish families are still tilling the soil. However, in many settlements the majority of households are no longer farming. Agriculture and sideline business are often mixed together. In some areas of Indiana, for example, Amish men work in large recreational vehicle factories.

In many settlements, the Amish have developed hundreds of small private businesses. These enterprises make fine indoor furniture, lawn furniture, gazebos, and storage sheds. Other Amish entrepreneurs operate greenhouses, construction crews, and machine shops. Amish women produce and sell lovely quilts, food preserves, and a wide assortment of handicrafts. Some of businesses are actually owned and operated by Amish women. The plentiful products of these shops are shipped and sold around the world by commercial distributors.

This growing Amish involvement in business signals an important social change that will likely alter Amish life and culture in the years to come. Business involvements will impact child-rearing practices, gender roles, leisure activities, lifestyles, the use of technology, and the speaking of English. Such involvements will bring broader exposure to the outside world. All of these changes will likely modify the traditional understanding of what it means to be separate from the world as the Amish interact with their non-Amish neighbors more frequently.

Donald B. Kraybill
Messiah College
GRANTHAM, PA

For Further Reading

Kraybill, Donald B. *The Riddle of Amish Culture, Revised Edition*. Baltimore, Md.: The Johns Hopkins University Press, 2001.

Kraybill, Donald B. and Carl Bowman. *On the Backroad to Heaven: Old Order Hutterites, Mennonites, Amish and Brethren*. Baltimore, Md.: The Johns Hopkins University Press, 2001.

Kraybill, Donald B. and Steve Nolt. *Amish Enterprise: From Plows to Profits*. Baltimore, Md.: The Johns Hopkins University Press, 1995.

Nolt, Steve. *A History of the Amish*. Intercourse, Pa.: Good Books, 1992.

Scott, Steve. *Why Do They Dress That Way?* Intercourse, Pa.: Good Books, 1986.

CONTENTS

BAKING CHART

Slow oven	250° - 325°
Moderate oven	350° - 375°
Moderate hot oven	375° - 400°
Hot oven	400° - 450°
Very hot oven	450° - 500°
Pastry Shell	450° - 12 to 15 min.
Custard pie	450° - 10 min.
reduce to	350° - 25 min.
Two crust pies with uncooked filling	450° - 10 min.
reduce to	350° - 30 to 40 min.
Two crust pies with cooked filling	440° - 450° - 30 min.
Meringue	350° - 10 to 12 min.
Yeast bread loaf	400° - 425° - 40 to 45 min.
Sweet rolls	375° - 15 to 20 min.
Biscuits	450° - 12 to 15 min.
Muffins	425° - 20 to 25 min.
Corn bread	425° - 20 to 30 min.
Gingerbread	425° - 40 to 50 min.
Angel and sponge cakes	325° - finish at 375°
Loaf cake	350° - 375° - 40 to 50 min. depending on size
Layer cake, or cup cakes	350° - 375° - 20 to 30 min.
Cookies	350° - 425° - 6 to 12 min. depending on size

Laura Miller (Grill Cook)

ABBREVIATIONS

c.	- cup	sm.	- small
T.	- tablespoon	pt.	- pint
t.	- teaspoon	med.	- medium
pkg.	- package	gal.	- gallon
lb.	- pound	sq.	- square
qt.	- quart (4 cups)	approx.	- approximately
lg.	- large (29 oz.)	min.	- minutes
oz.	- ounce		

Breads, Rolls, Doughnuts & Cereals

TABLE OF SUBSTITUTIONS

1 c. bottled milk equals ½ c. evaporated milk, plus ½ c. water.

1 c. sour milk equals 1 c. sweet milk into which 1 T. vinegar or lemon juice has been added.

1 square chocolate equals 3 T. cocoa.

1 T. cornstarch equals 2 T. of flour for thickening gravies.

1 t. baking powder equals ¼ t. soda plus ½ t. cream of tartar.

1 t. baking powder equals 1 t. soda with ½ c. sour cream or milk.

½ t. baking powder equals 1 egg

1 c. heavy cream equals ¼ c. milk and ¼ c. lard.

1 T. Clear-Jel equals 1 T. cornstarch

Butter, size of walnut equals 1 T.

Katie Miller (Gift Shop)

A RECIPE TO LIVE BY

Blend one cup of love and one half cup of kindness, add alternately in small portions one cup of appreciation and 3 cups of pleasant companionship into which has been sifted three teaspoons of deserving praise.

Flavor with one teaspoon carefully chosen advise.

Lightly fold in one cup of cheerfulness to which has been added a pinch of sorrow. Pour with tender care into small clean hearts and let bake until well matured. Turn out on the surface of society. Humbly invoke God's blessing and it will serve all mankind.

Katie Miller (Gift Shop)

A stale loaf of bread tastes almost fresh if you wrap it in a wet towel, set on a pan and bake in slow oven till towel is almost dry.

Breads, Rolls, Doughnuts & Cereals

BREAD HINTS

*Always have flour, when mixing bread or rolls, at room temperature before mixing. This will help keep the dough at a warm temperature and encourages it to rise.

*All milk used in bread recipes should be scalded, then cooled to lukewarm before using.

*For a finer textured bread, try letting dough rise in a place where it's a little cooler.

*Using milk instead of other liquid usually gives a softer crust which becomes a richer brown when baked.

*If bread is baked before it rises to double in size, it will not crumble so easily.

Mattie Yoder (Grill Cook)

Onion skin very thin
Mild winter's coming in
Onion skin thick and tough
Coming winter cold and rough.

AUTUMN BREAD

⅔ c. shortening
3 c. sugar
4 eggs, well beaten
1¾ c. pumpkin, grated
⅔ c. water
3½ c. flour
chopped nuts, if desired

½ t. salt
½ t. nutmeg
½ t. cloves
1 t. cinnamon
½ t. baking powder
2 t. baking soda

Thoroughly wash 3 16-oz. tin cans. Mix all ingredients and bake at 350° for 1 hour in the greased tin cans. Let cool 10 minutes. Remove from cans and roll in sugar.

Mary Ann Schlabach
(Waitress)
Betty A. Hershberger
(Grill Cook)

BROWN BREAD

1-1½ c. raisins
1 c. sugar
1 T. vegetable oil
3 T. molasses
1 t. vanilla

2 c. hot water
1 egg
½ t. salt
2 t. baking soda
2¾ c. flour

Pour the hot water over the raisins and let set until cool. Then add the other ingredients, mix, and pour into a loaf pan. Bake at 350° for 45 minutes.

Patty Kauffman (Grill Cook)

Happy is he that hath the God of Jacob for his help, whose hope is in the LORD his God: Which made heaven, and earth, the sea, and all that therein is: which keepeth truth for ever: Which executeth judgment for the oppressed: which giveth food to the hungry. The LORD looseth the prisoners: the LORD openeth the eyes of the blind: the LORD raiseth them that are bowed down: the LORD loveth the righteous....

Psa. 146:5-8

BUBBLE BREAD

1 c. milk, scalded
½ c. sugar
1 t. salt

Mix the above together and cool to lukewarm, add 2 pkg. yeast and 2 beaten eggs, then about 4½ c. flour. Knead till smooth and elastic, not sticky. Place in greased bowl and cover with damp cloth and let rise till double in size. Push down and let rise till double in size. Push down and let rise 10 min.

Meanwhile melt 1 stick butter or margarine in small pan. Mix together the ingredients.

1 c. sugar
1 T. cinnamon
½ c. pecans and raisins (optional)

Make dough size of walnut, roll each in melted butter then in sugar mixture. Place in greased angel food cake pan in staggered rows until all dough is used. Let rise and bake in 350° oven for about 45 min.

Mrs. Levi R. Miller

CINNAMON SPIRAL BREAD

1 c. warm water, (not hot)
1 pkg. yeast
2 c. lukewarm milk
¼ c. brown sugar, packed
2 eggs, beaten

1 T. salt
1 c. raisins
2 T. soft shortening
2 c. quick cooking rolled oats
5½-6 c. sifted Gold Medal flour

Dissolve yeast in water, in mixing bowl. Stir in milk, rolled oats, salt, brown sugar, egg, shortening, raisins, and half of flour. Mix with hand. Turn on board until light. Knead until smooth and elastic (about 5 min.) Round up in a greased bowl. Let rise till double in bulk (1½ or 2 hrs.). Divide into round balls. Roll out in oblong shape. Sprinkle with ½ c. brown sugar, 2 t. cinnamon. Roll up like jelly roll, sealing lightly at the end.

Millie Whetstone (Cook)

3

CORN BREAD

3 c. flour	2 t. soda
1 c. corn meal	4 eggs
¾ c. brown sugar	½ c. cooking oil
4 t. baking powder	

Enough milk to make a batter. Bake 425° 20-30 min. in 9x13 pan.

Elsie Rebecca Miller (Grill Cook)

CORN BREAD

3 c. corn meal	1 c. sugar
2 c. white flour	3 eggs
6 t. baking powder	2½ c. milk
½ c. lard	½ t. salt

Bake 425° 20-30 min. in 9x13 cake pan.

Katie Miller (Gift Shop)

CORN BREAD

Mix together:

2 c. flour	1 t. salt
2 c. corn meal	1 egg
1 c. sugar	1 round T. lard
4 t. baking powder	

Add milk and stir till nice and smooth. Bake at 350° 20-25 min. in 9x13 cake pan.

Mrs. Roseanna Chupp (Cook)

"Before you begin to give someone a piece of your mind, consider carefully whether you can spare any."

CORN BREAD

3 eggs
1¾ c. flour
1½ c. corn meal
2½ T. sugar

1 T. baking powder
¾ c. shortening
1¼ c. milk
pinch of salt

Mix all ingredients and pour in buttered pan. Bake at 375° oven for 20-25 min. or till done.

Sue Miller (Manager)

OATMEAL BREAD

2½ c. boiling water
2 c. oatmeal
1 c. honey or part karo
2 T. salt

¾ c. cooking oil
4 eggs, beaten
2 pkg. yeast
2 c. or more whole wheat flour

Dissolve yeast in 1 c. warm water. Pour boiling water over oatmeal and set aside to cool to lukewarm. Now beat all the above ingredients well together, being sure everything is just warm before adding yeast. Work in enough white flour (preferably unbleached) to make a nice spongy dough that is not sticky. Grease top and let rise twice after kneading it. Handle as other bread, bake as other bread. Bake at 400° for 10 min. Turn back to 350° for 25-30 min. Depending on size of loaves.

Elsie Rebecca Miller (Grill Cook)

SHORT ORDER COOK

When daddy cooks he doesn't read
The cookbooks mother seems to need;
He doesn't fuss with pies or cakes;
He never roasts or broils or bakes;
He doesn't use the rolling pin
Or measure level spoonfuls in;
He doesn't watch the oven clock;
He doesn't fill the cookie-crock;
We watch him with admiring eyes
While daddy fries and fries and fries!

PUMPKIN BREAD

1 c. vegetable oil
4 eggs
⅔ c. water
2 c. cooked pumpkin
3½ c. flour
1½ t. salt

1 t. nutmeg
2 t. baking soda
1 t. cinnamon
3 c. sugar
1 c. raisins (optional)
1 c. nuts (optional)

Cook raisins in 1½ c. water till soft; cool. Combine oil, eggs, water, and sugar. Sift together flour, salt, nutmeg, baking soda, and cinnamon. Make a well in the center of the mixture, then add the mixture of pumpkin, vegetable oil, eggs, water, and sugar. Blend till dry ingredients are moistened. Stir in raisins and nuts. Turn into three 8½"x2½" greased loaf pans. Bake at 350° for 1 hour.

Dorothy Chupp (Hostess)
Lucy Eash (Cook)

PUMPKIN BREAD

3 eggs
2½ c. sugar
1 c. vegetable oil
3 t. vanilla
2 c. cooked pumpkin
1 c. nuts, if desired

3 c. flour
1 t. baking soda
½ t. baking powder
1 t. salt
3 t. cinnamon

Combine eggs, sugar, oil, vanilla, and pumpkin; beat well. Sift together dry ingredients and stir into pumpkin mixture. Add nuts. Grease and flour 3 bread pans. Pour batter into pans. Bake for 1 hr. in a 350° oven. Eat it like bread or use it as pudding with whipped cream.

Katie Ann Lehman (Cook)

He hath given meat unto them that fear him: he will ever be mindful of his covenant.

Psa. 111:5

PUMPKIN BREAD

3 c. sugar	1 T. cinnamon
1 c. oil	⅔ c. cold water
4 eggs	2 c. pumpkin
1 t. salt	3½ c. flour
1 T. nutmeg	2 t. soda

Grease and flour 3 bread pans. Bake in 350° oven for 1 hr.

Mary Troyer (Dishwasher)

PUMPKIN BREAD

⅔ c. shortening	1½ t. salt
2⅔ c. sugar	½ t. baking powder
4 eggs	1 t. cinnamon
1 lb. pumpkin	1 t. cloves
⅔ c. water	⅔ c. nuts
3⅓ c. flour	⅔ c. raisins
2 t. soda	

Bake 65-75 min. at 350°. Makes 2 loaves 9x5x3 in.

Laura Miller (Grill Cook)

PUMPKIN PEANUT BREAD

⅓ c. shortening	½ t. nutmeg
1 c. brown sugar	2 t. baking powder
2 eggs	1 t. cinnamon
1 c. canned pumpkin	¼ t. allspice
2 c. flour	¾ c. chopped peanuts
½ t. soda	

Cream shortening and add sugar. Stir in eggs and pumpkin. Stir in remaining ingredients. Pour into a well greased loaf pan 9x5x3 in. Bake at 350° for 55 min to 1 hr. Cool slightly and unmold. Cool thoroughly before slicing.

Fannie Yoder (Cook)

7

WHITE BREAD

2½ c. milk
2½ c. water

Boil together, cool to lukewarm.

¼ c. lard   3 T. salt
⅓ c. sugar   ¼ c. yeast in 1 c. warm water

Mix all together, then work in enough flour, just so the dough is
a little sticky, (approx. 5 lbs.). Let set for ½ hr., then work down.
Set aside until double in size. Work out in pans. Let rise and bake
30 min. 350°. Makes 5 loaves.

Katie Cross (Waitress)

WHITE BREAD

2 c. water   ⅓ c. white sugar
1 c. milk   ⅓ c. shortening, scant
1 c. potato water, if possible   2 t. salt

Heat all together to boiling point. Cool, then add 2 pkg. yeast, and
10-11 c. Robinhood flour, adding about ⅓ of flour and beating
until smooth, then adding the rest. Have your dough a little sticky.
Cover with clean towel and let rise till double, about ½ hr. Knead
again. Makes 4 loaves. Let rise till double. Bake 350-375° approximately 1 hr.

Mrs. Amos R. Miller

A horse can't pull while kicking
This fact I merely mention
And he can't kick while pulling
Which is my chief contention
Let's imitate the good old horse
And lead a life that's fitting
Just pull an honest load
There'll be no time for kicking.

BREAD

Dissolve 2 pkg. dry yeast, and 1 t. sugar in ½ c. warm water. Let stand 10 min.
In large bowl dissolve 2 T. salt and 1/8 c. sugar in 3½ c. warm water. When dissolved add 1 heaping T. lard and the yeast.
Add 4 c. Robinhood flour, stir real good, then add 8 more c. flour.
Mix and knead well, put in greased bowl, and let stand 45 min.
Knead down and let rise 45 min. again.
Then work out in 4 loaves in greased pans.
Bake in oven at 350° for ¾ hr.
Put on cloth to cool, cover with cloth till just warm, then put in plastic bags.

Lucy Eash (Cook)

 PICK-A-BOO

Mrs. McTanish (*looking out of window*) — "Mac, here comes company for dinner.

Mr. McTanish — "Quick everybody! Grab a toothpick and get out on the porch."

HOMEMADE BREAD

½ T. sugar
2 pkg. yeast
¼ c. warm water

Mix and let rise, then add to the following:

2 T. sugar	¼ c. melted lard
2 T. salt	12-15 c. flour
3¾ c. warm milk	

Let rise, punch down and let rise again, make loaves and bake at 350°.

WHOLE WHEAT BREAD

Soak 1 pkg. yeast in ½ c. warm water
scald 1 c. milk   1 c. cool water
½ c. brown sugar   4 c. white flour
1 T. salt   2 c. whole wheat flour
¼ c. melted lard

Pour hot milk over sugar, salt, and lard. Stir till melted, then add yeast and water. Work in flour. If dough is still sticky, use a little more flour. Bake 350° 50-60 min. Makes 2 loaves.

Elsie Rebecca Miller (Grill Cook)

ZUCCHINI BREAD

2 c. sugar, granulated   3 eggs
1 c. salad oil

Stir really well, then sift together:

3 c. flour   1 t. salt
¼ t. baking powder   1 t. cinnamon
1 t. soda

Stir in with the first mixture.

Add:

2 c. grated raw zucchini   1 c. nuts

Put in 2 bread pans (greased). Bake in 350° oven for 40 min.

Elsie Miller (Grill Cook)

Why do they call him a "gentleman farmer?"
"Because he only raises his hat!"

BREAD STIX

1 envelope onion soup (cup-a-soup)
¼ lb. butter or margarine
bread slices

Mix soup and soft butter together, spread on bread slices and cut into 6 strips. Place on cookie sheet and toast in 350° oven till nice and brown. This is especially good using Hillbilly bread.

Elizabeth Miller (Noodles)

See that your kitchen fire be bright
And your hands be neat and skilled
For the love of man oft takes its flight
If his stomach be not well filled.

BUTTER HORNS (DINNER ROLLS)

Mix together:

1 pkg. yeast
1 T. sugar

Beat in 3 eggs with 1 c. warm water. Let stand 15 min.

Add:

½ c. sugar   ½ t. salt
½ c. shortening   5 c. flour

Knead well. Let stand in refrigerator overnight, divide in 2 parts and roll out in 12 in. circle, cut into 16 wedges, roll up starting with wide side, let rise 3-4 hours. Bake at 400° for 15 min. Brush with butter. Serve while warm.

Laura Miller (Grill Cook)

HOT ROLLS (Potato)

2 c. milk, scalded
½ c. sugar
2 eggs
1 T. salt
1 c. potatoes, mashed
½ c. shortening
2 pkg. yeast dissolved in ½ c. warm water
8 c. flour and (sometimes more)

Pour scalded milk over shortening, sugar and salt. Add mashed potatoes, cool to lukewarm. Dissolve yeast in warm water and add to first mixture. Then add eggs and flour. Knead until smooth. Let rise until double in bulk. Shape into rolls and let rise again. Bake 350° 20-25 min.

Mrs. Freddie S. Bontrager

Blessed is he that expects nothing
for he shall never be disappointed.

ICE BOX ROLLS

1 pkg. yeast
½ c. lukewarm water
1 t. sugar
1 c. lard
1 c. hot water

2 eggs, whipped
1 c. cold water
¾ c. sugar
8 c. flour

Mix the dough store in a cool place (can be kept for several days). Shape into rolls, let double in size. Bake 350° 15-20 min.

Lucy Eash (Cook)

12

LUNCH ROLLS

1 c. oatmeal	1½ t. salt
2 c. boiling water	2 pkg. yeast
3 T. butter	⅓ c. warm water
⅔ c. brown sugar, packed	5 c. flour
1 T. white sugar	

Cook first three ingredients and cool to lukewarm. Then add yeast soaked in the lukewarm water. Stir in rest of ingredients, cover and let rise in warm place until double in bulk (about 2 hr.). Then knead down and roll out. Spread with butter and brown sugar (not included in above amounts). Roll and cut as jelly roll. Let double in size. Bake 20-30 min. in 350° oven.

Katie Ann Lehman (Cook)

CINNAMON ROLLS

1½ c. milk, heat to lukewarm	2 eggs
1 c. mashed potatoes	2 pkg. yeast
2 t. salt	1 c. sugar
⅔ c. shortening	Approx. 7 c. Robinhood flour
½ c. water	

Let rise till double, punch down and roll out, spread with butter, sprinkle with brown sugar and cinnamon. Roll together like a jelly roll and cut in pieces. Let rise till double. Bake in greased pan 25-30 min. at 400°.

CINNAMON ROLLS

3 c. warm water	2 t. baking powder
¾ c. butter	dash of salt
1 c. sugar	8-9 c. flour
2 eggs	

Dissolve 1 pkg. yeast in 1 c. lukewarm water. Add 2 more cups water with shortening. Mix in beaten eggs, sugar and salt. Put in 6 cups flour with baking powder. Add remaining flour. Let rise until twice the size. Punch down and let rise again. Roll out and spread with butter, brown sugar and cinnamon. Cut and let rise again. Bake 400° 25-30 min.

Mabel Hershberger (Pie Baker)

13

CINNAMON ROLLS

½ c. lukewarm water
2 yeast cakes
Dissolve yeast cakes in water, and let set.
Scald 1½ c. milk
2 T. sugar
1 T. salt
Cool to lukewarm.
Add yeast and flour, 3 c. Robinhood flour, cover for ½ hr.
3 eggs, beaten
¾ c. sugar, beat well.

Mix together. Add ½ c. butter or oleo, melted. Add more flour, mix with a spoon. When you can't stir with a spoon it is enough, not with your hands. Let rise again, then roll out and spread with melted butter. Sprinkle with cinnamon and nuts if desired. (Takes about 6 c. of flour in all.) Let rise again. Bake 350° 20-30 min.

Ida Miller (Cook)

CINNAMON ROLLS

Beat 2 or 3 eggs in mixing bowl.

Add:

¾ c. sugar
1 t. salt
½ c. warm water

Dissolve 2 pkgs. yeast in another ½ c. warm water. Heat to scald 1 c. milk. Add ¼ lb. oleo or butter. Add milk after its hot. Then add 3 c. sifted flour and beat until smooth. Add 3 or more cups of flour. Knead till it can be handled. Let rise until double, then roll out. Take ½ of dough, roll out, spread with butter, brown sugar and cinnamon. Let rise again. Bake 350° 20-30 min.

Mrs. Tobias Hochetetler

14

APPLESAUCE PUFFS

Combine:

2 c. packaged biscuit mix	¼ c. sugar
1 t. cinnamon	

Add:

½ c. applesauce	1 egg, slightly beaten
¼ c. milk	2 T. salad oil

Beat vigorously for 30 seconds. Fill greased 2 in. muffin pans ⅔ full. Bake in hot oven, 400° for 12 min. or till done. Cool slightly; remove and dip tops in 2 T. melted butter or margarine. Then in ¼ c. sugar mixed with ¼ t. cinnamon. Makes 24 small muffins.

Mrs. Harley Miller (Miller's Orchard)
Applebutter

BISCUITS SUPREME

2 c. flour	2 t. sugar
½ t. salt	½ c. shortening
4 t. baking powder	⅔ c. milk
½ t. cream of tartar	

Sift dry ingredients together. Cut in shortening until mixture resembles course crumbs. Add milk all at once and stir until dough follows fork around bowl. Roll ½ in. thick. Cut with biscuit cutter. Place on ungreased cookie sheet. Bake at 450° for 10-12 min. Makes approximately 16 biscuits.

Katie Miller (Gift Shop)

EVER READY BISCUIT MIX

12 c. flour	2 T. salt
4 T. baking powder	2 c. lard

Mix crumbs with hands and store in tight container. When ready to use add a little water. Place on baking sheet. Bake 10-15 min. in 450° oven.

Laura Miller (Grill Cook)

BISCUITS

2 c. sifted flour
2 t. baking powder
½ t. cream of tartar
½ t. salt

2 T. sugar
½ c. shortening
1 egg
⅔ c. milk

Sift dry ingredients together, and cut in shortening. Pour milk in slowly. Add egg and stir. Knead on lightly floured surface. Pat or roll ½ in. thick. Place on baking sheet. Bake 10-15 min. in 450° oven.

Elsie Miller (Grill Cook)

 RECIPE FOR QUARRELING

Take a root of sassafras and steep in 1 pint of water and put into bottle. When your husband comes in to quarrel fill your mouth with it and hold it until he goes away.

A Sure Cure!

SOUTHERN GAL BISCUITS

2 c. sifted flour
4 t. baking powder
½ t. cream of tartar
½ t. salt

2 T. sugar
½ c. shortening
1 egg, unbeaten
⅔ c. milk

Sift all dry ingredients together. Add shortening and blend together. Pour milk into flour mixture slowly. Add the egg. Stir to a stiff dough. Drop by spoonfuls on cookie sheet and bake 10-15 min. at 450°.

Edna Nissley (Waitress)

16

BRAN MUFFINS

Delicious for breakfast.

Combine dry ingredients.

5 c. flour
2 t. salt
5 t. soda
3 c. sugar
1 pkg. (10 oz.) raisin bran flakes

Add:

4 eggs, beaten
1 c. salad oil (wesson)
1 qt. buttermilk

Mix well, keep in covered container in refrigerator (as long as 6 wks.). Fill greased muffin pans ¾ full, bake 15 min., 400° oven.

LaVerda Miller (Waitress)

SIX WEEK MUFFINS

1 box (10 oz.) raisin bran	1 qt. buttermilk
1 c. salad oil (crisco)	5 c. flour
3 c. sugar	5 t. soda
4 eggs, beaten	2 t. salt

Mix raisin bran, sugar, flour, soda and salt; add beaten eggs, crisco, and buttermilk. Use giant size mixing bowl and mix well. Store, covered in the refrigerator and use as desired. Keeps 6 weeks. Do not stir when putting mix into muffin tins. Bake at 400° for 15 min.

Sharon Nofziger (Waitress)

PULL BUNS

1 pkg. yeast dissolved in ¼ c. warm water
1 c. scalded milk   ½ t. salt
¾ c. white sugar   3 eggs, beaten
¾ c. butter, melted   about 3 c. flour

Add sugar, butter, salt to scalded milk. When lukewarm add yeast, eggs, and just enough flour to make a stiff batter. Cover and let rise. Roll small balls of dough about the size of a walnut and dip them in melted butter, then roll each ball in mixture of ½ c. nuts ground fine, 3 t. cinnamon, and ¾ c. brown sugar. Pile balls in an ungreased angel food pan and let rise for 30 min. Bake about 40 min. Bake until brown, turn pan upside down and remove right away. Serve warm, very good. I use Robinhood flour. Bake 350°.

Lucy Eash (Cook)

PLUCKETS

1 cake yeast dissolved in ¼ c. lukewarm water
1 c. scalded milk   3 eggs, well beaten
⅓ c. sugar   4 c. flour
⅓ c. butter, melted   ½ t. salt

Add sugar, butter, and salt to scalded milk. When lukewarm, add dissolved yeast, eggs and flour. Beat thoroughly. Cover and let rise until double. Stir down and let rise again, until double. Then take 1 t. of dough and dip in butter (melted), then roll in mixture of 1 c. sugar, ½ c. nuts, and 3 t. cinnamon. Pile balls loosely in ungreased angel food cake pan. Let rise 30 min. Bake at 400° for 10 min., and then at 350° for 30 min. When baked, turn the pan upside down immediately. Serve warm. The rolls will be stuck together and that's the way you serve them. Everyone plucks his roll from the central supply. These can be reheated in the oven if wrapped in foil. They are also good when served cold.

Betty A. Hershberger (Grill Cook)
Carol Pletcher (Waitress)

 Don't discourage the other man's plans,
unless you have a better one to offer.

POPOVER DONUTS

2 eggs, beaten	1 t. vanilla
1 c. granulated sugar	3 c. flour
1 c. sweet milk	3 t. baking powder
¼ t. salt	¼ t. nutmeg
2 T. butter or margarine, melted	¼ t. cinnamon

Combine ingredients in order given. Drop batter by soupspoonfuls into hot fat. When browned remove from fat and roll in sugar. These donuts turn themselves. You can mix the dough and fry part, then fry the rest later and have them fresh. I think adding powdered sugar to granulated sugar makes them ''sugar'' better. Dropping batter into hot fat eliminates rolling and cutting as for regular donuts.

Mary Ann Schlabach (Waitress)

LIGHT-AS-A-FEATHER DOUGHNUTS

¾ c. milk	¼ c. warm water
¼ c. sugar	1 pkg. yeast
1 t. salt	1 egg, beaten
¼ c. margarine	3¼ c. flour

Scald milk, stir in sugar, salt, and margarine. Cool to lukewarm. Measure warm water into large bowl. Sprinkle in yeast, stir until dissolved. Add lukewarm milk mixture, egg, and half the flour. Beat until smooth. Stir in enough additional flour to make a soft dough. Turn dough out onto a lightly floured board. Knead until smooth and elastic, about 10 min. Place in bowl, cover, let rise until double in bulk. Punch down, roll out about ½ in. thick and cut with donut cutter. Place on floured sheet pans. Let rise until double in size. Fry in wesson oil at 375°. Dip in glaze made of 2 c. powdered sugar, ⅓ c. milk and 1 t. vanilla.

Sharon Boley (Waitress)

SWEET DOUGHNUT RECIPE

¾ c. lard or shortening
¾ c. sugar
2 eggs
1 t. salt
1 pkg. yeast dissolved in 1 c. warm water
6-7 c. flour
1 c. mashed potatoes (use water if not enough potatoes)

Mix and let rise in warm place, until double in size. Punch down and roll out. Let rise again. Fry in deep fat. Dip doughnuts in glaze while still warm.

Doughnut Glaze

⅓ c. hot water
2 T. karo
1 t. vanilla
Powdered sugar to desired thickness (approx. 2½-2¾ c.).

Lydia Ann Miller (Cook)

SPRING MEDLEY   From an Old Magazine
Clean Confession

Oh welcome cupboard-sprucing time!
The time to toss away
The bit of this, the mite of that
I've saved for many a day:
The bag that holds the pinch of rice;
The cloves that lost their zip;
The crumb of cocoa, ages old,
That wouldn't make a sip;
The nearly empty box of starch
I arrange them on the floor—
Then carefully return them, as
I did the spring before!

—Marie Daerr

RAISED DOUGHNUTS

2 pkg. yeast	2 eggs
1 c. lukewarm water	½ t. salt
1 c. lukewarm milk	1/8 t. nutmeg
½ c. butter or oleo	1 t. lemon flavor
⅔ c. sugar	6 or 7 c. flour

Put yeast into lukewarm water. Scald milk and let stand to cool. Then blend together butter, sugar and well beaten eggs. Put in nutmeg and lemon flavor. Put the milk in the yeast and water and add 3 c. flour (till it is easy to handle). Put in a warm place. Let rise till double. Roll out and cut with doughnut cutter. Let rise again. Fry in deep fat. Frosting may be put on if desired. Makes approximately 50 doughnuts.

Doughnut Glaze

¼ lb. oleo
1 c. brown sugar
½ c. milk

Boil this 3 min. Then add powdered sugar (just enough so it's a little runny yet). Dip the doughnuts while frosting is still warm. Keep over *low* heat while dipping.

Katie Ann Lehman (Cook)

BREAKFAST CEREAL

5 c. quick-cook oatmeal	1 c. coconut, raisins or nothing
1 c. brown sugar	¼ t. cinnamon
½-⅔ c. light corn syrup	2 t. vanilla
1 c. wheat germ	½ t. salt

Put all dry ingredients together in a bowl and mix. Sprinkle vanilla and karo over mixture. Mix well. Pour into shallow pans. Toast at 200° for 20-30 min. (or until it starts to turn brown). Store in a tight container when cool. Serve with milk.

Elsie R. Miller (Grill Cook)

COLD CEREAL

1½ c. salad oil
¾ c. water
1½ t. vanilla
2 c. wheat germ

2 lbs. oatmeal
1½ c. honey
1 T. salt
2 c. flaked coconut

Mix in roasting pan and toast in oven 300° for 1 hr. Stir often, cool and refrigerate.

Sue Mullet (Bread Baker)

"Practice makes perfect, so be careful what you practice."

HOMEMADE COLD CEREAL

2 c. graham flour
2 c. quick oatmeal
1 c. brown sugar

½ c. butter, soft
1 t. salt
1 t. soda

Mix and make into crumbs. Put on trays and roast in oven 20 min. at 325°. Stir often for even roasting. Then cool.

Amanda Troyer (Waitress)

GRAPE NUTS

5 lb. brown sugar
8 lb. whole wheat flour
1¼ T. salt
2½ qt. buttermilk or sour milk

¾ lb. oleo, melted
1½ t. maple flavor
2 T. vanilla
2 T. soda

Put dry ingredients in bowl, except soda which should be added to milk. Just before adding the milk to the dry ingredients, mix well. The dough should be fairly thick. Put in pans, spread evenly. Bake in 350° oven until done.

Esther Nisley (Pie Baker)

The celebrated soprano was singing a solo when Bobby said to his mother, referring to the conductor of the orchestra: "Why does that man hit at that woman with a stick?"
"But he isn't hitting at her," replied the mother.
"Well, then, what's she hollerin' for"?

GRAPE NUTS

5 c. sour milk or buttermilk
1 c. sour cream or ½ c. melted oleo
1 c. sugar and 2 c. karo syrup
3 t. soda
3 t. salt
2 t. vanilla
11 c. whole wheat flour

3 c. brown sugar can be used instead of syrup. More milk or less flour must be used to account for moisture. Bake in loaf till done. When cool crumble fine. Dry and roast lightly brown in slow oven on cookie sheets. (Makes 8 qts.)

Susie W. Miller (Baby-sitter)

BUTTERMILK PANCAKES

1½ c. white flour
1½ c. whole wheat flour

Stir in enough buttermilk to make batter, set aside.

Then mix:

1 t. salt
2 t. soda, with cold water

Put this into batter just before frying.

Elsie R. Miller (Grill Cook)

WAFFLES

2 c. sifted flour	2½ t. baking powder
¾ t. salt	2 eggs, well beaten
1½ c. milk	5 T. melted shortening

Sift flour, measure, add baking powder, and salt; mix, add eggs and milk, then shortening. Mix only till smooth. Bake in hot waffle iron 3-5 min. or till done. Serve hot with butter and syrup.

Lydia Ann Miller (Cook)

WAFFLES

3 c. sifted flour	3 eggs, separated
1 t. baking powder	2 c. sour cream
1 t. soda	3 T. melted lard
1 t. salt	1½ c. water

Sift dry ingredients, drop in egg yolks, add sour cream and lard. Beat until smooth, add water. Fold in egg whites, beaten stiff. Bake in a hot waffle iron. Makes 12 waffles.

Barbara Bontrager (Cashier)

 TO MAKE A CAKE

Light oven; get out untensils and ingredients. Remove blocks and toy autos from table. Grease pan, crack nuts.

Measure 2 cups of flour; remove Johnny's hands from flour; wash flour off him. Remeasure flour.

Put flour, baking powder and salt in sifter. Get dustpan and brush up pieces of bowl Johnny knocked on floor. Get another bowl. Answer doorbell.

Return to kitchen. Remove Johnny's hands from bowl. Wash Johnny. Answer phone. Return. Remove ¼ inch salt from greased pan. Look for Johnny. Grease another pan. Answer telephone.

Return to kitchen and find Johnny. Remove his hands from bowl. Take up greased pan and find layer of nutshells in it. Head for Johnny who flees, knocking bowl off table.

Wash kitchen floor, table, walls, dishes. Call baker. Lie down.

Salads &
Salad Dressings

SERVES 100 PEOPLE

Baked beans	5 gals.	Meat loaf	24 lbs.
Beef	40 lbs.	Milk	6 gals.
Beets	30 lbs.	Nuts	3 lbs.
Bread	10 loaves	Olives	1¾ lbs.
Butter	3 lbs.	Pickles	2 qts.
Cakes	8	Pies	18
Carrots	3 lbs.	Potatoes	35 lbs.
Cheese	3 lbs.	Potato salad	12 qts.
Chicken pot pie	40 lbs.	Roast pork	40 lbs.
Coffee	3 lbs.	Rolls	200
Cream	3 qts.	Salad dressing	3 qts.
Fruit cocktail	2½ gals.	Scalloped potatoes	5 gals.
Fruit juice	4 #10 cans	Soup	5 gals.
Fruit salad	12 qts.	Tomato juice	4 #10 cans
Ham	40 lbs.	Vegetable	4 #10 cans
Hamburger	30 to 36 lbs.	Weiners	25 lbs.
Ice cream	4 gals.	Vegetable salad	20 qts.
Lettuce	20 heads	Whipping cream	4 pts.

Betty A. Hershberger (Grill Cook)

Put a little butter or lard in kettle of potatoes to keep from boiling over.

Onion odor may be removed from hands by rubbing them with dry salt.

Add ¼ t. soda to cranberries and they will not require much sugar.

When celery loses its crispness, place in a pan of cold water. Slice a raw potato and put it in a pan. Let stand for a while and it will regain its original crispness.

Salads & Salad Dressings

APPLE SALAD

6 or 8 apples, diced
1 can pineapple (tidbits)
1 doz. marshmallows

½ c. nuts
grapes, oranges (optional)

Combine diced apples and marshmallows with pineapple and nuts, grapes and oranges if desired. Mix ingredients for dressing and cool till thickened. When cooled, pour over apple mixture and stir until all fruit is coated. When ready to serve, whip the cream and mix lightly into the salad. (If using red apples, use half of them unpeeled for color and texture.) Serves 6 to 8.

Dressing

pineapple juice
2 eggs
¾ c. sugar

2 T. flour
2 T. butter
1 c. cream

Marilyn Bontrager (Waitress)

(Zu wenig and zu viel ist narran ziel)
(Too little and too much is the target of fools)

APPLE SALAD

4 apples (cored and diced)
2 bananas (sliced)
1 c. grapes (cut into fourths)
½ c. nuts (optional)

2 c. miniature marshmallows
½ c. sugar
½ c. salad dressing
2 T. milk

Combine the apples, marshmallows, bananas, nuts, and grapes. Then mix the salad dressing, sugar, and milk in a small bowl. Pour this over the fruit salad and combine throughly.

Mrs. Freddie S. Bontrager

But godliness with contentment is great gain. For we brought nothing into this world, and it is certain we can carry nothing out. And having food and raiment let us be therewith content.

1 Tim. 6:6-8

APRICOT SALAD

1 lg. can apricot halves,
    quartered
1 lg. can crushed pineapple
¾ c. miniature marshmallows

2 pkg. orange Jell-O®
2 c. boiling water
1 c. combined apricot &
    pineapple juices

Dissolve Jell-O® in boiling water. Stir in remaining ingredients. Pour into 9"x13" pan. When set, cover with topping.

Topping

½ c. sugar
3 T. flour
2 T. butter

1 egg, slightly beaten
1 c. combined fruit juices
1 pkg. Dream Whip®, prepared

Mix together all ingredients except butter and heat to boiling point. Take from burner and add butter. Cool. Fold the cooled mixture into 1 pkg. of whipped Dream Whip®. Pile onto Jell-O® and top with nuts.

Mrs. Freddie S. Bontrager

28

APRICOT PINEAPPLE SALAD

1 pkg. lemon jello
1 pkg. orange jello

Dissolve in 2 c. boiling water

Add:

1 c. apricot and pineapple juice
1 #2½ can apricot halves, cut up and drained
1 #2 can crushed pineapple, drained
¾ c. small marshmallows

Pour into 9x13 inch pan and chill until firm.

Topping

Place ½ c. sugar and 3 T. flour in saucepan. Blend in 1 egg and 1 c. apricot and pineapple juice. Cook until thick and add 2 T. butter. When cool fold in 1 c. whipped cream and spread on gelatin. Sprinkle with grated cheese or slivered almonds.

Edna Nissley (Waitress)

APRICOT SALAD

1 #2 can apricots
1 #2 can crushed pineapple
1 6 oz. pkg. orange jello
2 c. boiling water
2 c. fruit syrup

½ c. white sugar
2 T. flour
1 egg beaten
1 pkg. dream whip
grated american cheese

Drain fruit; reserve syrup. Dissolve jello in boiling water; add 1 c. reserved syrup. Chill until partially set. Chop apricots; add to jello with pineapple. Chill until firm. Mix sugar and flour; stir in remaining fruit syrup and egg. Cook in double boiler until thick, cool. Fold in dream whip. Spread over firm gelatin; sprinkle with cheese. Yield 8 servings.

Olive Bontrager (Cashier)

"O weary moms mixing dough
Don't you wish that food would grow?
A smile would come, I know, to see,
A cookie bush or donut tree."

CARROT SALAD

2 lbs. carrots, peeled, sliced or diced
1 green pepper, diced
1 onion, diced
½ c. salad oil

¾ c. vinegar
1 c. sugar
1 t. dry mustard
1 can tomato soup

Cook carrots in salt water until med. tender. Drain. Add onion and green pepper. Mix oil, sugar, and vinegar, and heat until sugar is dissolved (bring to boil). Add dry mustard and tomato soup. Mix and pour over vegetables. Cover and refrigerate. Keeps six weeks.

Mrs. Betty Graber (Waitress)
Lucy Eash (Cook)

CARROT SALAD

2 lbs. carrots, slice and cook in salt water. Do not over cook.

Sauce

1 small onion sliced
½ c. tomato soup
¼ c. vinegar
½ c. sugar
½ t. pepper

1 t. mustard
½ c. salad oil
1 t. worcestershire sauce
Green onion tops for color

Marinate overnight.

Martha Otto (Pie Baker)

MARINATED CARROTS

3 lbs. carrots
1 can tomato soup
1 c. sugar
½ c. oil
⅓ c. vinegar

1 t. salt
½ t. pepper
1 t. dry mustard
1 onion sliced
1 green pepper

Peel and slice carrots in ½ inch pieces. Cook just until tender and drain. Whip next 7 ingredients in blender for 5 min. Combine carrots, onions separated in rings and pepper sliced thin and pour dressing over carrots. Keeps for several weeks.

Elizabeth Miller (Noodles)

CARROT AND PINEAPPLE SALAD

1 pkg. lemon or orange jello
1 c. pineapple juice
1 c. boiling water

1 c. crushed pineapple
1½ c. ground raw carrots
½ c. nuts (optional)

Dissolve gelatin in hot water and add pineapple juice. Chill. When this begins to thicken, add other ingredients. Pour mixture into a mold and chill until set. Unmold on lettuce. Serve with mayonnaise. Serves 6.

Sue Miller (Manager)

CHICKEN SALAD

3 c. diced cooked chicken
½ c. celery thinly sliced
1 c. drained mandarin oranges
1 c. drained pineapple
½ c. grapes

¼ c. mayonnaise
¼ c. sour cream
½ t. lemon juice
1 t. sugar

Combine first five ingredients, combine mayonnaise, sour cream, lemon juice and sugar. Pour over chicken mixture; toss gently. Chill thoroughly. Serve on lettuce.

Olive Bontrager (Cashier)

HOT CHICKEN SALAD

2 c. diced cooked chicken
2 c. chopped celery
¾ c. slivered almonds
2 t. grated onions
½ c. grated american cheese

½ t. salt
1 t. lemon juice
1 c. mayonnaise
½ t. prepared mustard
1 c. finely chopped potato chips

Mix chicken, celery, almonds, onions, cheese and salt. Add juice and mustard to mayonnaise - fold into chicken mixture. Put into casserole - sprinkle with potato chips. Bake at 375° 15-20 min. Serves 6.

THE VEGETABLE GARDEN

First plant five rows of peas
Patience
Promptness
Preparation
Perseverance
Purity

Next plant three rows of squash
Squash gossip
Squash criticism
Squash indifference

Then plant five rows of lettuce
Let-us be faithful to duty
Let-us be unselfish
Let-us be loyal
Let-us be true to obligations
Let-us love one another

And no garden is complete without turnips
Turn-up for important meetings
Turn-up with a smile
Turn-up with good ideas
Turn-up with determination
to make everything count for something good and worthwhile.

Katie Miller (Gift Shop)

CRANBERRY CHICKEN SALAD

First Layer

1 envelope unflavored gelatin	½ c. evaporated milk
¼ c. cold water	2 c. diced chicken
1 c. hot chicken broth	1 t. salt
⅔ c. salad dressing	

Second Layer

1 envelope unflavored gelatin	1 c. finely chopped celery
½ c. cold water	½ c. chopped nuts
1 can whole cranberry sauce	½ c. orange juice
(melted)	

Soak gelatin in cold water and pour into hot chicken broth, add remaining first layer ingredients, pour into 9x12 glass cake pan. Chill until firm.

Soak gelatin for second layer. Stir into hot cranberry sauce. Cool; add celery, nuts and orange juice. Let set partially; pour over jelled chicken layer. When set cover with saran wrap and keep in refrigerator until ready to serve. Yield: 12 servings.

Mildred Two (Cake Decorator)

CINNAMON SWIRL SALAD

1 - 6 oz. box lemon jello	1 T. lemon juice
½ c. red cinnamon candies	½ c. coarsely chopped nuts
3 c. boiling water	1 - 6 oz. pkg. cream cheese softened
2 c. applesauce	¼ c. milk
dash of salt	2 T. mayonnaise or salad dressing

Dissolve jello and candies in boiling water; stir in applesauce, lemon juice, and salt. Chill until partially set. Fold in nuts. Put into mold or 8x8x2 inch pan.

Beat together creamed cheese, milk, and mayonnaise. Spoon over salad; swirl through to marble. Chill until firm. Yield: 8-10 servings.

Olive Bontrager (Cashier)

COLE SLAW

1 head cabbage
1 or 2 peppers
3 or 4 carrots

Grind all together into bowl, salt to taste. Let stand 1½ hour.

Cook together:

1½ c. sugar
¾ c. vinegar
½ c. wesson oil

Pour this while hot yet, over drained cabbage. If vinegar is too strong add a little water. This keeps for 4 weeks in a cool place.

Laura Miller (Grill Cook)

UNANSWERED PRAYER

"Give me, O God," I prayed,
  "Strength for my need."
But though I knew the laws of health,
  I paid no need.
"Send me, O God," I prayed
  "Someone to care."
And then I went my selfish way,
  Nor tried to share.
"Yield me, O God," I prayed,
  Keenness and skill,"
Yet never disciplined my mind,
  Nor trained my will.
"Grant me, O God," I prayed,
  "Wisdom to live,"
But what I had not worked to earn,
  He did not give.

Gertrude Lyon Sylvester

COLE SLAW

1½ c. sugar
½ c. hot water
½ c. vinegar

1½ t. salt
1 t. celery seed

Mix well and pour over 1 large head chopped cabbage. You may add chopped carrots also; this gives an extra color. Can be canned by heating all ingredients, and putting in cans and sealing.

Lydia ann Miller (Cook)

COLE SLAW CABBAGE

1½ c. sugar
¾ c. vinegar

¾ c. mazola oil
1 T. salt

Chop 1 head of cabbage, onion, celery. Heat sugar, vinegar, oil and salt to boiling point. Pour while hot over chopped cabbage, let set overnite. Keeps a few days.

Esther Nisley (Pie Baker)

EVERLASTING COLE SLAW

1 med. head cabbage
1 carrot
2 small onions
1 c. celery
1 green pepper

½ c. vinegar
1½ c. sugar
1 t. mustard seed
1 t. celery seed
salt and pepper to taste

Cut all of this fine and mix well. Store, covered in the refrigerator and use as needed. Will keep for quite a while.

Katie Cross (Waitress)

 "Little is much when God is in it."

It will be a hard winter if:
Squirrels begin gathering nuts early (middle or late September).
The north side of a beaver dam is more covered with sticks than the south.
Hoot Owls call late in the Fall.

CONFETTI SALAD

4 different flavors of jello (3 oz.)
Add 1½ c. water (boiling) to dissolve each pkg. and put in separate flat pans. Let set until hard.
Dissolve 2 pkg. (3 oz.) lemon jello with 2 c. hot pineapple juice. Let set until syrupy.
Then beat until real fluffy.
Add 2 boxes of dream whip or 1 pint of cream. (Whip Topping)
Cube the hardened jellos and add to whipped mixture.
Let set until firm.

Amanda Troyer (Waitress)

COTTAGE CHEESE AND PINEAPPLE SALAD

1 pkg. lemon or lime gelatin	¼ t. salt
1 c. hot water	1 c. cottage cheese
1 c. pineapple juice	½ c. chopped nuts
1 c. crushed pineapple	Strips of green and red pepper

Dissolve gelatin in hot water and add pineapple juice. Chill until liquid begins to congeal. Combine drained pineapple, cheese, nuts and salt and fold into gelatin mixture. Pour into mold and chill until firm. Unmold on lettuce and garnish with mayonnaise and strips of pepper. Serves 6.

Sue Miller (Manager)

"Old age is not of matter, but of mind. If you don't mind, it doesn't matter."
—*Author Unknown*

CRANBERRY SALAD

2 c. cranberries
1 c. sugar
1 lg. apple

½ c. walnuts
½ orange, peelings and all

Mix all together, let stand overnight.

Lucy Eash (Cook)

FRESH DANDELION SALAD (Spinach or Endive)

6 or 8 strips bacon (crumbled)
3 T. flour
water
3 T. sugar

1 T. vinegar
salt
3 eggs (hard boiled)
Fresh dandelion greens

Brown bacon and drain. Into the bacon grease stir in the flour. Add cold water and blend until smooth and to gravy consistency. Add sugar, vinegar and salt to taste. Simmer for 10 minutes; allow to cool for a few minutes while slicing eggs and crumbling bacon. Pour cooked dressing over cut up dandelion greens and top with eggs and bacon. You may use fresh endive or spinach instead of dandelion.

Sue Miller (Manager)

FINGER JELLO

3 boxes (pint size) jello
4 pkg. knox gelatin
4 c. boiling water

Let set till firm, cut in pieces and eat with fingers.

Mrs. Freddie S. Bontrager

Q. "Why do cows wear bells?"
A. "Because their horns don't work."

37

ICE CREAM SALAD

Pour 1 c. hot water over 1 box jello (choose your flavor). Add 1 pt. vanilla ice cream. After the cream melts, add 1 small can crushed pineapple and ½ c. nuts. Put into the refrigerator until solid.

Anita Miller (Busser)

 Put a smile in your food!

INSTANT FRUIT SALAD

1 pkg. vanilla instant pudding (dry)
1 large can fruit cocktail (not drained)
1 c. miniature marshmallows or less as desired

Blend together, refrigerate ½ hr. and add 1 container of cool whip, thawed (I like less cool whip and also less marshmallows).

You can vary this recipe with other pudding flavors and various canned fruits or fresh fruits. I like to add green grapes, bananas, pineapple, grapefruit and oranges.

Mildred Two (Cake Decorator)

LAYERED LETTUCE SALAD

1 head lettuce (in bite sized pieces)	1 sweet onion
1 c. celery (cut up)	8 slices bacon (fried and diced)
4 eggs (hard cooked and diced)	2 c. mayonnaise (½ Miracle Whip)
1 pkg. frozen peas (cooked)	4 oz. cheddar cheese (grated)
½ c. green pepper (diced)	2 T. sugar

Layer in a 9x12 inch dish the first seven ingredients. Mix mayonnaise and Miracle Whip salad dressing with sugar. Spread on top as frosting. Top with cheese, cover and refrigerate 8-12 hrs. At serving time garnish with additional bacon and parsley if desired.

Fannie R. Yutzy (Pie Baker)
Mrs. Freddie S. Bontrager

OVERNIGHT LEAF SALAD

1 head lettuce	2 c. mayonnaise
1 head cauliflower	⅓ c. parmesan cheese
1 sweet onion	¼ c. sugar
1 lb. fried bacon	

Put in layers and refrigerate overnight. Toss just before serving.

Mary Ann Schlabach (Waitress)

 GOD'S RECIPE AND OURS

God has a recipe for every one.
I am sure there is one for you.
Take 15 minutes the first of each day,
To lay on Him your burden as you pray.

Use a lot of His love as you open your heart
To the need of others about.
It will sweeten each hour, give strength for each task
And drive all bitterness out.

Take of His peace; it is promised you too.
A measure of joy and laughter is fine.
Blend this with faith, abundant and true
Add patience and meekness, to others be kind.

Yes, there is life abundant for every one.
It is promised in His book.
But for good things to eat and hints that are fine,
May make your work easier and save you time.
Then turn the page of this book —
Give it some attention, not just one look.

Read each recipe as you are going through.
You may find them helpful even to you.
Follow each recipe with care.
Your favorite one may be there.
For this book is made up of many good dishes.
And from our hearts to yours come our best wishes.

CAULIFLOWER SALAD

1 head lettuce, chunked
1 head cauliflower, sliced
a chopped onion
1 lb. bacon fried and crumbled

2 c. salad dressing
½ c. sugar
¼ to ½ c. parmesan cheese

Mix and chill.

Mrs. Betty Graber (Waitress)

When you "marinate" something, it means to let it stay in a mixture of ingredients until it soaks up and becomes the nature of the marinate. We all need to be "marinated" in Jesus, and stay there long enough to soak up His nature.

FRESH VEGETABLE SALAD

1 med. size head of lettuce
½ c. celery
¼ c. chopped onion
½ c. sliced green peppers

1 (10 oz.) pkg. frozen peas
2 c. mayonnaise
½ c. grated cheese
bacon bits

Layer first 6 ingredients in salad bowl. Let set in refrigerator overnight or at least 6 hrs. Just before serving sprinkle with grated cheese and bacon bits.

Mary Esther Miller (Waitress)

24 HOUR VEGETABLE SALAD

1 head lettuce, cut up
2 c. diced celery
1 lg. red onion

1 pkg. frozen peas (as is)
2 c. mayonnaise

Layer in pan in order as listed above. Sprinkle top generously with grated cheese and bacon bits. Put on lid and leave in refrigerator for 24 hrs.

Sharon Nofziger (Waitress)

HALF PRICE BOOKS

EST. 1972

Half Price Books #052
1375 W. Lane Ave
Columbus, OH 43221
614-486-8765

12-15-18 12:16 PM
Store #0052 / Cashier Huff K / Reg 1
Sale # 320295

SALE TRANSACTION

Lorenza's Pasta   230773434U
1 @9.99 $9.99
The Illustrated Book of Pres 235999694U
1 @8.49 $8.49
Amish-Country Cookbook   241794468U
1 @8.49 $8.49
Breakfast Heaven   240176560U
1 @9.99 $9.99

4 Items in Transaction

Subtotal $36.96
Sales Tax (7.5% on $36.96) $2.77
TOTAL $39.73

PAYMENT TYPE
MasterCard 1922 $39.73

Thanks for shopping at Half Price Books!

$5 Bonus with each $25 Gift Card!
Now through Monday, Dec. 24
We are bookish but have a social life.
Find us @halfpricebooks on
Facebook, Twitter & Instagram

H 0 2 0 0 5 2 0 0 1 3 2 0 2 9 5 1

3 LAYER SALAD

First Layer

3 eggs
3 T. flour
1 c. sugar
1 c. pineapple juice
Cook till thickens. Pour into 9x13 in. pan and chill.

Second Layer

1 - 8 oz. pkg. cream cheese
1 c. whipping cream (whipped)   Chill until set.

Third Layer

2 boxes lemon or lime jello
1 #2 can crushed pineapple, drained
½ c. nuts

Mrs. Mary Arlene Bontrager (Waitress)

Q. "On which side does a chicken have the most feathers?
A. "The outside."

---

12 LAYER SALAD

Jello (3 oz.) pkg. cherry-lime-lemon-orange-lime-strawberry
16 oz. sour cream

Add 1 c. boiling water to cherry jello, take out half and add to ⅓ c. sour cream (slowly). Pour in 9x13 inch pan. Chill 20 min. or till firm. Add 3 T. cold water to remaining jello and pour on top of first layer. Repeat the same with each following jello flavor. Fix jello in order given.

Betty A. Hershberger (Grill Cook)

THREE LAYER SALAD

2 (3 oz.) pkgs. lime jello
3¾ c. hot water
1 c. drained crushed pineapple

Let set till firm.

1 (8 oz.) pkg. cream cheese
1 c. whipped cream

Whip together and put on first layer.

Mix:
1 c. sugar   2 eggs
2 T. flour   ½ c. pineapple juice

Cook till thick, then let cool. Put this on top. Chill and serve.

Lizzie Ann Bontrager (Cook)

LEMON DELIGHT

Mix together:
1 stick oleo
1 c. flour
½ c. nuts

Bake at 375° in 9x13 in. pan for 15 min. Cool. Mix together with beater:

8 oz. pkg. cream cheese
1 c. powdered sugar
Fold in 1 c. cool whip. Put this layer on top of crust. Let chill 15 min.

Beat together till thickened:
3 c. milk
2 pkg. instant lemon pudding

Put on top of cream cheese layer. Chill 15 min. Top with rest of cool whip (use 9 oz. size cool whip). Sprinkle some nuts on top. It's scrumpdelicious!

Martha Otto (Pie Baker)

LIME JELLO SALAD

1 box (6 oz.) lime or orange jello	2 c. ice cream
1 c. hot water	½ c. drained pineapple
1 c. cold water	½ c. nutmeats

Mrs. Tobias Hochstetler

ORANGE CHEESE SALAD

3 oz. cream cheese	1 c. nuts
32 lg. marshmallows	1 c. crushed pineapple
1½ c. whipped cream	3 small boxes orange jello

Mix jello as directed on box. Put cheese, marshmallows and ½ c. jello mix in top of double boiler. Put on top of boiling water till melted. Put ½ of the remaining jello mix in pan approx. 2x6x12 inch size. Let set till hard. When marshmallow mix is cold, add nuts, pineapple and whipped cream. Pour on top of hard jello. When this has set, pour rest of jello on top.

Susie Bontreger (Grill Cook)

PEAR SALAD

1 lg. or sm. can pears	1 lg. or sm. cream cheese
1 lg. or sm. lime jello	1 lg. or sm. cool whip

Heat juice from pears and whip softened cheese, and jello. Put pears in blender and whip together. Let set then whip cool whip and jello mixture together. Let set.

Lois Buchtel (Dishwasher)

Q. "What do you get when you cross peanut butter with an elephant?"

A. "You either get peanut butter that never forgets or an elephant that sticks to the roof of your mouth."

Doctor: "I see you're coughing better this morning."
Patient: "Why not? I've been practicing all night."

PERFECTION SALAD

1 - 6 oz. box lime jello   ¾ c. grated carrots
½ c. crushed pineapple   1 c. grated cabbage

Prepare jello according to directions. Add pineapple, carrots, and cabbage. Let set until firm.

Sue Miller (Manager)

PINEAPPLE SALAD

chunk pineapple
raw apple, sliced
cheese, cubed

Take about the same amount of each. Take the juice from the pineapple and thicken with clear-jel. Cool, then mix.

Mrs. Tobias Hochstetler

PINEAPPLE SALAD

2 boxes lime jello dissolved in 3 c. hot water. Add 1 c. drained, crushed pineapple. Let set in bowl or dish.

Soften 1 - 8 oz. pkg. cream cheese with a little milk, add to 1 c. cream, whipped. Mix well. Spread on set jello layer.

1 c. sugar   2 egg yolks
3 T. flour   1 c. pineapple juice

Cook till thick. Cool; spread on top of cheese mixture. Garnish with maraschino cherries.

Sharon Boley (Waitress)

PINEAPPLE CHEESE SALAD

Mix in a saucepan 1 qt. pineapple and 1 c. sugar. When boiling stir in thickening of 4 lg. T. flour, and ½ t. salt. Add 1 c. water or more if sauce is too thick. Add ¼ c. cut up cheese, and 8 marshmallows. Beat and let cool. When ready to serve add salted peanuts, more cheese and marshmallows as you like.

Lucy Eash (Cook)

PINEAPPLE CHEESE SALAD

¾ c. pineapple juice
¾ c. sugar
1 c. water

1 T. butter
2 eggs, beaten
2 T. flour

Cook together into fine thick sauce, cool. Then add 1 c. finely chopped velveeta cheese, 5 or 6 finely cut marshmallows or just some miniature marshmallows, and 1 c. pineapple. Add nuts to suit your taste.

Vera Slabach (Dishwasher)

PINEAPPLE-CHEESE SALAD

1 can crushed pineapple, drained
1 c. velvetta cheese cubes, cut in small square size
1 c. planters peanuts
1 c. whipping cream, whipped

Measure liquid of drained pineapple and add additional pineapple juice to make 2 cups. Heat to a boil and sweeten to taste and thicken with either cornstarch or clear-jel. Boil to thicken, then cool. It is better if this is all mixed together shortly before serving. Mix whipped cream to the thickened juice then add pineapple, cheese, and peanuts.

Mattie Graber (driver)

PISTACHIO SALAD

1 box lime jello, dissolved in
1 c. hot water

Cool till jelled.

Mix 1 can fruit cocktail *undrained* and
1 box pistachio instant pudding and add to jello.

Then add ½ c. nuts and 1 c. miniature marshmallows
Fold in 1 - 9 oz. Cool Whip

Betty Hershberger (Grill Cook)

Mike: "I always do my hardest work before breakfast."
Sandy: "What's that?"
Mike: "Getting up."

POTATO SALAD

Cut up in small pieces 4 or 5 medium potatoes. Add sliced radishes, cut up celery, peppers, a little onion.

Salad Dressing

½ c. Miracle Whip
grate in a little onion
grate coarsely 2 or 3 radishes (if you don't want pink color, peel radish)
grate coarsely a little pepper
1-1½ T. vinegar
a little sugar for a sweet sour dressing.

Mildred Two (Cake Decorator)

Last night I dreamed I ate a five pound marshmallow.
When I woke up, my pillow was gone.

GERMAN POTATO SALAD

8 boiled potatoes	1 onion chopped
1 stalk celery diced	1 T. chopped parsley
2 hard cooked eggs	

Add together the above.

4 slices bacon, diced	½ c. cold water
2 eggs well beaten	¼ t. dry mustard
1 c. sugar	½ t. salt
½ c. vinegar	¼ t. pepper

Fry bacon in skillet until crisp and brown. Beat eggs, add sugar, spices, vinegar and water. Mix well. Pour mixture into the hot bacon fat and stir until mixture thickens (about 10 min.). Pour over the potato mixture and mix lightly. Let stand in a cold place several hours before serving.

Esther Nisley (Pie Baker)

Dentist: "What kind of filling would you like in your tooth?"
Boy: "Chocolate!"

SPRITE SALAD

5 pkgs. plain gelatin
½ c. cold water
3 c. hot water

juice from 1 lemon
1 c. sugar
32 oz. bottle of sprite

Dissolve gelatin in cold water. Immediately add hot water, lemon juice, and sugar. Cool and add sprite. Place in refrigerator. When it begins to jel add red grapes and pineapple chunks. Enough for large Tupperware jello mold.

Topping

Blend the pineapple juice with:

3 T. flour
½ c. sugar

2 well beaten eggs
2 T. butter

Cook until thickened. Cool and add 1 c. whipped topping.

Rosa Borntrager (Cook)

7-UP DELIGHT

2 boxes (3 oz.) lemon jello
2 c. boiling water
2 c. 7-UP

2 lg. bananas, diced
1 c. crushed pineapple

Dissolve jello in boiling water and add 7-UP. Chill until partly set, and add pineapple and bananas. Top with the following.

Boil together:

½ c. sugar
3 T. flour

1 egg, beaten
1 c. pineapple juice

When thick add 2 T. butter. Cool and add 1 c. whipping cream.

Mrs. Clara Ann Bontrager

48

TACO SALAD

1 head lettuce, shredded
1 can red kidney beans, drained
3 or 4 fresh tomatoes, chopped
1 c. cheese, grated

diced onions
1 pkg. Doritos, crushed
1 lb. hamb., fried in small pieces

Gently toss above and pour 1 small bottle french dressing over all.

Mabel Hershberger (Pie Baker)

TACO SALAD

1 head lettuce
2 tomatoes, chopped
1 can red kidney beans, drained
1 onion

1 lb. hamb., fried and drained
1 bag taco flavored Doritos
1 bag cheddar cheese, shredded
1 sm. jar Western dressing

Let hamburger cool and mix all together.

Carol Pletcher (Waitress)

TOSSED TACO SALAD

1 head lettuce, shredded
1 bunch green onions, chopped
4 tomatoes, chopped
1 pkg. (5½ oz.) taco chips
1 lb. ground beef
1 bottle (8 oz.) thousand island dressing
1 can red kidney beans, drained
12 oz. cheese, grated

Mix first six ingredients together. Brown ground beef and drain. Add to salad. Toss with dressing. Makes a large salad.

Jeannie Yoder (Waitress)

TACO SALAD

1 large head lettuce
1 c. grated cheese
1 lb. hamburger fried with onion, drained
1 pkg. taco chips
4 tomatoes, cut up
radishes
green pepper

Dressing

Blend:

1½ c. salad oil
½ c. vinegar
1½ c. sugar
½ c. ketchup

1 small onion
½ t. celery salt
½ t. paprika
1/8 t. pepper

Rosa Borntrager (Cook)
Lydia Yoder

THREE-WAY BEAN SALAD

1½ c. sugar
½ c. hot water
½ c. vinegar

1½ t. salt
1/8 c. salad oil

Mix well and add:

1 pt. green beans
1 pt. wax beans
1 pt. kidney beans

½ c. chopped celery
½ c. chopped onions

Sue Miller (Manager)

 Love your neighbor, it will drive him crazy!

WATERGATE SALAD

1 box instant pistachio pudding (3 oz.)
1 c. pecans, chopped
1 lg. container (12 oz.) Cool Whip®
1 can crushed pineapple w/ juice (20 oz.)
1½ c. miniature marshmallows

Mix dry pudding with crushed pineapple and juice. Stir in marshmallows and pecans. Fold in Cool Whip®. Refrigerate at least 1 hr. before serving.

Meda Bontrager (Waitress)

BLEU CHEESE DRESSING

½ c. mayonnaise
¼ c. lemon juice
½ t. Worcestershire sauce
1 clove garlic, minced or grated
6 oz. bleu cheese, crumbled
2 t. grated onion
½ t. Tabasco® sauce
1 can (6 oz.) evaporated milk, thoroughly chilled

Combine all ingredients except milk and chill. Whip milk to a soft peak. Fold into cheese mixture. This dressing is very thick and can also be used as a dip.

Leora V. Kauffman
(Purchasing)

FRENCH DRESSING

2 c. vegetable oil
2 c. white sugar
⅔ c. catsup
2 t. salt
1 onion, finely chopped
⅔ c. vinegar
2 t. celery seed

Combine oil, sugar, catsup, salt, and onion. Beat for 20 minutes. Add vinegar and celery seed, beat again until well mixed. Put in jar and store in refrigerator. You can also put in blender and blend covered for 5-10 minutes or until thick.

Carolyn Beechy (Cook)

FRENCH DRESSING

6 c. salad oil
6 c. sugar
2¼ c. catsup

2¼ c. vinegar
2 t. salt
4 t. worcestershire sauce

Mix well with mixer or blender. Makes approximately 4 qts.

Sue Miller (Manager)

FRUIT SALAD DRESSING

½ c. lemon or orange juice
½ c. pineapple juice
2 eggs
1½ T. flour

½ c. sugar
1 c. whipping cream
½ c. walnuts (Optional)

Combine juices and stir slowly into sugar and flour mixture. Cook in a double boiler until it thickens. Add beaten eggs and cook 1 minute longer; remove from heat and cool. Fold in whipped cream. Makes 2½ c. dressing.

Sue Miller (Manager)

 POPCORN

When the Sunday dinner dishes are all washed and put away.
    Comes a lull we don't experience on an ordinary day.
If you haven't any place to go, you sleep, or just look glum
    As you sit around a-wishin' that some company would come.

Have you felt that drowsy feeling when the dinner things are through?
    It sort of creeps upon you in spite of all that you can do.
And there's nothing that will quell it or dispel it quite as soon
    As a dishpan full of popcorn on a Sunday afternoon.

Popcorn really has a way of making everyone feel great.
    All the folks forget they're sleepy and sit up to have a plate.
So remember when it's raining on a Sunday afternoon.
    Just a dishpan full of popcorn puts the world right back in tune.

Harold Rowley

CREAMY FRUIT SALAD DRESSING

½ c. butter
2 T. flour
1 c. milk
3 egg yolks
1 t. mustard

½ c. vinegar
1 t. salt
3 egg whites
½ c. sugar
Fresh or canned fruit

Melt butter; stir in flour; add milk and cook, stirring, until thick. Beat egg yolks in top of double boiler. Thin mustard in a little of the vinegar, and add to egg yolks. Add salt and all of the vinegar, and the cooked mixture to the egg yolks. Stir and cook until thick; remove from stove and add beaten egg whites mixed with sugar. Cool. Mix with fruit when ready to serve. Will keep in refrigerator for several weeks.

Sue Miller (Manager)

GARLIC DRESSING

1 c. sharp salad dressing
1 c. mayonnaise
4 t. grated onion
4 t. chopped parsley
2 T. sweet pickles finely chopped
3 T. bleu cheese dressing
garlic to taste

Combine ingredients and refrigerate.

Sharon Comps

SALAD DRESSING

1 lg. onion, grated
1 c. sugar
1 t. salt

1 t. dry mustard
a little garlic salt
1 c. chili sauce (Del Monte)

Mix slowly and add: 1 pt. wesson oil. Beat well, Add ½ c. vinegar. Beat slowly.

Mrs. Ray E. (Susie) Miller (Cook)

SALAD DRESSING

Put in a bowl.

1 egg unbeaten
2 T. sugar
1¼ t. salt
¼ t. mustard

¼ t. paprika
¾ c. salad oil
½ c. vinegar

Mix well and take:

4 level T. clear-jel
¼ c. cold water and add to
1 c. boiling water. Cook until clear.

Add to mixture in bowl and beat until light. Beating every few minutes while cooling makes it smoother.

Lydia Yoder

SALAD DRESSING

⅔ c. vinegar
1¼ c. sugar

Heat till sugar is melted, then cool.

Add:

2 t. salt
2 t. dry mustard
1 t. celery seed

1 T. grated onions
1¾ c. salad oil

Add gradually, beat till creamy, put in refrigerator.

Mrs. Freddie S. Bontrager

A smooth tongue often hides sharp teeth.

HOMEMADE SALAD DRESSING

8 slices bacon or baco's   1 t. salt
3 hard cooked eggs (optional) 1 t. paprika
¾ c. oil   1 T. chopped onion
⅔ c. sugar   1 T. lemon juice
⅓ c. ketchup   1 t. worcestershire sauce
¼ c. vinegar

Either shake in shaker or blend in blender.

Sharon Nofziger (Waitress)

HOMEMADE SALAD DRESSING

Beat together:

1½ c. salad oil   4 t. salt
2 eggs   ⅔ c. sugar
1 T. mustard

Cook together till thick:

1⅓ c. flour   ¾ c. vinegar
⅔ c. sugar   2 c. water

Mix well with first part. Makes 1½ qt.

Mrs. Marie Miller

SWEET AND SOUR DRESSING

2½ c. sugar   ½ c. salad dressing
¾ c. vinegar   ¼ c. mustard
1½ t. celery seed   1½ c. salad oil
1½ t. black pepper   1 or 2 T. chopped onions
                     if you wish.

Mix well and put in blender for a few minutes.

Sue Miller (Manager)

THOUSAND ISLAND DRESSING

1½ qt. salad dressing   1½ t. salt
¾ c. pickle relish   ¼ c. sugar
¾ c. catsup

Mix by hand or with mixer. Makes approximately 2 qts.

Sue Miller (Manager)

VEGETABLE DIP

8 oz. sour cream   1 T. minced onion
1 c. real mayonnaise   1 T. parsley flakes
1 T. dill seed   1 T. Beau Monde spice

Mix until smooth and creamy. Serve with crackers, cauliflower, celery, chips, etc.

Rosalie Bontrager (Waitress)
Ida Miller (Cook)

VERSATILE SALAD DRESSING

½ c. light corn syrup   2 t. paprika
2 t. cornstarch   1 t. salt
¼ c. cider vinegar   2 t. celery seed
¼ c. orange juice   ¾ c. corn oil

Stir corn syrup, cornstarch, vinegar and orange juice in med. saucepan. Bring to boil over med. heat, stirring constantly, boil 1 min. Remove from heat. Stir in paprika, salt and celery seed. Add corn oil, ¼ c. at a time beating well with wire whip or rotary beater; or put in a blender, adding corn oil gradually. Chill. Good with fruit or mixed green salad. 1½ cups.

Sharon Comps

VINEGAR AND OIL DRESSING

2 c. salad oil   pinch of salt
1 c. vinegar   pinch of celery seed
3 T. sugar

Mix well. Makes approximately 3 cups.

Sue Miller (Manager)

Meat, Poultry & Main Dishes

HELPFUL HINTS

If you've over salted a pot of stew or soup, drop in a raw potato (quartered). It will absorb the salt.

When cooking noodles or macaroni, first bring your water to boiling point, then add noddles or macaroni and bring to a boil again having plenty of water, turn off and cover. Let set until tender. This keeps them from getting so mushy.

Lydia Ann Miller (Cook)

A little baking powder added to meat loaf will make it more fluffy and if you add about ½ c. milk to a lb. of hamburger - let it set for 1 to 1½ hrs. before using it, it will be more juicy.

*If a t. of baking powder is added to six eggs when making scrambled eggs or omelets them will be more fluffy.

*Add a t. of baking powder per quart of potatoes while mashing, and they will be fluffy, smooth, more tasty and will not bloat.

RECIPE FOR LIFE

1 c. of good thoughts   3 c. forgiveness
1 c. kind deeds   2 c. well-beaten faults
1 c. consideration for others

Mix thoroughly and add tears of joy, sorrow, and sympathy for others. Fold in 4 c. prayer and faith to lighten other ingredients and raise the texture to great heights of Christian living. After pouring all this into your daily life, bake well with the heat of human kindness. Serve with a smile.

Sharon Boley (Waitress)
Lydia Ann Miller (Cook)

Meat, Poultry & Main Dishes

BARBEQUED HAM

Cut the ham in slices, lay flat in frying pan; pepper each, then spread each slice with ¼ t. prepared mustard. Pour in vinegar in proportion of ½ t. per slice, fry quickly on both sides. When done take out and add to gravy in pan; ½ glass of wine, a tsp. sugar; boil up once and pour over meat.

Leora V. Kauffman (Purchasing)

BARBECUE SAUCE

2 c. water
2 c. vinegar
2 T. garlic salt
1 T. pepper
8 T. salt
1 stick butter (¼ lb.)
5 T. worcestershire sauce

Marilyn Joan Mast (Waitress)

(De mad mit dika boka hen hertza we do woka)
"Girls with fat cheeks have hearts like flint."

59

BARBECUE SAUCE

⅓ c. vinegar   1 T. worcestershire sauce
¼ c. catsup   1 t. mustard
2 T. salad oil   1 t. salt
2 T. soy sauce

Mix altogether and let come to a boil. Ready to use.

Wilma Hershberger

BARBECUE SAUCE FOR 8 CHICKENS

1 pt. water   8 T. salt
1 pt. vinegar   1 T. garlic powder
¼ lb. butter   5 T. worcestershire sauce
3 t. black pepper

Bring to boil. Keep it on chicken every time you turn it around. Delicious.

Mrs. Harley Miller (Miller's Orchard)
Applebutter
Katie Cross (Waitress)

BARBECUE SAUCE

For 10 chickens
¾ qt. water   ½ lb. butter
¾ qt. vinegar   1 T. garlic salt
½ T. sugar   5 T. worcestershire sauce
8 T. salt   1 large diced onion
2 to 3 T. pepper

For 3 chickens
1½ c. water   ½ of ¼ lb. butter
1½ c. vinegar   1 t. garlic salt
just a little sugar   1½ T. worcestershire sauce
2⅔ T. salt   ⅓ diced onion
¾ T. pepper

Simmer, then brush on chickens as you grill them.

Sharon Boley (Waitress)

BAKED CHICKEN

Sprinkle chicken with salt, then roll in flour. Put in baking dish in layers. Pour a little milk or cream over top (this will help make liquid and make it more golden brown). Cover and bake at 350° for 1-1½ hr. or until tender. Check once or so. If it needs liquid add a little water so it won't bake to bottom.

Lydia Ann Miller (Cook)

CRISP BAKED CHICKEN

Use young fryers.
Melt butter in saucepan.
Roll chicken in butter, then roll in fine soda cracker crumbs.
Season with salt and pepper.
Bake for 1½ hr. at 350°.

Do not cover chicken at all and do not put one piece on top of another.

Katie Miller (Hostess)

HUNTING CHICKEN

4 lb. chicken, stewed, and seasoned and cubed.
2 c. macaroni, cooked and drained
½ lb. cheese
½ T. flour
½ c. cream
4 c. broth
4 c. bread crumbs
2 T. butter

Thicken broth with flour. Mix chicken, macaroni, cheese, and broth. Put in greased pan. Brown bread crumbs in butter, add cream, spread on top of mixture. Bake 30 min. at 325°.

Jeannie Yoder (Waitress)

DELICIOUS FRIED CHICKEN

Shake it in jiffy or bisquick mix. Brown in oleo, sprinkle with paprika, salt, and pepper. Bake in oven at 350° till done. Chicken can be dipped in milk if desired.

Mrs. Harley Miller (Miller's Orchard)
Applebutter

PRESSED CHICKEN

3 lbs. chicken
3 c. water
1 t. salt
1 stalk celery, diced
1 T. plain gelatin, to each pint of broth
1 T. water
2 T. parsley, minced

Wash and cut chicken into serving pieces. Place in pressure cooker. Add water, salt and celery. Close cover securely; place pressure regulator on vent pipe and cook 15 min. with pressure regulator rocking slowly. Let pressure drop of its own accord, remove chicken from bones. Separate white and dark meat. Strain broth. Dissolve each T. of gelatin in 2 T. cold water, and add to boiling broth. Add minced parsley. Alternate layers of white and dark meat in dish or mold. Pour broth over chicken and cover dish. Place in a cool place to set. I cut up the chicken pretty fine. I also add some vinegar to broth.

Lucy Eash (Cook)

RICE KRISPIE CHICKEN

⅔ c. rice krispies   Lawry seasoning salt
⅓ c. flour   melted margarine

Roll chicken pieces in margarine then into rice krispie mixture. Arrange on shallow pan. Bake at 275° for several hours.

LaVerda Miller (Waitress)

RICE KRISPY CHICKEN

Set oven to 350°. Line cookie sheet (with sides) with aluminum foil.

1 chicken, cut up	Melt ⅔ c. oleo and add
4 c. crushed rice krispies	1 t. salt and ½ t. pepper

Dry chicken pieces and dip in seasoned oleo, roll in crumbs until well coated. Place in pan skin side up, do not crowd it. Bake about 1 hr. Do not cover or turn pieces while cooking.

Sue Mullet (Bread Baker)

CHICKEN RODEO

2 young chickens	1 T. paprika
½ c. flour	2 t. salt
½ c. cooking oil	dash pepper

Combine these ingredients and dip chicken in it. Arrange in shallow pan.

Cook to a boil:

¾ c. water	1 T. minced garlic
¾ c. catsup	1 T. minced parsley
2 T. grated onion	

Pour over chicken and bake 1 hr. in 300° oven.

Mrs. Clara Ann Bontrager

(Wannd dich ime busch ferlore hoscht, guk ame bam nuf.)
"When lost in the woods look up a tree."

SAVORY CRESCENT CHICKEN SQUARES

3 oz. pkg. cream cheese, softened
3 T. butter
2 c. cooked chicken, cubed
¼ t. salt
1/8 t. pepper
2 T. milk
1 T. chopped pimento
8 oz. can Pillsbury refrigerated quick crescent dinner rolls
¾ c. seasoned croutons, crushed

Preheat oven to 350°. Blend cream cheese and 2 T. butter until smooth. Add the next 5 incredients, mix well. Separate crescent dough into 4 rectangles. Firmly press perforations, to seal. Spoon ½ c. meat mixture into center of each rectangle. Put 4 corners of dough to top center of chicken mixture, twist slightly, and seal edges. Brush top with reserved 1 T. butter and dip in crouton crumbs. Bake on ungreased cookie sheet 20-25 min. until golden brown.

Mushroom Sauce

Heat together 1 can mushroom soup, and ½ to 1 c. milk and serve with chicken squares.

Lavera Hooley (Waitress)

Doctor: "Are you still taking the cough medicine I gave you?"

Patient: "No, I tasted it and decided I'd rather have the cough."

CHICKEN AND DRESSING

½ c. milk
3 c. herb-seasoned croutons
½ c. celery, diced
1 T. minced onion
3 c. cooked chicken
3 eggs, beaten
1 can cream of chicken soup
1 c. milk

1 t. salt
½ t. poultry seasoning
½ t. marjoram flakes
½ c. flour
¼ c. parmesan cheese
¼ c. butter
½ c. almonds

Pour ½ c. milk in greased 9x13 inch pan. Combine croutons, celery, and onion. Spread in dish. Sprinkle chicken over croutons. Combine eggs, soup, 1 c. milk, salt, poultry seasoning and marjoram. Pour over chicken. Combine flour, cheese, and butter, blending until crumbs form. Sprinkle over casserole, top with almonds. Bake at 375° for 40 min.

Esther Hershberger

CHICKEN DRESSING

2 - 1 lb. loaves of cubed toasted bread
1 med. sized onion
1-1½ c. each of chopped celery and carrots
½ c. chopped parsley
1 T. celery seed
1 T. seasoned or spiced salt
1 t. pepper
1 qt. chicken and broth mixed
1 med. potato (cooked and diced)
6 eggs, beaten
Salt to taste

Put all dry ingredients in large mixing bowl and pour liquids over top. If bread is toasted real hard you may need more liquid of which you can use more broth, milk, or just hot water. I prefer water or broth before much milk. This can be frozen for later use.

Lydia Ann Miller (Cook)

MUSHROOM DRESSING

½ to 1 lb. fresh mushrooms,
    coarsely sliced
8 slices white bread, buttered
½ c. chopped onion
½ c. chopped celery
½ c. chopped green pepper
½ c. mayonnaise

¾ t. salt
¼ t. pepper
2 eggs, slightly beaten
1½ c. milk
1 can cream of mushroom soup,
    undiluted
grated cheddar cheese

Sauté mushrooms in butter, just enough so they begin to smell like mushrooms. Cut three slices of buttered bread into 1" cubes and put in a greased casserole dish. Combine mushrooms with onion, celery, and green pepper. Add mayonnaise, salt, and pepper to vegetables and pour over bread. Place three more cubed slices of buttered bread on top. Combine beaten eggs with the milk and pour over the top. Refrigerate 1 hr.

An hour before serving, spoon mushroom soup over top of casserole. Sprinkle with remaining 2 slices of buttered bread cubes. Bake 60-70 minutes at 325°. Sprinkle with grated cheese in last 10 minutes of baking time.

Millie Whetstone (Cook)

CHICKEN AND SPAGHETTI CASSEROLE

1 chicken (5-6 lbs.)
1 can tomatoes (8 oz.)
1 can mushrooms (8½ oz.)
1 lb. grated cheese
salt to taste

1 lb. canned chili without beans
1 lg. pkg. spaghetti (2 lb.)
2 or 3 onions
2 or 3 green peppers

Cook chicken in water, seasoning with salt to taste. When well done, remove chicken to cool slightly. Save broth and remove meat from bone; cut into bite-size pieces. Use 2/3 of broth to cook spaghetti; do not rinse. Chop onions and peppers, then cook in remainder of broth until tender.

In a large buttered roasting pan, layer half the chicken, half the spaghetti, and half of the onions and green peppers with broth. Spoon over this mixture half the chili, half the tomatoes, half the mushrooms, and half the grated cheese. Add second layer the same way. Cover with aluminum foil and bake for at least 2 hours at 325°. Add water if needed.

Leora V. Kauffman
(Purchasing)

HAMBURGER VEGETABLE CASSEROLE

3 lbs. hamburger
3 onions, chopped
3 c. potatoes, cubed
3 c. celery, sliced
3 c. carrots, diced
3 cans peas (6 oz. each)

3 c. spaghetti, cooked and drained
2 cans cream of mushroom soup
(6 oz. each)
9 slices bacon
1 qt. tomato juice
1 lb. cheese, shredded

Brown hamburger and onions, drain. Cook vegetables and drain.

In a roasting pan, place hamburger, cooked vegetables, and cooked spaghetti. Pour mushroom soup over top. Fry bacon and lay it over top. Pour tomato juice over all and sprinkle with cheese.

Bake 1½ hours in a 350° oven.

Amanda Troyer (Waitress)

CREAMY HAMBURGER CASSEROLE

1 lb. hamburger
2-3 small onions
1 can (6 oz.) cream of chicken soup
1 can (6 oz.) cream of celery soup
Canned beans or peas (optional)

3 c. macaroni, cooked and drained
1 c. cheese, shredded
1 c. bread crumbs
1 can (6 oz.) cream of
mushroom soup

Brown the hamburger in a pan with the diced onions. Drain grease. Add the cooked macaroni, along with cooked beans or peas if desired.

Put the meat, vegetables, and macaroni in a casserole dish. Combine soups in a bowl, milk to dilute until the mixture pour easily. Add cheese and bread crumbs on top. Bake at 350° until done (about 1½ hr.).

Mabel Hershberger
(Pie Baker)

Nevertheless he left not himself without witness, in that he did good, and gave us rain from heaven, and fruitful seasons, filling our hearts with food and gladness.

Acts 14:17

HAMBURGER CASSEROLE

2 lbs. hamburger	1 8 oz. pkg. fine noodles, cooked
1 c. chopped onions	1 10 oz. can cream of chicken soup
1 pt. peas	2 10 oz. cans cream of mushroom soup

Fry onions in oil, and add hamburger. Stir till all is heated, add peas and cooked noodles. Then add soups. Top with buttered bread crumbs. Bake ½ hr. at 350° then top with cheese. Then take another ½ hr.

Lizzie Ann Bontrager (Cook)

HAMBURGER AND CHEESE CASSEROLE

1 lb. hamburger	4 c. noodles uncooked
½ c. onion	8 oz pkg. cheese
16 oz. tomato sauce	1 c. cottage cheese
1 t. sugar	¼ c. sour cream
¾ t. salt	¼ c. green peppers
¼ t. garlic salt	¼ c. parmesan cheese
¼ t. pepper	

Combine onion and meat till brown. Stir in tomato sauce, sugar, salt, garlic salt, and pepper. Remove from heat. Meanwhile cook noodles and drain. Combine cheeses and sour cream and peppers. Spread half of noodles in a 11x7'' pan. Top with some of meat sauce and then top with all of cheese mixture. Add remaining noodles and meat sauce. Last top with parmesan cheese. Bake at 350° for ½ hour.

Betty A. Hershberger (Grill Cook)

I do not understand Christianity, I do not understand electricity, but I don't intend to sit in the dark until I do.

HAMBURGER PIE WITH ONION BISCUITS

1 med. onion (chopped)
1½ lb. ground beef
salt and pepper to taste
1 can tomato soup

Put hamburger in skillet, stir fine and fry. Add salt and pepper. Add soup and heat. Pour into greased baking dish.

Onion Biscuits

1½ c. sifted flour
1½ t. baking powder
½ t. salt
¼ c. shortening
1 egg (beaten)
⅓ c. milk
1 t. celery seed
½ c. onions (chopped)

Sift flour, salt and baking powder. Stir in celery seed, cut in shortening, mix and add onions. Combine egg and milk and add to flour mixture. Put out and use donut cutter. Then put donut rings on top of meat and bake until biscuits are done.

Mrs. Noah Hershberger

JACK POT CASSEROLE

1 lb. hamburger
2 T. fat
¼ c. onion
1.- 11 oz. can tomato soup
1½ c. water

1 can corn
¼ c. olives
1 c. cheese
½ (8 oz.) pkg. noodles
salt and pepper

Brown meat in fat, add onion, cook till golden brown. Add tomato soup, water and noodles. Cook until noodles are tender. Season to taste. Add corn, olives and cheese. Put in casserole and bake at 350° for 45 min.

Mrs. Freddie S. Bontrager

(Hund as gautze beisse net.)
"A barking dog seldom bites."

HUNGRY BOY'S CASSEROLE

Saute in large skillet:

1½ lbs. ground beef   ½ c. chopped onions
1 c. sliced celery   1 clove minced garlic (optional)
1 c. diced carrots

Simmer together while preparing biscuit dough.

¾ c. catsup   1 t. paprika
¾ c. water   1 lb. pork and beans
1 t. salt   1 lb. chick peas or lima beans

Biscuit Dough

2 c. sifted flour   4 T. cold shortening
3 t. baking powder   ¾ c. milk
½ t. salt

Sift dry ingredients together and cut in shortening. Add milk to make a soft dough. Place on a floured board and knead lightly a few seconds, using as little flour as possible on board. Spread 1 c. of vegetables, that were simmered together, on top of dough, rolled out. Roll up like a jelly roll and cut into 1 inch thick sections. Mix meat and remaining vegetables in baking dish, top with biscuits. Bake at 425° about 20 min.

Meda Bontrager (Waitress)

(Falle is nix, abers ufschte)
"To fall is nothing — but to get up"

LASAGNA CASSEROLE

1 lb. hamburger
2 cloves garlic or 1 t. garlic powder
1 - 8 oz. can tomato sauce
1 - #2 can tomatoes
8 oz. lasagna noodles, cooked
¾ lb. cottage cheese

½ lb. mozzarella cheese
2 T. salad oil
1½ t. salt
¼ t. oregano
½ c. parmesan cheese

Saute hamburger and garlic in oil. Add tomato sauce, tomatoes, salt and oregano. Simmer for 20 minutes. Cook noodles. Alternate layers of noodles, mozzarella cheese, cottage cheese, meat sauce and parmesan cheese, ending with sauce and parmesan cheese. Bake 375° for 1 hour. This fills a 13x9 inch loaf pan.

Sharon Nofziger (Waitress)

CHURCH SUPPER LASAGNA

1 pkg. 13 oz. lasagne noodles
2 T. salad oil
1 lb. ground beef
2 T. instant minced onion
¼ c. chopped celery
2 T. chopped parsley

¼ t. garlic powder
1½ t. salt
3 cans (8 oz. each) tomato sauce
4 sliced boiled eggs
1 lb. sliced Mozzarella cheese
1 pt. lg. curd cottage cheese

Cook noodles; rinse under cold water and drain. Heat oil and brown beef in large skillet. Stir in onion, parsley, celery, garlic powder, salt and tomato sauce. Cover and simmer 15 min. Reserve a few egg slices for garnish. In 13x9x2 inch oiled pan, layer about ⅓ each of the noodles, Mozzarella cheese, cottage cheese, eggs and meat sauce. Repeat layers twice ending with meat sauce. Bake in 350° oven 30 min. Garnish with egg slices. Makes 10-12 servings.

Mrs. Mary Arlene Bontrager (Waitress)

 We always have time enough — if we but use it right.

CHINESE "GLOB"

1 lb. hamburger, browned
1 c. diced celery
1 c. chopped onion
1¼ c. minute rice, uncooked

1 can cream of chicken soup
1 can cream of mushroom soup
1⅓ can of water
2 T. soy sauce

Mix all ingredients, bake at 350° for 45 min. Put a can of Chow Mein noodles on top and bake another 15 min. Serves 6 to 8.

Sue Mullet (Bread Baker)

MOCK CHOW MEIN CASSEROLE

2 lbs. of hamburger browned with
2 med. sized onions and
2 c. chopped celery

Place in casserole dish and add:

1 can chicken rice soup
1 can mushroom soup
1 c. rice (cooked)
1 c. water

2 T. soya sauce (drained)
1 can bean sprouts (drained)
1 can chop suey vegetables (drained)

Mix well and bake 1 hr. at 375°.
Last 10 min. cover with 1 can chow mein noodles and brown.

Mary Esther Miller (Waitress)

BALLARD BISCUITS

½ lb. hamburger
1 c. chopped onions
1 can mushroom soup
1 can chicken soup

1 pkg. (8 oz.) cream cheese
¼ c. milk
1 t. salt
¼ c. catsup

Fry the onion, hamburger and salt together till done. Add the two kinds of soup, cream cheese, milk and catsup. Pour in loaf pan and put in oven till bubbly. Remove from oven and put biscuits on top. Bake at 375° for 15 to 20 min.

Carolyn Beechy (Cook)

BURGER FOR A BUNCH

½ c. potato flakes	1 t. soda
2 T. melted butter	⅓ c. butter
2 c. flour	½ c. milk
1 T. sugar	¼ c. mayonnaise
1 t. cream of tartar	½ c. shredded cheese

Combine ¼ c. of potato flakes with melted butter and set aside. In a large mixing bowl combine ¼ c. potato flakes, flour, sugar, cream of tartar and soda. Cut in the butter until mixture resembles coarse crumbs. Add milk and mayonnaise, blend until a soft dough forms. Divide half and shape into balls. Roll out one ball on floured board to a 9 inch circle. Place on greased cookie sheet. Spread either hamburger or tuna filling to within ½ inch of edges, sprinkle with cheese. Roll out top crust and place on filling, seal edges, brush with milk, sprinkle with buttered potato flakes. Bake 20 to 25 min. at 375°

Ida Kauffman

HAMBURGER FILLING

1 lb. ground beef	1 egg
2 T. instant minced onion	¼ c. catsup
1 t. salt	1 T. mustard
¼ t. pepper	¼ c. relish
¾ c. potato flakes	

In a large skillet saute ground beef, onion, salt and pepper until brown. Add remaining ingredients and blend well.

Ida Kauffman

TUNA FILLING

2 cans tuna (7 oz.)	¾ c. potato flakes
drained and flaked	1 egg
2 T. minced onion	10½ oz. can of celery soup
¼ t. pepper	1 T. lemon juice

Ida Kauffman

SHRIMP CORN CASSEROLE

3 T. butter
3 T. flour
1½ c. milk
¾ c. cheese
2 cans whole kernel corn, drained

1 T. grated onion
½ t. celery seed
¼ t. onion salt
1 lb. shrimp
parsley

Melt the butter, stir in the flour and cheese. Stir until melted. Add rest of ingredients and bake at 350° for 30 min. Garnish with parsley.

Leora V. Kauffman (Purchasing)

RICE KRISPIE HOT DISH

6 c. rice krispies
1 onion, chopped fine
2 lbs. ground beef

2 cans chicken and rice soup
2 cans cream of mushroom soup

Mix altogether and bake 1 hr. in 350° oven. Serves 8 people.

Polly Yoder (Cook)

A hungry little boy was beginning to eat his dinner when his father reminded him that they hadn't prayed.
"We don't have to," said the little boy, "Mommy is a good cook!"

TUNA MACARONI

1 lb. elbow macaroni — cook according to directions. Pour part of the macaroni into a greased casserole dish. On top of this place cut up tuna chunks. Over this pour ⅓ can mushroom soup. Repeat procedure until dish is full. Pour milk over all until it covers the macaroni. Top with crumbs. Bake 1 hr. in moderate oven. Cheese slices may be put on top for last 10 min. of baking, instead of bread crumbs.

Esther Yoder (Cook)

TUNA MACARONI CASSEROLE

Add 2 c. macaroni to 2 qts. of water. Add 2 T. salt and stir. Cook 8 min. then drain. Do not rinse!

Add 4 T. butter or margarine and ¼ c. milk. Add ¾ c. cheese. Pour into baking dish and blend:

1 - 6½ oz. can tuna
1 c. cooked peas
2 T. finely chopped onions

Place in 350° oven for 20 min. or until thoroughly heated. I usually put more onions and peas in than what it says. If you wish, you can put in 1 diced pepper.

Edna Mae Schmucker (Dishwasher)

BAKED NOODLES AND TUNA WITH MUSHROOMS

½ lb. noodles	1 c. canned tuna
1½ qts. boiling water	1 10½ oz. can mushroom soup
1½ t. salt	¼ c. buttered crumbs

Cook noodles in salt water until tender and drain.
Flake the tuna with a fork.
Mix with noodles and mushroom soup.
Turn into a greased baking dish.
Sprinkle with crumbs and bake at 350° for 40 min.
Serves 6.

Sue Miller (Manager)

Parents spend the first part of a child's life urging him to walk and talk, and the rest of his childhood making him sit down and be quiet.

PORK CHOP CASSEROLE

2 c. noodles
½ c. catsup
4 lg. pork chops
1¼ c. water

salt and pepper to suit your taste
½ c. chopped onion
1 c. buttered and toasted bread crumbs

Cook noodles in boiling water for 8 min., drain and blanch. Brown pork chops on both sides. Fry until nearly done, season with salt and pepper. Mix onion, noodles, catsup. Put chops in buttered casserole, cover with noodle mixture and top with bread crumbs. Bake in oven at 350° for 45 min.

Lucy Eash (Cook)

SAUSAGE CASSEROLE

6 eggs
2 c. milk
6 slices white bread
1 t. salt

4 oz. mild cheese, cubed
1 t. dry mustard
1 lb. bulk sausage (not smoked)

Brown sausage and drain. Beat eggs; add mustard, milk, and salt. Mix in bread cubes, cheese and sausage. Refrigerate overnight. Bake at 350° for 45 min. Remove and let set a few minutes before serving.

Esther Hershberger

"Papa, are you growing taller all the time?"

"No my child. Why do you ask?"

"Cause the top of your head is poking up through your hair."

Be honest!

LAYERED MEAT AND VEGETABLE DISH

1 layer of stew meat cut up   1 layer of carrots sliced
1 layer of onions sliced   1 layer of potatoes sliced

Pour over tomato juice with 3 T. tapioca. Bake in 350° oven until it boils then 300° for 2 more hours.

Mildred Two (Cake Decorator)

YAMESETTA

1 lb. hamburger   1 can tomato soup
½ lb. noodles   2 slices of butter bread
1 can mushroom soup

Cover with slices of cheese.

Brown hamburger, soak noodles in boiling water for 10 min. Then put the following in. Mushroom soup, tomato soup, put brown hamburger in bottom of baking dish. Bake in 350° oven till done.

Betty Schrock (Angel Food Cakes)

"What dainty morsels rumors are. They are eaten with great relish!"
Proverbs 18:8

YA - MA - ZETTA

1½ lbs. hamburger, brown and season
1 pkg. noodles, cook till tender

In loaf pan put:

1 layer noodles
1 layer hamburger

In between put:

1 can tomato soup	1 c. diced celery
1 can vegetable soup	½ lb. velveeta cheese
1 can cream of chicken soup	1 can cream of mushroom soup

Bake 1 hr. in 375° oven.

Lydia Ann Miller (Cook)

YUMSETTI

1 lg. pkg. cooked noodles	2 qt. mushroom soup
3 lbs. hamburger,	1 can chicken or celery soup
fry in butter and 1 onion	1 c. sour cream
1 pt. peas	½ loaf bread, toasted in butter

Mix all the soup and cream together and pour over the other mixture in a large container. Mix and pour into roaster, and bake 1 hr. at 350°.

Idella Yoder (Bus Girl)

ZUCCHINI CASSEROLE

Wash and slice or dice one zucchini, boil till almost done. Drain. Brown 1 lb. hamburger and one onion; layer squash and meat. Put small can of tomato sauce over each layer plus ½ c. catsup. Sprinkle with bread crumbs and permesan cheese over top. Bake 30 min. at 350°.

Sharon Nofziger (Waitress)

MEAT LOAF

2½ lb. hamburger
2 eggs
salt
pepper

¼ lb. crackers (crumbled)
½ c. catsup
1 T. steak sauce
¼ c. onions

Mix and bake at 300° 2 to 2½ hr.

Lydia Ann Miller (Cook)

MEAT LOAF

2 lbs. ground beef
2 eggs
2½ c. dry bread crumbs
¾ c. ketchup

1 t. accent
½ c. warm water
1 pkg. onion soup mix

Mix thoroughly. Put into loaf pans. Cover with 2 strips of bacon. Pour 1 can of tomato paste over top. Bake for 1 hr. at 350°.

Katie Miller (Gift Shop)

SIMPLE MEAT LOAF

3 lbs. hamburger
2 eggs
4 c. bread crumbs

2 c. milk
3 t. salt
3 t. fine cut onions

Soak bread crumbs in milk, mix together and bake in rather slow oven uncovered. When nearly done add mixture of:
½ c. catsup
3 T. brown sugar
½ T. prepared mustard

Spread on top and bake a little longer.

Mattie Graber (Driver)

PIZZA MEAT LOAF

1½ c. canned pitted ripe olives
1½ lb. ground lean beef
1 (10½ oz.) canned pizza sauce
½ c. fine soft bread crumbs
2 T. chopped parsley

1 t. salt
½ t. garlic powder
½ t. pepper
½ c. grated cheddar cheese

Drain olives. Slice ½ cup set aside finely chopped remaining olives and mix with beef, ⅔ c. pizza sauce, crumbs, parsley, salt, garlic powder and pepper. Shape into an eight inch circle on pizza pan or shallow baking pan. Bake in moderate hot oven 375° for 15 min. Remove from oven; pour off any excess fat that may have accumulated in pan. Pour remaining pizza sauce over the top. Sprinkle with olive slices and cheese. Return to oven and bake 10-15 min. longer.

HAM LOAF

2 lbs. ground beef
2 lbs. ground ham
4 slices bread, cut up
¼ lb. soda crackers, crushed
1 small onion
2 cans tomato soup

4 eggs
1 t. salt
½ t. pepper
4 T. prepared mustard
2 T. worcestershire sauce

Mix well and add just enough milk to give a soft consistency. Bake in preheated oven at 350° for 2 hrs.

Rosa Borntrager (Cook)

Some people who say 'Our Father' on Sunday go around the rest of the week acting like orphans.

BAR-BE-QUE LOAF

1 lb. ground beef
¾ c. oatmeal
1 T. chopped onions

¾ c. milk
salt and pepper to suit your taste.

Fry in pan with grease.

Sauce

1 c. tomatoes
1 T. onions
½ T. chili powder

1½ t. vinegar
1½ t. sugar

Bake 1 hour in hot oven.

Lucy Eash (Cook)

ONION PATTIES

¾ c. flour
1 T. sugar
1 T. cornmeal
2½ c. finely chopped onion

2 t. baking powder
1 t. salt
¾ c. milk

Mix dry ingredients together, then add milk. Batter should be fairly thick. Add onions and mix thoroughly. Drop by spoonfuls into deep fat. Flatten slightly when you turn them.

Edna Nissley (Waitress)

SALMON PATTIES

1 - 1 lb. can salmon
1 egg
¾ c. milk
¾ c. cracker crumbs

1 t. chopped onions
1 T. lemon juice
1 T. flour

Mix. Melt oleo in skillet and brown on both sides before serving.

Sue Miller (Manager)

POOR MAN'S STEAK

2 lbs. hamburger
2 c. cracker crumbs
2 c. milk

Add onions, salt and pepper to taste. Mix and press in cookie sheet. Put in refrigerator overnight, then cut in squares and roll in flour. Then fry till brown. Put in roaster or casserole. Pour 1 - 10 oz. can mushroom soup (diluted with 1 can water) over meat. Bake in slow oven for 2 hrs.

Lizzie Ann Bontrager (Cook)

POOR MAN'S STEAK

1 lb. hamburger
1 c. milk
¼ t. pepper

1 c. cracker crumbs
1 t. salt
1 small onion chopped fine

Mix well and shape in a narrow loaf. Let it set for at least 8 hours, or overnight. Slice in pieces and fry till brown. Put slices in layers in a roaster and spread mushroom soup on each piece. Use 1 can of soup. Bake 1 hr. at 325°.

Sue Miller (Manager)

MEAT BALLS

1 lb. hamburger
½ c. bread crumbs
½ c. milk

1 small onion
salt and pepper

Form in balls, brown in a skillet and top with sauce and bake 1 hr. at 350°.

Sauce

1 c. catsup
2 T. mustard
2 T. vinegar

½ c. sugar
¾ t. salt

Serves 6 or 7.

Rosalie Bontrager (Waitress)

(Wammer flucht iberm fische fangt mer nix.)
"If you swear while fishing, you will not catch any fish."

MEAT BALLS IN GRAVY

4 lbs. hamburger	4 eggs
1 c. diced celery	3 t. salt
1 med. onion	1 t. pepper

Mix well. Make into balls. Brown in oleo or bacon grease. Arrange in roaster. Pour 1 can of mushroom soup, 1 can milk that has been heated, over meat balls. Bake for 45 min. Makes gravy right with meat balls. 350°

Mrs. Harley Miller (Miller's Orchard)
applebutter

BEEF AND RICE DINNER

2 T. oleo	1 t. salt
¼ c. chopped onions	¼ c. molasses
2 T. mustard	1 lb. ground beef
1 can tomatoes (1 lb.)	1 c. raw rice

Melt oleo in skillet, add onions and cook till tender, not brown. Add ground beef and half of salt. Brown beef breaking it in bits, while beef is browning. Combine molasses and mustard, add beef mixture with tomatoes, adding salt. Gradually add rice, cover, reduce heat and simmer 25-30 min. or till tender.

Mrs. Robert W. Miller

SAVORY RICE AND BEANS

½ c. chopped onion
½ t. thyme leaves, crushed
2 T. butter or margarine
1 can 16 oz. pork and beans with tomato sauce
1 can (13¾ oz.) chicken broth
1 c. diced celery
1 c. raw regular rice

In a saucepan cook onion with thyme in butter until tender. Add remaining ingredients. Bring to a boil, reduce heat, cover and simmer for 25 min. or until done. Stir occasionally. Makes about 5 cups or 8 servings.

Edna Nissley (Waitress)

SPANISH RICE

Melt 2 T. butter in frying pan.

Add:

½ c. dry rice   1 onion, minced
½ c. green pepper   ½ -¾ lb. ground beef

Let brown until rice is lightly browned and the meat golden, stirring to prevent over browning in spots.

Add:

1 c. water   ½ t. celery salt
¾ t. salt   1/8 t. pepper
1 - #2 can tomatoes

Let simmer slowly until all the liquid is absorbed and the rice is tender, about 30 min.

Betty Schrock (Angel Food Cakes)

SPANISH RICE

1 c. uncooked rice	¼ c. oleo or butter
1 med. onion thinly sliced	1 t. salt
½ med. green pepper diced	1 c. water
2 c. stewed tomatoes with juice	dash of pepper

Melt butter, or oleo in saucepan. Add onions, green peppers, and rice. Cook and stir over high heat until browned. Add tomatoes, water, salt, and pepper. Mix well. Bring gently to a boil. Cover tightly, lower heat and simmer 30 min. Serves 4-6.

Lydia Ann Miller (Cook)

 Seven prayerless days makes one weak.

SWEET AND SOUR PORK WITH RICE

2 T. cooking oil
1 lb. boneless pork, cut up in 1 in. cubes
1 can (15¼ oz.) pineapple chunks
½ c. light corn syrup
¼ c. vinegar
2 T. soy sauce
1 clove garlic, minced
2 T. cornstarch
½ c. red and green pepper slices

Heat cooking oil in skillet. Brown pork. Add next 5 ingredients. Bring to boil, simmer 10 min. or until done. Mix cornstarch and 2 T. water; add to pork with the peppers. Boil 2 min. stirring constantly. Serve over rice. Serves 4

Elsie Miller (Grill Cook)

ROASTED BEEF OR ROUND STEAK

Brown on both sides. Roast for about 1 hr. Then pour 1 can of mushroom soup over it. Bake till done. Will give a good broth for gravy and makes a delicious steak. Add salt and pepper as desired.

Mrs. Harley Miller (Miller's Orchard)
Applebutter

BAR-B-Q SANDWICHES

3 lbs. hamburger
3 lbs. beef (boiled) or 1 qt. chunk canned beef
1½ c. catsup
1 onion, chopped
¼ c. Worcestershire Sauce
¼ c. brown sugar
2 cans chicken gumbo soup
salt & pepper to taste

Brown hamburger and onion. Drain. Boil beef until tender and break into stringy bits. Combine beef and hamburger and add other ingredients. Simmer for 45 minutes to an hour over slow heat. This lets the flavor become savory throughout. This can be frozen for use later.

Esther Hershberger

CHIP CHOP HAM SANDWICHES

2 lb. chipped ham
3 T. brown sugar
1 c. catsup
¼ c. vinegar
1 c. water
1 T. worcestershire sauce

Cut meat into bite size pieces. Fry a little in butter. Sprinkle a little flour over it and add the rest of the ingredients. Simmer one hour at 250° F. Makes 15-20 delicious sandwiches.

Sue Miller (Manager)

BIG BOY CHEESE BURGERS

1 lb. ground beef	¼ c. finely chopped onion
1 t. salt	½ c. corn flake crumbs
½ t. pepper	⅓ c. evaporated milk
1 T. worcestershire sauce	hamburger buns
¼ c. catsup	american cheese

Mix ground beef, salt, pepper, worcestershire sauce, catsup, onion, cornflake crumbs, and evaporated milk in a 2 qt. bowl. Mix lightly but thoroughly. Spread the mixture on hamburger buns, covering to edges. Bake in oven at 400° for about 25 min. or until beef is done. Top with cheese the last few min. of baking.

Mary Esther Yoder (Pie Baker)

SLOPPY JOE

2½ lb. hamburger
1 med. onion, chopped
2½ T. worcestershire sauce
⅓ c. brown sugar
½ c. catsup
1 T. mustard
1 small can (10¾ oz.) cream of mushroom soup

Fry hamburger with salt, pepper and onions. Drain grease and add worcestershire sauce, sugar, catsup, mustard and mushroom soup. Heat and serve.

Sue Miller (Manager)

(Dr schaffmann is sei lu waert.)
"The laborer is worthy of his hire."

SLOPPY JOES

2 T. shortening
3 lbs. ground beef
3 large onions - chopped
1 T. salt
½ t. pepper

1 t. worcestershire sauce
¾ c. flour
1 bottle catsup
1¼ c. cooked tomatoes

Melt shortening in large, heavy skillet. Add beef and onions, fry until lightly browned. Add seasonings. Sprinkle flour over the hot mixture blending well. Add tomatoes and catsup. Let simmer for 10-15 min. till thickened.

Susie Bontreger (Grill Cook)

SLOPPY JOE SAUCE

1 peck tomatoes
12 onions
8 peppers (grind)
1 c. salt

Mix well and let stand 24 hrs. Drain well, and add:

6 c. sugar
4 c. vinegar
2 T. powdered mustard

Let stand a few hrs. and can cold, no need to seal.
Add some sauce to fried hamburger to suit taste.

Katie Ann Lehman (Cook)

"Soldiers of the cross do their best fighting on their knees!"

SUPPER SANDWICH BAKE

12 slices bread
butter or margarine
1 lb. lean ground beef
¼ c. ketchup
1 t. salt

6 frankfurters
2 medium onions, sliced
6 slices american cheese
2 beaten eggs
1 c. milk

Spread six slices bread with butter; arrange in bottom of greased 13x9x2 inch pan. Toast in moderate oven (350°) about 15 min. Combine beef, ketchup, and salt and spread over toast (⅓ c. per sandwich). Top with frankfurters cut almost in half lengthwise, onion, and cheese slices. Combine eggs and milk; pour over bread. Bake in moderate oven about 50 min. Makes 6 servings.

Debbie Oesch (Waitress)

MOCK PIZZA

1 t. oregano leaf
1 large onion
½ lb. cheese (cubed) any kind
1 lb. hamburger

1 can tomato soup (size 10¼ oz.)
½ can milk (size 10¼ oz.)
¼ lb. soda crackers (scant)

Brown hamburger and onions, put a layer of coarsely crumbled crackers into a well greased 9x13 inch pan. Spread cheese over crackers, then hamburger and onions mixture. Pour soup, milk and oregano leaf over the other mixture. No salt because crackers and cheese provide enough salt. Bake 30-45 min. in 350° oven.

Katie Ann Lehman (Cook)

 Do you run on batteries, or are you plugged in?

PIZZA CRUST

½ c. warm water
½ t. sugar
1½ c. sifted flour

1 pkg. active dry yeast
1 T. cooking oil or shortening
½ t. salt.

Dissolve yeast and sugar in warm water and let stand for 5 minutes. Stir in the salt and oil. Add flour and knead until it forms a smooth ball.

Let rise in a greased, covered bowl in a warm place (about 80°) until the dough ball has doubled in size.

Pat dough in a greased 12″ pizza pan, pressing the dough up on the sides. Put on the pizza sauce, cheese, and other toppings you desire. Bake 20-30 minutes at 400°.

Mrs. Ray E. (Susie) Miller
(Cook)

Who can find a virtuous woman? for her price is far above rubies.

The heart of her husband doth safely trust in her, so that he shall have no need of spoil.

She will do him good and not evil all the days of her life.

She seeketh wool, and flax, and worketh willingly with her hands.

She is like the merchants' ships; she bringeth her food from afar.

She riseth also while it is yet night, and giveth meat to her household, and a portion to her maidens.

Prov. 31:10-15

PIZZA CRUST

2 c. flour
2 t. baking powder
1 t. salt

¼ c. oil
⅔ c. milk

Combine dry ingredients. Add oil and milk, and stir together to form dough. Roll out on pizza sheet.

Karen Lehman (Waitress)

PIZZA DOUGH

4½ c. flour
½ t. pepper
½ t. salt

1 t. sugar
1¾ c. warm water
1 pkg. yeast

Mix yeast with dry ingredients. Add water to yeast mixture and mix together, only long enough to fully mix the dough. Let rise 1½ hrs. Can be frozen unbaked. Makes 3 large pizzas.

Esther Hershberger

PIZZA DOUGH

Dissolve 1 T. yeast in 2 T. lukewarm water.
Melt ½ c. oleo, add 1 t. salt and 1 t. sugar.
1 c. cold water, then add yeast and approximately 3 c. flour.

Mary Troyer (Dishwasher)

"The wages of sin is death, but by receiving Christ you can leave before payday."

PIZZA

Dough

Heat 1 c. milk with ¼ c. sugar, 4 T. butter, 1 t. salt until melted. Cool. Soften 1 pkg. yeast in 1/8 c. lukewarm water. Beat 1 egg, add to cooled milk and yeast and pour all at once in 4 c. flour. Beat till mixture is smooth. Let rise in a warm place.

1 pt. tomato juice   1 T. worcestershire sauce
½ t. oregano   1 garlic bud or garlic salt
1 t. prepared mustard

Cook mixture. Then spread on dough that has been spread in pizza pan. Add sausage, hamburger, cheese on to suit taste. Bake at 400° for 20 min.

Jeannie Yoder (Waitress)

EASY HOMEMADE PIZZA

Combine in bowl:

4 c. flour
6 t. baking powder
2 t. salt

Combine:

1⅓ c. milk
⅔ c. wesson oil
Pour all at once over flour mixture. Mix with fork, shape into ball. Knead until smooth. Roll out on greased cookie sheet.

Pizza Sauce

4 - 6 oz. cans tomato paste 1 t. garlic powder
⅔ c. wesson oil   1 t. salt
⅔ c. water   1 t. pepper
2 t. oregano

Put on top of crust, add hamburger, cheese or sausage, onoins or green peppers. Bake at 400° for 20-25 min. Makes 3 round sheets.

Polly Yoder (Cook)

PIZZA SAUCE

3 gal. tomato juice
a little parsley
3-4 med. size onions

Cook and add:

1 c. sugar	2 T. oregano
1 t. paprika	½ c. salt
2 T. garlic salt	1 T. chili powder

Make thick with 2 c. clear-jell. Cold pack 30 min.

Mrs. Leroy J. Yoder

PIZZA SAUCE

4 qt. tomato juice	1 t. black pepper
1 onion cut up fine	½ t. tabasco sauce
1 t. garlic salt	2 T. salt
1 t. oregano	2 heaping T. sugar

Cook ½ hr. Cold pack 20 min. Thicken with clear-jell if needed.

Mrs. Ray E. (Susie) Miller (Cook)

PIZZA SAUCE (to can)

1 qt. drained tomato juice	2 t. salt
½ c. wesson oil (optional)	1 large t. pepper
2 t. oregano	½ c. chopped onions
2 scant t. garlic powder	⅓ t. cloves

Boil all together. If thickening is needed use a little cornstarch or clear-jell. Put boiling sauce in cans and seal.

Katie Miller (Hostess)

BEEF LOG

5 lbs. hamburger
2½ t. pepper
5 rounded t. Morton's Tender Quick Salt
2½ t. garlic salt
2½ t. whole mustard seed
2 t. celery seed
1 t. dill seed
2½ t. liquid smoke

Mix in bowl, cover and refrigerate. Remove once a day for 3 days and knead well for 5 minutes. On the 4th day, divide into 6 sausage-like rolls. Lay rolls on drip pan of broiler pan and bake 9 hrs. at 160°. Turn once at 4½ hrs. At end of 9 hrs. remove and wrap in paper towels to remove grease. Wrap and store in refrigerator or freeze. It will keep in the refrigerator 3 weeks.

Esther Hershberger

BEEF LOG or SUMMER SAUSAGE

5 lbs. hamburger (not too lean)
2½ t. garlic salt
2½ t. mustard seed
2½ t. coarse pepper
2½ t. liquid smoke
5 t. (heaping Mortons Tender Quick salt)

Mix one day and knead every day for four days (knead about 5 min.). On the fifth day put into rolls and bake at 150° for 8 hrs. Bake 4 hrs., turn over and bake 4 more hrs. Bake on broiler rack so drippings can drain off. When done wrap in paper towel to soak up grease, then wrap in handiwrap. Slice thin and serve. Will freeze well.

Arlene Miller (Cook)
Mrs. Betty Graber (Waitress)

 What goes into your mind comes out of your mouth.

TO SUGAR CURE BEEF STEAK

To every 5 lb. steaks add:

1 t. salt petre	5 t. gran. sugar
1 t. black pepper	5 t. salt

Sprinkle some on each slice on each side of meat, wring a cloth out of vinegar and lay on top. Let stand 7 to 10 days in a cool place. Fry and can, add 1 c. water or beef broth to each quart. Boil 2½ hours.

Mrs. Tobias Hochstetler

HOMEMADE CHICKEN BOLOGNA

Cut off meat from chicken bones (as for hamburger). To 25 lbs. of fresh chicken and 1 lb. tender quick, and grind twice. Let set 24 hrs.

Add the following:

1 oz. black pepper	2 t. salt petre
½ c. sugar	2 t. garlic
3 T. liquid smoke	

Grind again.

Mix well, put in cans and process as for any other meat (cold pack 3 hrs.). This can also be put in cloth bags, cooked and put in freezer. Hamburger can also be used.

Lydia Mae Troyer (Cook)
Mrs. Robert W. Miller
Edma Mae Schmucker (DIshwasher)

Prayer should be the key of the day and the lock of the night.

BOLOGNA

60 lbs. beef
40 lbs. pork
3 lbs. tender quick
1½ oz. mace
4 or 5 drops smoke flavor to each lb. meat
3 oz. black pepper
1½ to 2 oz. garlic powder
1½ oz. ground corinder seed

Mix the tenderquick to the meat and grind with coarse plate. After grinding, spread meat in cool place and let cure 48 hrs. Then grind again 2 times thru fine plate (1/8 in. hole). Add the seasoning and mix well; 6 or 7 qts. of water added to meat makes mixing easier. This is good either frozen and fried in patties for sandwiches or canned as you would hamburger. To slice and use for sandwiches, either hot or cold. To can cold pack in hot water 2 to 3 hrs. Pressure cooker makes it too dry.

Mrs. Clara Miller

The secret or success in conversation is to be able to disagree without being disagreeable.

SMOKE BRINE FOR TURKEY

Put turkey in crock and cover with the following:

¼ lb. Morton's Tender Quick Salt)
3 T. liquid smoke
1 gal. water.

Cover and let stand 24 hrs.

Katie Ann Lehman (Cook)

Nowadays you'll find almost everything in the average American home . . . except the family.

BOLOGNA

To 25 lbs. fresh meat add 1 lb. tenderquick, and grind twice. Let set 24 hrs.

To 2 qts. water add:

1 oz. black pepper	½ c. brown sugar
½ oz. salt petre	1 t. garlic
1 soup spoon corinder	3 t. liquid smoke
7/8 oz. mace	

Mix and add all together to meat and grind again. Mix well and put in cans and process as any other meat (may add some pork if you like).

Mrs. Amos R. Miller

The wider the black band on the woolly worm the harder the winter.
If he's brown at both ends and orange in the middle, the winter will be mild.

HARVARD BEETS

1 qt. cooked cubed red beets

Drain and heat, then add: ¼ c. sugar
                                      2½ T. vinegar
Thicken with 1 T. cornstarch mixed with a little cold water.
Add beets and heat all together.

Sue Miller (Manager)

BROCCOLI CASSEROLE DISH

1 c. rice
1 c. mushroom soup
1 small jar cheese whiz
½ c. onion
½ c. celery

1 pkg. frozen chopped broccoli
¼ c. pimento
mushroom sauteed (optional)
½ c. almonds

Cook rice as directed. Add undiluted soup and cheese. Saute onions, celery and add. Pour boiling water over frozen broccoli, and drain. Add almonds, pimento, and broccoli to rice mixture. Put in casserole, and bake at 325° for 45 to 60 min. Serves 6 to 8.

Lavera Hooley (Waitress)

SCALLOPED CARROTS

12 carrots
4 T. butter
4 T. flour
2 c. onion
¼ t. salt

¼ t. celery salt
½ c. diced velveeta cheese
1 t. mustard
1/8 t. pepper
crushed potato chips

Dice carrots. Cook until tender but not too soft. Make white sauce with the butter, flour and milk. Add onion, salt, pepper, mustard and cheese. Pour carrots into casserole. Top with crushed potato chips. Bake at 350° for 45 min.

Esther Yoder (Cook)

CREAMED SWEET CORN

Mix 2 T. sugar with 2 t. flour, add to 4 T. melted butter.
Add this all together to 1 qt. heated sweet corn.
May add a pinch of salt.

Lydia Ann Miller (Cook)

FRIED CUCUMBERS

Beat 1 egg and add 1 c. milk. Peel and slice 2 or 3 cucumbers. Dip in about 2 c. cracker crumbs. Lay out to dry a little, then dip in egg-and-milk mixture and then again in cracker crumbs and fry. Sprinkle with salt to taste.

Esther Yoder (Cook)

COOKED MUSH

Heat 16 c. water to boiling point.
Add 4 c. corn meal and 2 to 3 T. salt, stirring while adding corn meal. Cook 20 to 30 minutes over low heat or on asbestos pad. Pour in 9x12 inch cake pan to cool. Let set over night. Slice in pieces and fry in deep fat fryer or skillet. 1 c. milk may be added to make it golden brown when frying.

Lydia Ann Miller (Cook)

 You can "take the day off," but you can't put it back.

TOMATOES SCALLOPED

Stew and season a quart of tomatoes to your taste; add some butter and a little chipped onion, then grated bread crumbs till like a stiff batter. Pour into buttered baking dish. Strew the top with more bread crumbs and bake 20 min.

This is nice as a breakfast dish or a dinner vegetable. If any are left over, make into round croquettes and fry nice and brown and you have another dish.

Leora V. Kauffman (Purchasing)

VEGETABLE CASSEROLE WITH HERBS

2 or 3 carrots
1 medium onion
1 small head cabbage
Bay leaves, caraway seed, or
    sweet basil (optional)

2 or 3 medium potatoes
1 lg. stalk celery
1/3 c. rice (brown or instant white)

Soak rice 2-3 hours. Drain and put in well-buttered casserole dish.

Slice the carrots, potatoes, and onions in thick slices and cut the celery stalk into fairly large pieces. Place these vegetables in layers on top of rice. Sprinkle each layer generously with dried minced garlic and season with pepper and parsley.

Add a pinch or two of bay leaves, caraway seed, or sweet basil. Lay cabbage wedges over top and pour the following mixture over all:

1/2 can cream of mushroom soup
1 T. beef base

3 T. sour cream
1½-2 c. water

Bake in 350° oven until vegetables and rice are done (about 1½ hours).

Leora V. Kauffman
(Purchasing)

BAKED POTATOES

½ lb. bacon
9 potatoes, boiled and mashed,
    seasoned with milk, butter,
    salt and pepper
3 slices lightly toasted bread

3 eggs, beaten
3 T. grated Parmesan cheese
1 medium onion, finely chopped
1 pkg. (8 oz.) grated Cheddar
    cheese

Fry bacon, then drain and dice it. Mix all ingredients thoroughly. Place in casserole dish and top with buttered bread crumbs and parsley. Bake at 350° until golden brown. Serves 6-8 people.

Barbara Bontrager (Cashier)

DUTCH POTATOES

Slice cooked potatoes and fry in butter or oleo. Sprinkle with flour, and add salt and pepper to your taste. When nice and brown add milk, enough to thicken. Simmer over low heat. Before serving top with shredded cheese. Keep simmering until cheese is melted.

Sue Miller (Manager)

GOLDEN PARMESAN POTATOES

6 large potatoes, raw
¼ c. sifted flour
¼ c. grated parmesan cheese
¾ t. salt

1/8 t. pepper
⅓ c. butter
chopped parsley

Pare and quarter potatoes. Combine flour, cheese, salt, and pepper in a bag. Moisten potatoes with water and shake a few at a time in the bag, coating potatoes well with cheese mixture. Melt butter in a 9x13 inch baking pan, place potatoes in pan. Bake at 375° for about 1 hr. turning once during baking when golden brown.

Mrs. Harley Miller (Miller's Orchard)
Applebutter

MASHED POTATO CAKES

5 c. mashed potatoes
2 eggs

15 individual crackers
enough flour to hold together

Beat well and fry in skillet with a little butter or oleo, till golden brown.

Sue Miller (Manager)

"Faults are like headlights on a car; those of others always seem more glaring then our own."

POTATOES ALA TIMBALE

Cook, drain and mash, pass through sieve 2 qts. of Irish potatoes.

Put in sauce pan with:

6 oz. butter	pepper
2 whole eggs	nutmeg
yolks of 6 eggs	a little sugar
salt	

Have a plain 2 qt. mold well buttered and sprinkled with fresh bread crumbs. Put potato mixture in it with a little more bread crumbs, and bits of butter on top. Bake for half an hour in a moderately hot oven. Pass a knife blade between potatoes and mold, turn over carefully and in a few minutes take the mold off.

Leora V. Kauffman (Purchasing)

STUFFED GREEN PEPPERS

Combine:

3 lb. ground meat	3 eggs
1½ c. instant rice	½ c. cracker meal
½ c. sugar	salt and pepper

Make into balls, filling 12 peppers.

Heat:

1 can (large) tomato juice
1 can tomato soup
1 small can water

Add meat balls and pepper. Simmer 1½ hrs. Add ¾ c. sugar. Simmer ½ hr. till done. Stir often as it will burn with that much sugar in it.

Mildred Two (Cake Decorator)

SWEET SOUR BAKED BEANS

8 slices of bacon
4 large onions, peeled and sliced
1 c. brown sugar
1 t. dry mustard

1 t. salt
½ t. garlic powder
½ c. cider vinegar

Brown bacon, drain and crumble. Empty frying pan and put onions and remaining ingredients in skillet and simmer covered 20 min. Meanwhile put in 3 qt. greased casserole:

2 - 15 oz. can dried lima beans, drained
1 - 1 lb. can green lima beans, drained
1 - 1 lb. can dark red kidney beans, drained
1 - 11 oz. can New English baked beans, undrained

Stir in onion mixture and bake at 350° 1 hr. Substitute 1 can green and 1 can wax beans for 1 of the lima beans. If you can't get the New English baked beans, add a little molasses. Can be frozen.

Mildred Two (Cake Decorator)

OLD FASHIONED OMELET

10 T. flour
1 t. salt

1½ qts. milk
6-7 eggs

Heat the skillet, add some shortening, mix eggs, flour, milk, and salt. Pour in skillet and bake. Can be baked in oven at about 350° or on top of stove turning occasionally.

Lydia Ann Miller (Cook)

If you see a friend without a smile,
Please give him one of yours.

BRUNCH

Serves 4 or more

2 c. toasted bread croutons
1 c. cheddar cheese, grated
4 eggs
2 c. milk

½ t. salt
¼ t. dry mustard
1/8 t. onion salt
bacon or sausage

Grease 11x7 inch casserole, beat eggs, milk and seasonings. Crumble bacon or sausage into eggs and milk mixture. Put croutons on bottom, next the grated cheese, pour egg mixture over it. Bake at 325° for 50 min.

LaVerda Miller (Waitress)

People who cough incessantly never seem to go to a doctor — they go to banquets, concerts, and church.

CHEESE SOUFFLE

8 slices of bread
1 lb. cheese, grated
6 eggs, beaten
¼ c. margarine
cubed ham, bacon or mushrooms

2 c. milk
1 T. onion salt
salt
pepper

Cube bread, put in bottom of casserole. Combine cheese, margarine and meat. Sprinkle over bread cubes. Mix eggs, milk and seasoning. Add over top of the other ingredients. Refrigerate overnite. Bake at 325° for 45 min.

Esther Nisley (Pie Baker)

Cakes
& Frostings

CAKE, THE INGREDIENTS

The sugar we use, the taste to please.
Shortening is needed, the toughness to ease.
The flour, we add to make it firm.
Also the eggs, under the same term.

Milk is required, for some that we make.
While this all depends on the quality of cake.
A dash of salt, the taste to improve.
Flavoring as desired, then may be used.

The leavening is added to make it light.
But recipes are required to do it right.
You prefer a nice cake, then you must trust.
The accurate measurements are also a must.

Katie Miller (Gift Shop)

A LOVE CAKE FOR MOTHER

1 can of "obedience"
several lbs. of "affection"
1 pt. of "neatness"
some holiday, birthday, and everyday "surprises"
1 can of "running errands" (willing brand)
1 box powdered "get up when I should"
1 bottle of "keep sunny all day long"
1 can of "pure thoughtfulness"

Mix well, bake in a hearty warm oven and serve to "mother" every day. She ought to have it in big slices.

Arlene Miller (Cook)

A different, good frosting is to mash a small boiled, hot, potato. Add vanilla and enough powdered sugar to have it spread nicely.

Add a t. of vinegar to cooked icing. This will keep it from cracking when it is cut.

Cakes & Frostings

AMERICAN BEAUTY CAKE

2 oz. red food coloring
2 T. cocoa
½ c. shortening (non-liquid)
1½ c. granulated sugar
2 eggs
1 c. buttermilk

½ t. salt
2½ c. sifted flour
1 t. vanilla
1 T. vinegar
1 t. baking soda

Mix food coloring with cocoa and let stand. Cream shortening with sugar. Add eggs and color mix. Beat very well. Add buttermilk, flour, salt, and vanilla, beat again. Remove from mixture and add vinegar and soda. Mix by hand. Pour in 2 greased and floured 9 inch pans. Bake 350°-375° for 30-35 min.

Icing

4 T. flour
1 c. milk
1 c. sugar
pinch salt

½ c. butter
½ c. shortening
2 t. vanilla

Mix flour and milk and cook until it thickens to consistency of cream. Mix well sugar, shortening and vanilla, and slightly cooked flour mixture and beat until fluffy.

ANGEL FOOD CAKE

1¾ c. egg whites
¼ t. salt

1½ t. cream of tartar
½ t. almond flavoring

Beat 1⅓ c. sugar in egg whites after they are beaten quite stiff. Fold in 1¼ c. sifted cake flour, sifted 3 times with ½ c. sugar. Bake 35 min. at 375° in tube pan.

Betty Schrock (Angel Food Cakes)

APPLE CAKE

3 eggs
1¾ c. sugar
1 c. salad oil
2 c. flour
1 t. soda

1 t. salt
1 t. cinnamon
2 c. chopped apples
1 c. chopped nuts if desired

Beat eggs, sugar, and salad oil. Sift flour, soda, salt, and cinnamon. Stir into first mixture until blended. Fold in apples and nuts. Bake in 13x9x2 inch greased pan at 350° for 40-50 min.

Topping

1 T. cornstarch
½ c. white sugar
½ c. brown sugar

1 c. water
1 stick margarine
1 t. vanilla

Mix cornstarch and sugars together. Add water, margarine and vanilla. Cook until thickened. Serve warm over square servings of cake. Amen.

Mrs. Harley Miller (Miller's Orchard)
Applebutter

 It will rain if leaves turn inside out or show their backs.

FRESH APPLE CAKE

½ c. shortening or oil
2 c. sugar
2 eggs
2 c. flour
2 t. soda
½-1 t. salt

2 t. cinnamon
½ t. nutmeg
4 c. chopped apples
1 c. nuts
½-1 c. cooked raisins

Cream shortening; add sugar and beat until fluffy. Add eggs; beat. Combine all dry ingredients and add to egg mixture. Stir in apples, nuts and raisins. Pour into greased 9x13 inch pan. Bake 45 min. at 350°.

Olive Bontrager (Cashier)

Are you fun to live with?

RAW SLICED APPLE CAKE

2 c. sliced peeled apples
1 c. sugar
1 egg
1 spoon (soup) cooking oil

Topping for Cake

1 c. flour
1 t. soda
1½ t. cinnamon
½ c. chopped nuts
(raisins optional)

½ c. brown sugar
¼ c. sugar
2 T. flour

1 c. water
¼ c. oleo
1 t. vanilla

Mix sugar and apples together, let set till melted. Add egg and oil and beat well. Add dry ingredients and pour in 9 inch square loaf pan and bake at 375° till done (approx. 40 min.). Immediately cover with cooked hot sauce or topping. May be topped with a little coconut. This cake will be real moist and won't dry out so quick. For a big loaf pan size double the recipe.

Mattie Graber (Driver)

APPLE BLOSSOM CAKE

1¼ c. oil
2 c. sugar
2 eggs
1 t. vanilla
1 c. chopped nuts
3 c. chopped apples peeled

3 c. flour
½ t. salt
1½ t. baking soda
1 t. cinnamon
1 t. nutmeg

Combine oil, sugar, eggs, and vanilla, and beat. Stir in nuts and peeled apples. Sift together flour, salt, baking soda, cinnamon, and nutmeg, and add to other ingredients. Bake in 9x13 in. greased pan at 350° 30-40 min.

Mix together and sprinkle on top of unbaked cake.

½ c. sugar
1 t. cinnamon
½ c. chopped nuts

Marilyn Bontreger (Waitress)

APPLE NUT CAKE

1¼ c. oil
2 c. sugar
3 eggs

Mix together.

3 c. flour
1 t. soda
1 t. salt
1 t. cinnamon

2 t. vanilla
3 c. cubed apples
1 c. nuts

Mix all ingredients together. Pour into a greased 9x13 in. pan and bake in 350° oven. Start in **cold** oven. 40-45 min.

Topping

1 stick butter
¼ c. Carnation milk
1 c. brown sugar

Bring to a boil and pour on cake while still warm.

Sharon Boley (Waitress)

APPLE-WALNUT CAKE

4 c. apples coarsely chopped
2 c. sugar
2 eggs
2 t. vanilla
2 c. all purpose flour

½ c. vegetable oil
2 t. baking soda
1½ to 2 t. cinnamon
1 t. salt
1 c. chopped walnuts

Combine apples and sugar - let stand. Beat eggs, and add oil and vanilla. Mix and sift flour and baking powder, cinnamon and salt. Stir in alternately with apple sugar mixture. Add walnuts. Pour into greased and floured 13x9x2 inch pan. Bake t 350° 45 min. to 1 hr., or until cake is done. Let stand in pan to cool. Ice with lemon butter icing or whipped cream.

Icing

1 stick of margarine, melted
1 c. brown sugar, packed
1 t. vanilla or lemon extract
½ c. evaporated milk or whole milk

Combine all, bring to rolling boil and pour over cooled cake.

Mildred Two (Cake Decorator)

APPLEBUTTER CAKE

½ c. shortening
1 c. sugar
4 eggs beaten
2½ c. flour
1½ t. soda
½ t. salt

1 t. cinnamon
½ t. cloves
½ t. nutmeg
1 c. sour or buttermilk
1 c. applebutter

Beat together shortening and sugar, add eggs. Sift together dry ingredients. Add alternately with milk, mix applebutter in well. Bake in greased loaf pan at 325° for 40 min. or until done.

Meda Bontrager (Waitress)

The human brain is a wonderful thing. It operates from the moment you're born until the first time you get up to make a public speech.

KNOBBY APPLE CAKE

1 c. sugar
½ c. shortening (I use Crisco.)
2 eggs
1½ c. sifted flour
1 t. soda

1 t. vanilla
2½ c. chopped apples
½ c. soaked raisins
½ c. pecans or nut meats

Cream sugar and shortening and eggs, beat well. Add the rest, mix well. Bake in 9x13x2 inch pan. Bake at 350° for 40-45 min.

Mrs. Harley Miller (Miller's Orchard)
Applebutter

KNOBBY APPLE CAKE

3 T. butter or oleo
1 egg beaten
½ t. nutmeg
1 t. baking soda
3 c. diced apples
1 t. vanilla

1 c. sugar
½ t. cinnamon
½ t. salt
1 c. sifted flour
¼ c. chopped nuts

Cream butter and sugar, add eggs, mix well. Sift dry ingredients together, add to creamed mixture. Stir in diced apples, nuts and vanilla. Pour in greased 8x8x2 inch pan. Bake at 350° for 40-45 min. Serve hot or cold.

Lydia Ann Miller (Cook)

A word of advice — don't give it.

BANANA CAKE

2 c. flour
½ t. baking powder
1¼ c. sugar
¼ c. sour cream

¾ t. soda
½ c. butter or shortening
2 eggs
1 c. mashed bananas

Sift flour, soda, and baking powder. Cream butter or shortening and sugar. Add eggs and beat well. Add sour cream to the bananas. Add the flour and banana mixtures alternately to the butter and sugar mixture. Bake in greased loaf pan at 375° oven, 30 min. or till done.

Lydia Ann Miller (Cook)

If you can't see the bright side, then polish the dull side; stop living on Grumble Corner; move to Thanksgiving Street!

BEST EVER CAKE

1 c. shortening
2 c. brown sugar
2 eggs
1 T. vinegar
2½ c. flour

2 t. soda
½ t. salt
½ c. cocoa
1 t. vanilla
1 c. hot water

Mix ingredients in order and pour into 9x13 in. pan. Bake at 350° for 40-45 min.

Esther Yoder (Cook)

BLACK MAGIC CAKE

1¾ c. flour
2 c. sugar
¾ c. Hershey's Cocoa®
2 t. baking soda
1 t. baking powder
½ c. vegetable oil

1 c. buttermilk or sour milk
1 t. vanilla
1 t. salt
2 eggs
1 c. strong black coffee, or
    2 t. instant coffee plus
    1 c. boiling water

Combine dry ingredients, then add the rest. Beat at medium speed for 2 minutes. Batter will be thin. Bake at 350° for 35-40 minutes in oblong pan. Moist!

Marilyn Bontrager (Waitress)

BUNDT CAKE

1 box yellow cake mix
1 box instant vanilla pudding
3 eggs
1 t. butter flavoring
2 t. cinnamon

¾ c. vegetable oil
¾ c. water
1 t. vanilla
⅓ c. sugar
⅓ c. nuts

Mix cake mix, oil, pudding, and water. Add 3 eggs and beat well at high speed for 5 minutes. Add vanilla and butter flavoring. Grease Bundt pan well with oleo. Mix sugar, cinnamon, and nuts. Put half of this mixture in the bottom of the pan. Add half of the cake batter, then the rest of the dry mixture, followed by the rest of the batter. Bake 40-50 minutes at 350°.

Mary Esther Miller
(Waitress)

When thou makest a dinner or a supper, call not thy friends, nor thy brethren, neither thy kinsmen, nor thy rich neighbours; lest they also bid thee again, and a recompence be made thee. But when thou makest a feast, call the poor, the maimed, the lame, the blind: And thou shalt be blessed; for they cannot recompense thee: for thou shalt be recompensed at the resurrection of the just.

Luke 14:12-14

BUTTERSCOTCH TORTE

6 eggs separated
1½ c. sugar
1 t. baking powder
2 t. vanilla

1 t. almond extract
2 c. graham cracker crumbs
1 c. chopped nuts

Beat egg yolks well, slowly adding sugar, then baking powder and flavoring. Mix well. Beat egg whites until they hold stiff peaks: Fold in yolk mixture, crumbs and nuts. Bake in slow oven 325° 30-35 min.

Sauce

Add ¼ c. water to ¼ c. melted butter in saucepan. Blend in 1 c. brown sugar and 1 T. flour. Add 1 egg well beaten, ¼ c. orange juice, and ½ t. vanilla. Mix well. Bring to boil and cook until thickened.

This can be served in the pan or fixed like date pudding.

Vera Slabach (Dishwasher)

CARROT CAKE

2 c. sugar
1½ c. mazola oil
4 eggs
2 c. sifted flour
1 t. cinnamon

2 t. soda
1 t. salt
3 c. finely grated carrots
½ c. chopped nuts

Using electric mixer, combine sugar and cooking oil. Add eggs and beat until well mixed. Mix in flour which has been sifted with cinnamon, salt, soda. Slowly mix in carrots and nuts. Pour into greased and floured pan. Bake in 300° oven for 35-40 min. or until done.

Icing

1 (8 oz.) cream cheese
1 lb. powdered sugar
½ c. coconut (optional)

2 t. vanilla
¼ lb. oleo

Soften cream cheese, blend in butter, then add all other ingredients. Keep in refrigerator.

Edna Nissley (Waitress)

CARROT CAKE

2 c. granulated sugar
1½ c. salad oil
4 eggs

Stir really well, then sift together:

2 c. cake flour
2 t. baking powder
2 t. soda

2 t. cinnamon
1 t. salt

Cream the two mixtures together, and fold in 3 c. raw grated carrots and ½ c. chopped nuts if desired. Bake 300° 35-40 min.

Elsie R. Miller (Grill Cook)

CARROT CAKE

2 c. sugar
4 eggs beaten
1 t. cinnamon
1½ c. mazola oil
2½ c. flour

2 t. soda
2 c. finely grated carrot
1 t. salt
½ c. nuts preferred

Combine sugar and oil. Add eggs, beat well. Mix in flour, sifted with cinnamon, soda, and salt. Slowly mix in carrots. Bake 40-60 min. Oven 300°.

Fannie Yoder (Cook)

CARROT PECAN CAKE

1½ c. salad oil
2 c. sugar
2 c. sifted flour
2 t. baking powder
1 t. soda

2 t. cinnamon
1 t. salt
4 eggs
3 c. grated raw carrots
1 c. finely chopped pecans

Bake in 9x13 in. pan at 325° 35-40 min.

Mary Troyer (Dishwasher)

CHOCOLATE TOWN SPECIAL CAKE

1¾ c. sugar
⅔ c. shortening
2 eggs
1 t. vanilla
2½ c. sifted cake flour

1½ t. baking soda
½ t. salt
1 c. buttermilk
½ c. cocoa
½ c. boiling water

Bake at 350° 20-30 min.

Lizzie Ann Bontrager (Cook)

3 HOLE CHOCOLATE CAKE

3 c. bread flour
2 c. sugar
3½ T. cocoa
2 t. soda
2 t. salt

2 t. vanilla
2 T. vinegar
⅔ c. vegetable oil
2 c. water

Sift flour, sugar, cocoa, soda and salt together. Put in oblong cake pan, make 3 holes and add the liquid ingredients and mix with a fork. Bake at 350° - takes a little longer than other cakes.

Mrs. Amos R. Miller

COLONIAL JIFFY CHOCOLATE CAKE

1 egg
1 c. sugar
½ c. cocoa
½ c. shortening
1 t. soda
½ t. baking powder

1½ c. flour
1 t. vanilla
½ t. salt
½ c. milk
½ c. boiling water

Put ingredients in bowl in order given. Beat with beater for 3 min. Put in greased 8x8x2 inch pan and bake in slow oven 325° for 40-50 min.

Lydia Ann Miller (Cook)
Edna Nissley (Waitress)

117

HAPPY VALLEY CHOCOLATE CAKE

3 c. flour
2 c. white sugar
2 t. baking soda
6 T. cocoa
1 t. salt

2 c. cold water
2 t. vanilla
2 t. vinegar
10 T. vegetable oil

Mix dry ingredients, add remaining ingredients. Bake at 375° for 35 min. or until done.

Katie Miller (Gift Shop)

CRAZY CAKE

2 eggs
½ c. cocoa
1 c. shortening
3½ c. flour
1 c. sour milk

2 t. soda
2 c. sugar
1 c. boiling water
Dash of salt

Mix all together and stir. Makes a large cake.
Bake 350°-375° 30-40 min.

Mary Troyer (Dishwasher)

CHOCOLATE PUDDING CAKE

1 c. shortening
2 c. sugar
2 eggs
1 t. vanilla
1 c. buttermilk or sour milk

3 c. flour
2 t. soda
1 t. salt
½ c. cocoa

Cream shortening and sugar together, add eggs then mix well, add the rest of ingredients. Pour into 13x9 inch cake pan.

Mix:
1½ c. sugar
2 T. cocoa
¾ to 1 c. hot water

Pour over cake batter, bake in 350° oven for 50-60 min. Nuts may be added to batter if desired.

Laura Miller (Grill Cook)

CHOCOLATE SHEET CAKE

Put in a large mixing bowl, 2 c. flour and 2 c. sugar, mix well.

Mix and melt together:

½ c. oleo   4 T. cocoa
½ c. crisco   add 1 c. of water and boil

Pour over flour and sugar mixture.

Add:

2 beaten eggs   ¼ t. salt
½ c. buttermilk or sour milk   1 t. vanilla
1 t. soda

Pour on a greased cookie sheet and bake at 350°.

Frosting

Bring to boil:

½ c. oleo
4 T. cocoa
6 T. milk

Pour over 1 lb. powdered sugar, beat well and add nuts if desired.
A delicious sheet cake.

Mrs. Harley Miller (Miller's Orchard)
Applebutter

 Some people carve their careers . . . others chisel.

TEXAS CAKE

2 c. flour
2 c. sugar
2 eggs

½ c. sour cream
½ t. soda
½ t. baking powder

Mix in mixer bowl.

Bring to a boil:

2 sticks margarine
1 c. water
2 T. cocoa, heaped

While hot, add to flour mixture. Cream well. Pour into greased and floured jelly roll pan. Bake 20 min. at 350°. Frost while warm.

Frosting

1 stick margarine
6 T. milk
2 T. cocoa

Bring to a boil. Remove from heat and add all at once to:

1 box powdered sugar
1 t. vanilla
1 c. chopped nuts

Esther Nisley (Pie Baker)

One pastor said that his church people would be the first to go up in the rapture. He gave his reason: "The Bible says: 'The dead in Christ shall rise first.' "

COOKIE SHEET CAKE

Sift together:

2 c. flour
2 c. sugar
½ t. salt

Melt and bring to brisk boil:

2 sticks oleo
1 c. water
4 T. cocoa (heaping)

Pour over dry ingredients.

Mix and add to above:

½ c. sour milk or buttermilk - sour cream
1 t. soda
1 t. vanilla
2 eggs
1 t. cinnamon (optional)

Pour into greased cookie sheet. Bake 20 min. at 400°.

Icing

1 stick oleo   5-6 T. milk
2-4 T. cocoa   1 t. vanilla

Mix and bring to a brisk boil and add:

1 box powdered sugar
1 c. nuts

Spread icing on hot cake when it comes from oven.

Mary Ann Schlabach (Waitress)
Mrs. Clara Ann Bontrager
Katie Cross (Waitress)
Mary Troyer (Dishwasher)
Jeannie Yoder (Waitress)

COCOA CAKE

2 c. brown sugar
½ c. butter, cream well or stir well with 2 eggs
½ c. sour milk
⅓ c. cocoa mixed in ½ c. warm water
1 level t. soda
2 c. flour

Mix sour milk alternately with flour and pour into 2 cake pans or 9x13 in. pan. Bake 325° 40-45 min.

Lucy Eash (Cook)

CHOCOLATE SALAD DRESSING CAKE

1 c. sugar
1 c. salad dressing
1 c. warm water
2 t. soda

1 t. vanilla
2 c. flour
4 T. cocoa
½ t. salt

Mix sugar and salad dressing together thoroughly. Then mix warm water and soda together and pour into first mixture. Add vanilla. Sift flour, cocoa, and salt and gradually add to other mixture. Pour into greased pan and bake in 350° oven 35-40 min.

Ida Miller (Cook)
Lydia Mae Troyer (Cook)

COFFEE CAKE

1 c. sugar   ⅓ c. butter
2 c. flour   salt   Cream together - take out ½ c.

Add:
1 c. milk
½ t. soda
1 t. baking powder   Pour into a 9x12 inch pan.

Sprinkle on top:

½ c. flour mixture   1 t. cinnamon
½ c. brown sugar   2 round T. butter or more

Bake at 350° about ½ hr.—until done.

Mildred Two (Cake Decorator)

122

BLUEBERRY COFFEE CAKE

⅔ c. sugar
⅓ c. liquid shortening
1 egg
½ c. milk
2 t. baking powder

½ t. salt
1½ c. flour
1 c. blueberries
1 c. nuts (optional)

Beat together sugar, shortening and egg. Sift baking powder, salt, flour and add alternately with milk. Add blueberries and nuts if desired. Pour into a 9 in. square pan.

Topping
½ c. brown sugar
½ c. butter
nuts (optional)

Spread on cake and bake at 350° for 25-30 min.

Meda Bontrager (Waitress)

DANISH COFFEE CAKE

1 stick soft margarine
1 c. flour

¼ t. salt
1 t. sugar

Add 2 T. water and mix like pie dough. Roll thin or pat out onto cookie sheet. Set aside.

Boil 1 stick oleo and 1 c. water, remove from heat and add 1 c. flour. Blend well. Beat in 3 eggs one at a time. Add 1 t. almond extract and 1 t. vanilla.

Spread onto crust (unbaked) and smooth out evenly. Bake 30 min. at 400°.

After cooled spread with butter frosting and sprinkle with nuts.

Dorothy Chupp (Cashier)

 Don't praise the bread before it's baked.

You can live without music, you can live without books,
But show me the one who can live without cooks.

CRUMB CAKE

2½ c. flour
½ c. shortening

1½ c. brown sugar
flavor with spice or extract

Mix as a pie dough and save out 1 c. crumbs. Mix 1 t. soda to 1 c. buttermilk or sour milk, mix well. Add this to remaining crumbs and mix well. Pour in greased 9x9 in. pan and sprinkle rest of crumbs over top and bake 350°-375° 25-30 min.

Lydia Ann Miller (Cook)

CRUMB CAKE

2½ c. flour
¾ t. salt

1½ c. brown sugar
½ c. shortening

Mix together into crumbs and save 1 c. of crumbs for top. Add 1 t. soda and 1 c. sour milk and add to rest of crumbs. Add vanilla and spice to taste.

½ t. cinnamon
½ t. cloves
1 t. vanilla

Bake in moderate oven 350°-375° 25-30 min.

Katie Miller (Gift Shop)

CRUMB CAKE

Mix together to form crumbs:

2 c. flour
1 c. sugar

½ c. lard
1 t. salt

Save ½ c. for topping.

Add:

1¼ c. sour milk
½ t. cinnamon
½ t. cloves

½ t. vanilla
½ t. lemon flavor
1 t. soda

Mix well, bake at 350° about 30 min. or till done.

Mrs. Marie Miller

The first twelve days after Christmas indicate what each month in the next year will be like.

GERMAN CREAM CAKE

1 c. butter
3 c. sugar
6 eggs
1 c. sour cream

3 c. flour
¼ t. baking powder
1½ t. vanilla

Cream the butter and blend in the sugar. Add the eggs one at a time and beat well after each addition. Blend in sour cream. Sift the flour with baking powder, and add to first mixture in 3 or 4 parts. Add vanilla, blend well. Bake at 350° for 1 hr. and 25 min. or until tests done. Remove from oven, let stand 5 min., invert and cool. When cool wrap in saran or foil and leave for 24 hrs. at room temp.

Leora V. Kauffman (Purchasing)

SELF FROSTING DATE CAKE

1 c. chopped dates
1½ c. boiling water
1 t. soda

Sprinkle soda over dates, then pour boiling water over all.

Cream:

½ c. shortening
2 beaten eggs
1 c. sugar

Then add to date mixture and sift:

2 c. flour
½ t. salt
¾ t. soda

Mix well and add to date mixture. Pour into a greased 9x13 inch pan. Spread with the following topping.

Topping

1 - 6 oz. pkg. chocolate chips
½ c. brown sugar
½ c. chopped nuts

Mix and sprinkle over cake. Bake at 350° for 35 min.

Fannie R. Yutzy (Pie Baker)

GRANDPA CAKE

2 c. brown sugar
½ c. butter beaten with 2 eggs
1 c. sour milk
1 t. soda
1 t. baking powder
3 c. flour
vanilla

Mix sour milk alternately with flour mixture and pour into cake pans. Bake 350° 30-40 min.

Lucy Eash (Cook)

GREEK BREAD (or cake)

2 c. sugar
1½ c. Mazola® oil
4 eggs
1 t. vanilla
3 c. sifted flour

1½ t. baking soda
½ t. cinnamon
1 can Milnot®
1 can almond filling
½ c. walnuts and raisins, chopped

Beat together the oil, sugar, and eggs. Beat well for about 20 minutes. Add the almond filling while still beating; then add the vanilla, flour, baking soda, and Milnot®. Still beating the batter, add nuts and raisins. Bake in a greased and floured angel-food cake pan for 1 hour and 15 minutes at 350°.

Sue Kauffman

HOT FUDGE SUNDAE CAKE

1 c. flour
2 t. cocoa
¼ t. salt
2 t. salad oil
1 c. nuts, chopped

¾ c. sugar
2 t. baking powder
½ c. milk
1 t. vanilla
1 c. brown sugar

Mix these ingredients except brown sugar and pour into a buttered cake pan. Sprinkle brown sugar and an additional ¼ c. cocoa on top of batter. Then pour 1⅓ c. hot water over batter to make the chocolate sauce. Bake 40 minutes at 350°. Delicious to eat with ice cream.

Lizzie Ann Bontrager (Cook)

HICKORY NUT CAKE

1½ c. sugar
whites of 4 eggs, beaten
1½ c. milk
½ c. butter
1 c. nuts, chopped

3 t. baking powder
3 c. flour
1 t. vanilla
½ c. lard

Cream together the butter, lard, and sugar. Add egg whites. Add dry ingredients alternately with milk. Fold in vanilla and nuts. Bake at 375° for 40-45 minutes.

Lucy Eash (Cook)

ITALIAN CREAM CAKE

1 stick oleo
½ c. crisco
2 c. sugar
5 egg yolks
2 c. flour
1 t. soda

1 c. buttermilk or sour milk
1 t. vanilla
1 c. chopped nuts
1 can coconut
5 egg whites (beaten stiff)

Cream oleo and crisco. Add sugar, then eggs; combine flour and soda, add to mixture alternately with milk. Stir in nuts, vanilla, and coconut. Fold in egg whites. Bake at 350° for 25-30 min.

Cream Cheese Frosting

½ stick oleo
1 - 8 oz. pkg. cream cheese

1 box powdered sugar
1 t. vanilla

Marilyn Bontreger (Waitress)

MILKY WAY CAKE

8 - 1¾ oz. Milky Ways
2 c. sugar
2½ c. flour
1¼ c. buttermilk
1 c. pecans

3 sticks butter
4 eggs well beaten
¼ t. baking soda
1 t. vanilla

Melt Milky Ways with 1 stick butter. Remove from fire and let cool. Cream remaining 2 sticks butter with sugar. Add eggs and cooled chocolate mixture. Sift flour and baking soda together. Alternately add flour and buttermilk to the batter blending well. Add vanilla and nuts. Grease and dust with powdered sugar. Three 9 inch pans or 1 loaf pan. Bake at 325° to 350° for 30-45 min.

Icing for Milky Way Cake

2½ c. sugar
1 stick butter
1 - 6 oz. pkg. chocolate chips

1 c. evaporated milk
1 c. marshmallow cream
1 c. pecans (chopped)

Combine sugar and evaporated milk. Cook to a soft ball stage. Remove from heat and add butter, marshmallow cream and chocolate chips. Stir until all have melted. Add pecans. Spread on cake, let cool.

Amanda Troyer (Waitress)

MOM'S LETTER CAKE

1 c. heavy sour cream
2 eggs
2 c. brown sugar

Beat very well, add:

½ c. sweet milk
1 t. soda
½ t. cream of tartar
2 c. pastry flour (sifted once before measuring)
½ c. walnut meats (sprinkle over top)

Bake in loaf pan at 350° for 25-30 min.

Lucy Eash (Cook)

OATMEAL CAKE

Pour 1¼ c. boiling water over 1 c. quick oatmeal, let stand 15 min.

Cream together:

1 c. butter
1 c. brown sugar
1 c. white sugar

Beat 2 eggs - mix all to oatmeal mixture and add:

1⅓ c. flour   1 t. cinnamon
½ t. salt   1 t. soda

Bake at 350°.

Topping

6 T. butter
⅔ c. brown sugar
1 c. coconut

Melt and put on cake when baked. Bake about 10 min. at 350°.

Laura Miller (Grill Cook)

OATMEAL CAKE

1 c. quick oatmeal
Pour 1¼ c. boiling water over oatmeal, let stand 15 min.

Cream:

½ c. oleo or shortening
1 c. brown sugar
1 c. white sugar

Add to oatmeal, also add:

2 beaten eggs

Sift together:

1⅓ c. flour   1 t. cinnamon
¼ t. salt   1 t. soda

Bake at 375° in 9x13 in. pan. Remove cake from oven when done and frost; return to oven until it browns. If watched carefully you can brown frosting in the broiler.

Frosting

6 T. butter or oleo, melted   1 c. coconut
⅔ c. brown sugar   Chopped nuts if desired
5 t. cream

Mary Ann Schlabach (Waitress)
Barbara Bontrager (Cashier)
Marilyn Joan Mast (Waitress)

Getting rid of ourself is like peeling an onion, layer by layer, and it is often a tearful process.

"Better is a dinner with herbs where love is, than a fatted ox and hatred with it."
Proverbs 15:17

OATMEAL CAKE

1 c. quick rolled oats
1¼ c. boiling water

Mix in bowl and let stand 20 min. Add:

1 c. granulated sugar
1 c. brown sugar
½ c. wesson oil or other vegetable oil
1 egg

Beat together well and add:

1⅓ c. flour   1 t. cinnamon
1 t. soda   1 t. nutmeg, if desired
½ t. salt

Pour into prepared 9x13 in. pans and bake for 35 min. at 350°.

While cake is still warm put on topping of:

5 T. butter or oleo   ¼ c. cream or milnot
1 c. brown sugar   ½ c. pecans
1 c. Bakers Angel flake coconut

Mix and put on cake and return to oven for 10 min.

Mary Esther Yoder (Pie Baker)
Karen Lehman (Waitress)
Lizzie Ann Bontrager (Cook)
Mattie Yoder (Grill Cook)
Lydia Ann Miller (Cook)
Betty Schrock (Angel Food Cakes)

MOCHA OATMEAL CAKE

2 T. instant coffee powder
1⅓ c. boiling water
1 c. oatmeal
  (quick or old fashioned uncooked)
¾ c. butter (softened)
1 c. white sugar
1 c. brown sugar (firmly packed)

2 eggs
1½ t. vanilla
2 c. sifted flour
1¼ t. soda
¾ t. salt
3 T. cocoa

Combine coffee powder and boiling water. Pour over oatmeal; stir to combine. Cover and let stand 20 min. Beat butter till creamy. Gradually add sugars, beating until fluffy. Beat in eggs, one at a time. Blend in vanilla. Add oatmeal mixture; blend well. Sift together flour, soda, salt, and cocoa. Add to creamed mixture. Blend well. Pour batter into greased and floured tube pan. Bake 50-55 min. at 350°.

Frosting for Mocha Oatmeal Cake

1½ T. butter or margarine (soft)
1 c. sugar
dash of salt

½ t. vanilla
1½ T. coffee powder

Beat butter until creamy. Add sugar, salt, vanilla, and coffee. Beat until smooth. Drizzle over cake. Nut meats may be sprinkled over frosting if desired.

Dorothy Chupp (Cashier)

PENNSYLVANIA SPONGE CAKE

4 eggs
1 T. cold water
1¼ c. sugar
pinch of salt

2 c. cake flour
2 t. baking powder
2 t. vanilla
12 T. hot water

Break and separate eggs; add cold water to yolks and beat well. Sift sugar, add to yolks and beat well, then beat egg whites until stiff and add to mixture. Add cake flour and salt in which baking powder has been sifted. Add vanilla. Last of all add water (just below boiling point). The batter will be quite thin.

Lydia Mae Troyer (Cook)

PUDDING CAKE

2½ c. flour -
  keep part to put nuts in
3 t. baking powder
1 c. sugar

½ t. salt
¼ t. nutmeg
¾ t. vanilla
1¼ c. milk

Bake in pan over syrup:

1 c. brown sugar
1¼ c. water

Cook together.

Melt 1 T. butter in cake pan, then add the boiling hot syrup, or bring to boil in pan, add dough and bake at 350° for 50-60 min.

Laura Miller (Grill Cook)

PUMPKIN CAKE ROLL

3 eggs
1 c. sugar
⅔ c. pumpkin
1 t. lemon juice
¾ c. flour
1 t. baking powder

2 t. cinnamon
1 t. ginger
½ t. nutmeg
½ t. salt
nuts

Filling

1 c. powdered sugar
8 oz. cream cheese, softened

4 T. butter
½ t. vanilla

Beat eggs on high speed for 5 min. Gradually beat in sugar. Stir in pumpkin and lemon juice. Combine flour with rest of dry ingredients. Fold into pumpkin. Spread in a 10x15 inch pan lined with waxed paper. Top with nuts. Bake for 10-15 min. at 375°. Do not overbake! Loosen edges with a knife then turn out onto a towel sprinkled with powdered sugar. Starting at a narrow end, roll towel and cake together. Beat filling together until fluffy. Spread over cake and roll. Chill.

Esther Hershberger

QUEEN ELIZABETH CAKE

Pour 1 c. boiling water over 1 c. chopped dates and add 1 t. soda. Let stand while the following is mixed in the usual manner.

1 c. sugar
1 beaten egg
½ c. butter
1½ c. sifted flour

1 t. vanilla
1⅓ t. salt
1 t. baking powder
½ c. nuts

Add these ingredients to above mixture and pour into a 9x12 inch pan. Bake for about 35 min. at 350°.

Icing

5 T. brown sugar
5 T. cream
2 T. butter

Boil for 3 min. Spread on cake and sprinkle with shredded coconut and nuts. This is supposed to be the only cake the queen makes herself.

Wilma Weaver (Waitress)

RAISIN COOKIE CAKE

1½ c. sugar
3½ c. flour
2 t. soda
2 beaten eggs
1 c. chocolate chips

½ c. shortening
2 t. nutmeg
½ t. salt
2 t. cinnamon
2 c. raisins (Cook in 1 c. water)

Dissolve soda in water raisins were cooked in. Add to the dough. Then spread dough on cookie sheet. Dough will be thick but try and spread rather thin. Bake in 9x13 in. pan 350° for 30 min. Frost with favorite frosting or dust with powdered sugar.

Fannie Yoder (Cook)

RED VELVET CAKE

½ c. shortening
1½ c. sugar
2 eggs
¼ c. red food color
1 t. salt
1 c. buttermilk

2¼ c. flour
2 t. soda
1 t. vanilla
1 T. vinegar
2 t. cocoa

Mix vinegar and soda, let stand. Cream sugar and shortening. Add eggs, mix well. Add cocoa, food color, then add buttermilk, salt and flour. Last add vinegar and soda mixture. Bake at 350° 20-30 min.

Frosting (very good)

1 c. milk
3 T. flour

Mix this together and cook till thick. Cool! Be sure it is cold before adding to rest of mixture.

Cream:

1 c. granulated sugar
1 stick oleo or butter

Whip together till fluffy like whipped cream. Either layer or loaf pan.

Mrs. Harley Miller (Miller's Orchard)
Applebutter

ROCKY MOUNTAIN CAKE

2 c. cake flour
1 T. baking powder
1 t. cinnamon
½ t. allspice
7 eggs separated
¾ c. cold water

1½ c. sugar
1 t. salt
½ t. nutmeg
½ t. ground cloves
½ c. salad oil
½ t. cream of tartar

Mix oil, sugar and egg yolks. Add flour and spices alternately with water. Fold in beaten egg whites. Bake at 375° 40-50 min.

Lydia Mae Troyer (Cook)

RHUBARB CAKE

This cake keeps well and is very moist.

1½ c. rhubarb (cut fine)
½ c. sugar
2 c. flour
½ c. vegetable oil
1 c. sour milk

1 t. cinnamon
1½ c. sugar
1 t. soda
1 t. vanilla
2 eggs, beaten

6 T. butter or oleo
⅔ c. brown sugar
1 c. nuts

1 c. coconut
¼ c. milk

Combine rhubarb with ½ c. sugar and set aside. Mix flour, sugar, oil, egg, sour milk, soda, cinnamon and vanilla. Add the rhubarb and sugar mixture. Stir until well blended. Pour into greased and floured 9x13 inch pan. Bake at 350° for 1 hr. or until done. Combine the last 5 ingredients and cook 3 min. Pour topping over cake while still warm.

Katie Cross (Waitress)

SHOOFLY CAKE

4 c. flour
2 c. brown sugar

¾ c. shortening
1 t. salt

Mix together like pie dough and reserve 1 c. of crumbs for topping.

Add to crumbs:

1 c. dark corn syrup
1 T. soda
2 c. boiling water

Mix syrup, water, and soda before adding to the crumbs. Grease and dust with flour a 9x13 inch cake pan. Spread batter evenly into pan and top with the 1 c. remaining crumbs. Bake at 350° for 45 min.

Dorothy Chupp (Cashier)

SKILLET CAKE

¾ c. sugar
3 T. butter
1 egg

½ c. sweet milk
1½ c. flour
2 t. baking powder

Cream together sugar, butter and beaten egg, sweet milk, flour into which baking powder has been sifted. Pour in skillet in which 1 c. brown sugar and 3 T. butter has been melted. Bake in moderate oven. When done turn on a plate bottom side up. Serve hot or cold with whipped cream or plain.

Polly Hershberger

SPICE CAKE

Sift together:
2 c. flour
1⅓ c. sugar
3½ t. baking powder
1 t. salt

1 t. cinnamon
½ t. nutmeg
¼ t. cloves

Add:

½ c. vegetable shortening
1 c. milk
1 t. vanilla

Beat 2 eggs and add. Makes a loaf cake. Bake 40-45 min. at 350°.

Mrs. Roseanna Chupp (Cook)

SPICE CAKE

1½ c. sugar
½ c. butter or lard
2 eggs
½ c. sour milk or buttermilk
½ c. applebutter
1 t. allspice

1 t. cinnamon
1 t. vanilla
1 t. soda
½ t. baking powder
1 t. cloves
2½ c. flour

Put spice in applebutter and fill cup with cold water.
Bake in 9x13 in pan 325°-350° 30-40 min.

Amanda Troyer (Waitress)

137

WARM SPICE CAKE

3 eggs
1½ c. sugar
½ c. butter
1 c. maple syrup
pinch of salt
1 t. soda

3 level t. baking powder
1 t. cloves
1 t. allspice
1 t. cinnamon
1 c. hot water
3 c. flour

Measure your flour before you sift it. Make the cups level.
Bake in 9x13 in. pan 325° 40-45 min.

Lucy Eash (Cook)

SUGAR PLUM SPICE CAKE

Sift together:

2½ c. flour
1 t. soda
¾ t. cinnamon

1 t. baking powder
¾ t. salt
¾ t. cloves

Cream together:

1 c. sugar
½ c. shortening   Mix with dry ingredients, then add:

⅔ c. brown sugar
2 eggs, beaten
1¼ c. sour milk

Pour into greased pan and bake 25-30 min. at 375°.

Lydia Ann Miller (Cook)
Katie Miller (Gift Shop)

Do you know where you can get a good chicken dinner for 15 cents?
"No, where?"
"At the feed store."

SOUR CREAM CAKE

Break 2 eggs in a cup; fill up with sour cream. Put in a mixing bowl, beat well with egg beater or mixer.

Add:

1 c. sugar
1 c. flour
1 t. soda, sifted in.

Add 1 t. vanilla. Mix and pour in 8x8 in. pan. Bake at 350° until done.

Lydia Ann Miller (Cook)

TWO EGG CAKE

1 c. sugar
½ c. shortening
2 eggs
1 c. milk

2 c. flour
2 t. baking powder
½ t. salt
1 t. vanilla

Mix ingredients in order given and bake 325°-350° 25-30 min.

Esther Yoder (Cook)

VELVET SUNSHINE CAKE

1½ c. sugar
1¼ c. cake flour
1½ c. water
½ t. salt

6 eggs beaten separately
½ t. cream of tartar
vanilla

Method: Sift flour once then measure. Sift together 4 times with salt and cream of tartar. Boil sugar and water together until it spins a long thread. Pour syrup slowly over beaten egg whites; continue beating using wire whip until mixture cools. Beat egg yolks with rotary egg beater until thick and lemon color. Fold egg yolks into egg white mixture, same as for angel food cake. Pour in a large ungreased tube cake pan and bake 1 hr. at 325°.

Lucy Eash (Cook)

139

UPSIDE DOWN PEACH CAKE

Melt ⅓ c. butter in heavy 10 inch skillet or baking dish. Sprinkle with ½ c. brown sugar. Arrange drained cooked peach slices over sugar.

Cake Batter

Beat 2 eggs until thick (5 min.). Gradually beat in ⅔ c. sugar. Beat in at once 6 T. peach juice, and 1 t. vanilla.

Sift together and beat in all at once:

1 c. flour
⅓ t. baking powder
¼ t. salt

Pour the batter over fruit and bake at 350° for 45 min. Invert on plate or cookie sheet. Serve warm with milk.

Mrs. Levi R. Miller

WACKY CAKE

1½ c. flour   1 t. baking soda
1 c. sugar   3 T. cocoa
½ t. salt

Sift this together three times and place in baking dish. Then make three holes. In one put 1 t. vinegar, in second put 1 t. vanilla, and in third put 5 T. melted shortening. Over all of this pour 1 c. of water. Mix well all the ingredients. Bake in 8x8 in. pan 35 min. at 350°.

Mary Troyer (Dishwasher)
Patty Kauffman (Grill Cook)

 If an ant builds its hill high it will be a hard winter.

WHITE CAKE

Sift together in bowl:

2-1/8 c. flour	1 t. salt
4 t. baking powder	1½ c. sugar

Add:

½ c. shortening
1 c. milk
1 t. vanilla

Beat for 2 min. and add ½ to ⅔ c. egg whites (unbeaten). Beat 2 min. more. Bake for 30-35 min. at 350°.

Laura Miller (Grill Cook)

WALNUT SPONGE CAKE

6 eggs, separated	1¼ c. sifted flour
½ c. cold water	¾ t. cream of tartar
1½ c. sugar	½ t. salt
½ t. vanilla	¾ c. walnuts chopped fine

Beat egg yolks until thick and lemon color. Add water and beat well. Beat in sugar and gradually add flavoring. Fold in flour, salt and nuts. Beat whites and cream of tartar till stiff, then fold into yolk mixture. Bake in tube pan at 325° for 60 min.

Lucy Eash (Cook)

"The Lord God made to grow every tree that is pleasant to the sight and good for food."   Genesis 2:9

 A good cook adds a pinch of love.

WATERMELON CAKE

whites of 4 eggs, beaten slightly	½ c. butter
1½ c. sugar	2 c. flour
½ c. sour milk	

Cream the butter and sugar well, together. Then add the milk with a scant ½ t. soda; immediately stir in a little flour, then a little egg white, alternately, till all flour and egg are added. Take another bowl and put in:

1½ c. pink sugar	scant t. soda
½ c. sour milk	2 c. flour

Flavor this pink batter with any flavoring you wish. Add ¼ lb. seeded raisins that have been floured. Spread bottom and sides of your cake pan with the white batter, fill up with the pink, save enough of the white to cover over the top. Bake in moderate oven till done. 350°-375° 20-30 min.

French Frosting

½ lb. powdered sugar	juice of 1 lemon
4 spoonfulls rose water or vanilla	whites of 2 eggs

Beat all together well. Apply to half cooled cake with pastry brush. Set in a cool oven to dry the icing. It will be set in 1 hr.

Leora V. Kauffman (Purchasing)

 We should always swap problems; everyone knows how to solve the other fellow's.

YUM YUM CAKE

½ c. butter
1 c. sugar
2 eggs separated
1 t. vanilla
1 t. baking powder

1 t. soda
1 t. salt
1 c. sour cream
2 c. sifted flour

Cream butter and sugar until light and fluffy. Add vanilla. Add egg yolks. Add sifted dry ingredients alternately with sour cream until smooth. Fold in stiffly beaten egg whites.

Spread half into greased 9x9 inch pan. Mix topping well and sprinkle half on top of batter. Cover with remainder of batter and sprinkle rest of topping. Bake at 350° approx. 40 min.

Topping

⅓ c. brown sugar
¼ c. sugar

1 c. chopped nuts
1 t. cinnamon

Mrs. Tobias Hochstetler

FROSTING FOR ANGEL FOOD CAKE

1 (8 oz.) pkg. cream cheese
2 c. powdered sugar

Mix well, beat 1 c. whipped topping until stiff and fold in cream cheese mixture. Put on angel food cake.

Sauce

1 T. instant clear-jel mixed with 2 T. sugar. Add to 1 pt. fresh strawberries, stirring constantly. Put on top of frosted cake and let drip over the sides. Very good and looks delicious.

Lydia Ann Miller (Cook)

"Faults are thick where love is thin."

More lives are ruined over a cup of coffee than by the shot of a gun.

CARAMELSCOTCH FROSTING

(Enough for 8x12x2 inch loaf cake)

1 c. brown sugar, packed	¼ t. salt
3 T. shortening	⅓ c. milk
2 T. butter or margarine	1½ c. powdered sugar, sifted

Put brown sugar, shortening, butter and salt in saucepan and cook over med. heat until mixture begins to bubble. Stir constantly. Add milk, mix well. Continue cooking over med. heat until mixture boils, stirring constantly. Boil vigorously 1 full min. Remove from heat and cool to lukewarm. Add powdered sugar all at once and beat until creamy and thick enough to spread. If it becomes too thick, soften over hot water.

Sharon Cemps

CREAM CHEESE FROSTING

3 oz. pkg. softened cream cheese	1 t. milk (more if needed)
6 T. soft margarine	¾ lb. powdered sugar
1 t. vanilla	

Katie Miller (Gift Shop)

The lazy man aims at nothing and generally hits it.

PINEAPPLE FROSTING

For angel food cake.

1 pkg. cool whip
1 box instant vanilla pudding
1 can crushed pineapple

Mix all together and spread on cake.

Katie Miller (Gift Shop)

FROSTING

½ c. butter   ¼ c. milk
1 c. brown sugar   1¾ to 2 c. powdered sugar

Melt butter and add sugar, boil 2 min., stirring constantly. Add milk and bring to boil, stirring constantly. Cool to lukewarm. Then add powdered sugar and if it gets too stiff, add a little hot water.

Ida Miller (Cook)

BAKE-ON CAKE ICING

10 T. brown sugar   6 T. melted butter
5 T. cream   ½ c. coconut
1 t. vanilla   ½ c. nut meats

Spread on hot cake and return to oven or place under broiler till it bubbles. Take out and cool.

Mrs. Leroy J. Yoder

A little bit of this and a little bit of that, makes you big and fat.

If you are thick and tired . . . cut out the rich food and late hours.

BROWN BEAUTY ICING

Set bowl in ice water. Mix thoroughly:

1⅓ c. sifted powdered sugar
¼ t. salt
¼ c. milk
¼ c. soft shortening

3 sq. (2 oz.) unsweetened
  choc. melted
1 t. vanilla

Add 1 egg (or 3 egg yolks); beat until thick enough to spread.

Lydia Ann Miller (Cook)

BUTTER ICING

⅓ c. soft butter
3 c. sifted confectioners sugar
3 T. cream

1½ t. vanilla
1 egg yolk

Blend butter and sugar. Stir in cream and vanilla. Add egg yolk.

Arlene Miller (Cook)

ICING

3 fun size Milky Way bars
½ c. butter or margarine
2 c. powdered sugar

1 t. vanilla
milk or cream

Melt bars in butter. Add sugar and vanilla. Blend in just enough milk or cream to make it spreadable.

Arlene Miller (Cook)

The Christian life is like tea. Its full strength comes out when it's in hot water!

FROSTING FOR CAKE AND FLOWERS

¾ c. crisco   2 t. clear vanilla
3 or 4 egg whites - room temp.   ½ t. cream of tartar
dash salt

Add ⅓ of 2 lb. box powdered sugar and beat well.

Add water and powdered sugar until right for decorating or frosting. Water for frosting about ½ c. depending on egg whites. Less of course for decorating. Keep covered at all times, as it will harden. Do not put cake under Tupperware until after cut.

Mildred Two (Cake Decorator)

LACE ICING

Flow frosting for cake decorating

1 egg white - break up with fork and add:
6 to 9 oz. of sieved powdered sugar - 1 T. at a time, stirring well with each addition. Then add: 2 drops lemon juice or acetic acid 10% solution and 1 T. white corn syrup.

Hand mix this until perfect consistency to put through the small Australian tube - pipe pattern of lace or figures on paper and do tube work on waxpaper over design. To flow - dilute with water until when held and dropped back into dish - it will disappear on count of ten.

Mildred Two (Cake Decorator)

ROYAL ICING FOR MAKING FLOWERS

For cake decorating

3 egg whites, room temp.   1 lb. powdered sugar
½ t. cream of tartar   1 t. clear vanilla

Beat 5 to 7 min. until right consistency. Keep covered at all times as it dries very quickly.

Mildred Two (Cake Decorator)

Cookies, Snacks & Candies

A HAPPY HOME RECIPE

4 cups of love
2 cups of loyalty
3 cups of forgiveness
1 cup of friendship

5 Tablespoons of hope
2 Tablespoons of tenderness
4 quarts of faith
1 barrel of laughter

Take love and loyalty, mix thoroughly with faith. Blend it with tenderness, kindness, and understanding, add friendship and hope, sprinkle abundantly with laughter. Bake it with sunshine. Serve daily with generous helpings.

Katie Miller (Gift Shop)

Measure shortening before molasses in baking and it will not stick to cup.

To keep cookies soft, put a slice of bread in cookie jar.

Katie Miller (Gift Shop)

Cookies, Snacks & Candies

ANGEL CRISP COOKIES

1 c. brown sugar
1 c. white sugar
1 c. lard
1 c. butter
2 eggs

2 t. vanilla
2 t. soda
1 t. salt
2 t. cream of tartar
4 c. flour

Roll in balls. Dip balls in cold water, then dip in white sugar. Flatten and bake.

Katie Miller (Gift Shop)

ANGEL CRISP COOKIES

½ c. white sugar
½ c. brown sugar
1 c. shortening, half butter
1 t. soda

1 t. cream of tartar
1 egg
½ t. salt
2½ c. flour

Make little balls on cookie sheet, press down with fork, bake at 425° 8-10 min.

Lucy Eash (Cook)

God grinds the axes He means to use!

Good character — like good soup is usually homemade.

FRESH APPLE COOKIES

½ c. shortening
1⅓ c. brown sugar
1 egg
⅓ c. sweet or sour milk
1 t. soda
½ t. nutmeg
½ t. salt

1 t. cinnamon
1 t. cloves
1 c. unpared finely
 chopped apples
1 c. raisins
½ c. nuts
2 c. flour

Mix all together and drop on baking sheets, bake 400° for 11-14 min.

Sue Mullet (Bread Baker)

GLAZED APPLE COOKIES

½ c. shortening
1⅓ c. brown sugar
1 egg
2 c. Robin Hood flour
1 t. soda
½ t. salt
1 t. cinnamon

1 t. cloves
½ t. nutmeg
½ c. nuts
1 c. raisins (if desired)
¼ c. apple juice or milk
1 c. chopped raw apples

Beat sugar, shortening and egg, and cream well. Add ½ dry ingredients, nuts, apples, raisins, blend in juice or milk. Add remaining flour mixture. Mix well. Drop on cookie sheet and bake in 400° oven. Spread with glaze while cookies are hot.

Vanilla Glaze

1½ c. powdered sugar
2½ T. apple juice or milk

1 T. butter
salt and vanilla

Martha Otto (Pie Baker)

GLAZED APPLE COOKIES

2 eggs	1 t. cinnamon
2½ c. brown sugar	1 t. cloves
1 c. lard	½ c. milk
1 t. salt	4 c. flour
2 t. soda	2 c. apples, chopped

Bake 375°-400

Icing

3 c. powdered sugar	3 T. milk
1 T. butter	flavoring

Put on while cookies are still warm.

Lydia Mae Troyer (Cook)

When butterflies migrate early, winter will be early, or when they gather in bunches in the air, winter is coming soon.

BLACK WALNUT COOKIES

1 c. shortening	4 c. brown sugar
½ c. oleo	4 eggs
1 t. salt	2 t. soda
2 t. cinnamon	1 t. nutmeg
6 c. sifted flour	1 c. walnuts

Cream shortening, oleo, and sugar; add eggs and salt. Sift together: soda, cinnamon, nutmeg, and flour. Add to shortening mixture. Mix well, add nuts. Drop on greased cookie sheet. Press down with glass bottom dipped in white sugar. Bake in 350° oven till done.

Mrs. Urias U. Miller

BUTTER COOKIES

1 lb. butter	2 c. powdered sugar

Cream together until creamy. Add:

2 t. vanilla	5 c. flour
1 egg, beaten	½ t. salt

Mix well and put them in cookie press and press them on cookie sheets and bake in 375° oven.

Mrs. Harley Miller (Miller's Orchard)
Applebutter

BUTTERMILK COOKIES

2½ c. white sugar	2½ t. soda
2½ c. brown sugar	(dissolved in buttermilk)
2½ c. lard	5 t. baking powder
5 eggs, beaten	2½ t. vanilla
3 c. buttermilk	1 t. nutmeg
	8½ c. flour

Drop on cookie sheets and bake at 425°.

Katie Miller (Gift Shop)

BUTTERSCOTCH COOKIES WITH ICING

½ c. shortening	1 t. soda
1½ c. brown sugar	½ t. baking powder
2 eggs	½ t. salt
1 t. vanilla	1 c. sour cream
2½ c. flour	⅔ c. nuts, optional

Cream shortening and sugar. Add vanilla and eggs. Sift together dry ingredients. Then add alternately with sour cream. Add nuts. Use ½ c. more flour if needed. Drop by teaspoonfuls on cookie sheet. Bake 10 min. at 350°. Cool and frost with the following.

Brown Butter Icing

¼ c. butter (no substitute)	3 T. boiling water
2 c. powdered sugar	½ t. vanilla

Brown butter, pour over sugar, then add water and vanilla. Mix.

Arlene Miller (Cook)

CHOCOLATE CHIP COOKIES

2 c. shortening
1½ c. brown sugar
1½ c. white sugar
3 eggs
2 T. water

1½ t. soda
2 t. vanilla
5¼ c. flour
1 pkg. chocolate chips
½ c. walnuts

Bake 325° 8-10 min.

Katie Miller (Gift Shop)

CHOCOLATE CHIP - PEANUT BUTTER CRISPS

½ c. granulated sugar
½ c. brown sugar, packed
½ c. peanut butter
¼ c. butter or margarine, softened
¼ c. shortening

1 egg
½ t. baking soda
½ t. baking powder
4 c. rice crispies
1 pkg. (6 oz.) chocolate chips*

Heat oven to 325°. Mix sugars, peanut butter, shortening, egg, baking soda, and baking powder in 4 qt. bowl thoroughly. Stir in cereal and chocolate chips. Shape dough slightly by rounded T. Place about 2 inches apart on ungreased cookie sheet. Bake until golden, 10-12 min. Cool 5 min. before removing from cookie sheet. About 3½ dozen.

*You can substitute butterscotch chips for chocolate chips.

Mary Ann Schlabach (Waitress)

CHOCOLATE CRINKLES

1 c. cocoa
½ c. vegetable oil
2 c. white sugar
4 eggs

2 c. flour
2 t. baking powder
2 t. vanilla
½ t. salt

Mix oil, cocoa, and sugar. Blend in eggs one at a time. Add vanilla, flour, baking powder, and salt. Chill dough several hours or overnight. Drop by spoonfuls or make balls, roll in powdered sugar, then in granulated sugar. Bake in 350° oven very slowly. Will easily burn at bottom if oven is too hot.

Lizzie Ann Bontrager (Cook)

CHURCH COOKIES

4 c. white sugar
4 c. lard (3 c. lard and 1 c. oleo)
6 to 8 eggs
2 T. vanilla
1 T. lemon flavor
13 c. flour

4 c. brown sugar
4 c. sour milk
4 t. soda
8 t. baking powder
pinch of salt

Esther Nisley (Pie Baker)

AUNT SUSIE'S CHURCH COOKIES

2 tincups lard
4 tincups sugar (3 c. brown and 1 c. white sugar)
2 tincups sour or buttermilk or sweet milk with vinegar added
8 or 9 eggs
6 soup spoons baking powder
3 or 4 soup spoons soda
salt
flavor and flour

Mrs. Clara Ann Bontrager

COFFEE COOKIES

4 c. brown sugar
2 c. lard
4 eggs
2 t. vanilla

2 t. soda
6 t. baking powder
2 c. coffee (as you drink it)
8 c. all-purpose flour

These may either be dropped or rolled and cut. Top with frosting made of:

1 c. confectioners sugar
a pinch of salt

1½ T. Spry or Crisco
½ t. vanilla

Gradually add 3 or 4 T. boiling water.

Lizzie Ann Bontrager (Cook)

"Most of the people who are now buying margarine, have seen butter days."

COFFEE COOKIES

3 c. brown sugar
1½ c. lard
1½ c. coffee, a little strong
1½ t. soda

4½ t. baking powder
vanilla and lemon
4 eggs
6 c. flour

Mix coffee and flour alternately. Bake 350°.

Lucy Eash (Cook)

COWBOY COOKIES

2 c. flour
½ t. baking powder
1 t. soda
½ t. salt
1 c. shortening
1 c. brown sugar

1 c. white sugar
2 eggs
2 c. rolled oats
1 - 6 oz. semi-sweet choc. pieces
1 t. vanilla

Sift together flour, baking powder, soda and salt and set aside. Blend shortening and sugars, add beaten eggs. Add flour mixture, oats, chocolate pieces and vanilla. Drop from teaspoon onto lightly greased baking sheet. Bake at 350°.

Susie Bontrager (Grill Cook)

There are only two ways to handle a woman and nobody knows either of them.

DATE PINWHEELS

Cook together until thick, about 10 min.

2½ c. dates
1 c. water
1 c. sugar
cool and add 1 c. nuts

Mix together:

1 c. shortening   ½ t. salt
4 c. flour   ½ t. soda
2 c. brown sugar   3 eggs, beaten

Divide dough into 2 parts, roll out and spread with date mixture. Roll up like jelly roll and chill several hours, slice ¼ in. thick and bake at 375° for 10-12 min.

Laura Miller (Grill Cook)

DROP COOKIES

2 c. brown sugar   2 eggs
1 c. shortening   1 c. seedless raisins
½ c. water   4 c. flour
½ c. coffee   3 t. baking powder
1 t. soda   vanilla

Bake 350° 8-10 min.

Lydia Mae Troyer (Cook)

"Don't just be good — be good for something!"

BROWN DROP COOKIES

Cream

1 c. shortening
2 c. sugar

Add and cream well:

3 eggs

Sift together:

4 c. flour	1 t. cinnamon
¼ t. salt	1 t. cloves
1 t. soda	1/8 t. ginger

Add flour mixture to creamed things with 1 c. sour milk. Sprinkle 1 c. nuts and 1 c. raisins with a little flour. Add last and drop on floured cookie sheets and bake 350°-375°.

Sue Mullet (Bread Baker)

If you enjoyed today, it wasn't wasted.

NUT DROP COOKIE

A soft cookie.

1 c. brown sugar	1 t. soda
1 c. granulated sugar	1 t. cinnamon
1 c. butter and lard	1 t. cloves
1 c. sour milk	1 c. chopped nuts
3 eggs, beaten	1 c. chocolate chips
3½ to 4 c. flour (just according what kind of flour used)	

Mix in given order an bake at 425°.

Mary Ann Schlabach (Waitress)

MOM'S DUTCH COOKIES

Beat together until well creamed:

3 c. lard	4 eggs
2½ c. brown sugar	3 c. milk*
2½ c. white sugar	3 t. vanilla

*sour milk or buttermilk makes cookies delicious

Sift together:

11 c. flour	3 t. soda
6 t. baking powder	3 t. salt

Add milk and dry ingredients alternately, beating well after each addition. Drop on greased cookie sheet and bake at 350°.

Dorothy Chupp (Hostess)

 "In the tears of His saints God sees a rainbow."

GOLDEN NUGGETS

Here is an old recipe found in an old cookbook that we really enjoy. Here's how it goes.

Take a measuring cup and spoon in half a cup of sugar. Then from a karo syrup bottle measure enough to make another half cup. Place the two ingredients in a saucepan on a very low flame. Stir constantly until dissolved. Next add a cup of peanut butter. (We prefer chunky.) Stir until well blended. Remove pan from stove and pour over 3½ c. corn flakes. Blend until well coated but not crushed. Let pan cool slightly until the heat does not scorch the hands. Then take portions about the size of hen eggs and work rapidly into balls.

Jeannie Yoder (Waitress)

HEART COOKIES

6 T. butter
6 T. confectioners sugar
1 egg yolk

1 t. vanilla
1 c. sifted flour

Cream the butter and sugar together thoroughly. Add the egg yolk and vanilla, beat well. Stir in flour. On a lightly floured surface, roll out dough 1/8 to ¼ inch thick. Cut out hearts with a cookie cutter and place on an ungreased cookie sheet. Decorate with candy sugar. Bake for 15-30 min. at 350°.

Esther Yoder (Cook)

HONEY CHIP COOKIES

⅓ c. shortening
½ c. honey
1 egg
1 t. vanilla
½ c. nuts

1¼ c. flour
½ t. soda
¼ t. salt
1 small pkg. chocolate chips

Drop by teaspoon on greased cookie sheet. Bake at 375° for 12-15 min.

Karen Lehman (Waitress)

MAPLE SYRUP COOKIES

1¾ c. syrup
¾ c. lard
3 eggs, beaten
3 c. flour, heaping
¼ t. salt
1 t. cinnamon

1 t. soda
1 t. baking powder, rounded
½ t. nutmeg
½ t. cloves
½ c. nutmeats
½ c. chocolate chips

Mix syrup, lard, eggs, and salt. Sift dry ingredients and add. Stir in nutmeats and chocolate chips. Drop by teaspoon on to greased cookie sheet. Bake in a moderate oven until they spring back when lightly touched. Bake 350°-375°

Elsie R. Miller (Grill Cook)

MEXICAN CINNAMON COOKIES

1 c. butter, softened
½ c. confectioners sugar
2¼ c. flour, sifted
1 t. cinnamon

1 t. vanilla
¼ t. salt
½ c. granulated sugar
½ t. cinnamon

Beat butter at high speed till light and fluffy. At a low speed beat in sugar, flour, cinnamon, vanilla and salt until just combined. Dough will be stiff. Shape into ball, and wrap in waxed paper. Refrigerate 30 min. Preheat oven to 400°. Ball cookies into ¾ in. balls, or if flat cookies are preferred, 1 in. balls, ¼ in. thick. Place 1½ in. apart on ungreased sheets. Bake 10 min. until cookies are golden or brown. Combine sugar and cinnamon. Roll hot cookies in mixture. Place on wire rack to cool. Sprinkle with remaining mixture. 5 doz. ball cookies, 3 doz. flat.

Meda Bontrager (Waitress)

"It's a wise husband who will buy his wife such fine china that she won't trust him to wash the dishes."

SOFT MOLASSES COOKIES

1 c. shortening
1 c. sugar
1 c. molasses
1 c. sour milk
6 c. flour
3 t. soda

2 t. ginger
2 t. cinnamon
½ t. cloves
½ t. nutmeg
1 t. salt

Cream shortening and sugar, and add molasses. Sift flour with soda, spices, and salt. Add alternately with sour milk to form soft dough. Chill in refrigerator overnite or several hrs. Roll out about ½ inch thick, cut and put raisin in center of each cookie. Bake in 350° oven, 5-8 min. Put icing on, made with powdered sugar, milk, shortening, and vanilla.

Mrs. Harley Miller (Miller's Orchard)
Applebutter

SOFT MOLASSES COOKIES

1 c. shortening
1 c. sugar
1 egg
½ c. light molasses
1 t. vinegar

3 c. flour
1½ t. cinnamon
1 t. ginger
2 t. baking powder
salt

Bake at 350° 15 min.

Millie Whetstone (Cook)

MONSTER COOKIES

12 eggs
4 c. brown sugar
4 c. white sugar
1 T. vanilla
1 T. karo

8 t. soda
1 lb. margarine
3 lbs. peanut butter
18 c. oatmeal (2 lb. 10 oz.)
1 lb. M&Ms or 1 lb. butterscotch
   chips

Mix in order given, in large fix and mix bowl. Bake 12 min. at 325°.
Let set 1 or 2 min. before removing from pan. Makes a 30 lb. lard
can full of cookies.

Mrs. Freddie S. Bontrager
Edna Mae Schmucker (Dishwasher)
Mrs. Ray E. (Susie) Miller (Cook)

OATMEAL COOKIES

1 c. shortening
1 c. brown sugar
2 eggs, beaten
1 t. vanilla
1 c. white sugar

1½ c. flour
1 t. soda
1 t. salt
3 c. oatmeal, Quick Mothers
½ c. nuts

Sift flour, soda and salt together. Mix all ingredients in order given.
Chill thoroughly. Fix in rolls to chill, slice and bake at 375°.

Mrs. David Perry Yoder

OATMEAL COOKIES

½ c. butter
½ c. lard
3 c. brown sugar
4 eggs, beaten
2 t. vanilla
3 c. reg. oatmeal
¾ c. milk

1 c. raisins
 (soak in water beforehand)
3½ c. flour
4 t. baking powder
4 t. cinnamon
1 t. salt
1 t. soda
1 t. cloves

Drop on greased cookie sheets. Bake 350°-375°

Mrs. Calvin H. Yoder

OATMEAL COOKIES

1 c. brown sugar
1 c. white sugar
2 c. oatmeal
1 c. cooked raisins
1 c. lard, pour lard hot over above
1 t. cinnamon
1 t. cloves

½ c. hot water, with 1 t. soda
3 eggs
4 T. sweet milk
3 c. flour
2 t. baking powder
½ c. walnuts

Lucy Eash (Cook)

OATMEAL COOKIES

2½ lbs. sugar (½ brn., ½ wh.)
1¼ lbs. lard
1 lb. raisins
1 lb. quick oats
4 eggs

1 pt. buttermilk
2 lbs. flour
3 t. soda
1 t. salt
2½ t. nutmeg

Drop on cookie sheet and bake 350°-375°

Katie Miller (Gift Shop)

164

SOFT OATMEAL COOKIES

Part 1

2 c. soft sugar	4 eggs
1 c. butter and lard	1 t. cinnamon
3 c. flour	2 t. baking powder

Part 2

4 c. rolled oats	1 t. soda
1 c. hot water	½ t. salt
1 box raisins	

Cream sugar and shortening and add eggs. Cook water and raisins together, till raisins are soft. Add to shortening and eggs while hot. Then add the rest of the ingredients. Put in 350° oven, bake till done.

Wilma Weaver (Waitress)

It's the little things that bother
And put us on the rack
You can sit upon a mountain
But you can't sit on a tack.

PEANUT BUTTER COOKIES

1 c. brown sugar
1 c. white sugar
1 c. lard
2 eggs

½ c. peanut butter
1¾ t. soda
1 t. vanilla
3½ c. flour

Mix sugar and lard, then peanut butter and eggs. Then flour and soda sifted together. Form balls with dough and press with fork. Bake 375° 10-15 min.

Amanda Troyer (Waitress)

PRIDE OF IOWA COOKIES

1 c. brown sugar
1 c. white sugar
1 c. shortening
2 eggs
2 c. flour
½ t. salt

1 t. soda
1 t baking powder
1 t. vanilla
1 c. coconut or a pkg. choc. chips
3 c. quick rolled oats
½ c. chopped nuts

Blend sugar and shortening, add beaten eggs. Sift together dry ingredients and add to first mixture. Stir in vanilla, coconut, oats and nuts. Mix well and drop by teaspoonfuls on greased cookie sheet. Flatten with bottom of glass. Bake at 375° until light brown (about 8 min.).

Mrs. Harley Miller (Miller's Orchard)
Applebutter

A sure cure for a man who is too lazy to think for himself is marriage.

PUFF COOKIES

1 c. shortening, rounded
1 c. brown sugar
½ c. white sugar
2 eggs
2¾ c. flour

1 t. cream of tartar
1 t. soda
1 t. baking powder
½ t. salt

Mix shortening, sugar and eggs thoroughly. Mix dry ingredients and add to sugar mixture. Chill. Form into balls and roll into mixture of 2 T. sugar and 2 t. cinnamon or add chocolate chips. Press balls with hand. Bake at 375° for 8-10 min. on ungreased cookie sheet. Cookies will puff, then settle down and look crinkly.

Katie Miller (Gift Shop)

RANGER COOKIES

1 c. granulated sugar
1 c. brown sugar
1 c. shortening, scant
2 eggs and 2 T. water
2 c. flour (pastry)
2 c. quick oats

2 c. rice crispies
1 c. coconut
1 t. soda
½ t. baking powder
½ t. salt
1 c. nut meats, cut up

Cream sugar and shortening, add beaten eggs, beat until fluffy. Add soda in water (above). Add dry mixture, and drop by teaspoonfuls on cookie sheet. Bake at 375°. Do not over bake.

Mattie Graber (Driver)

RUSSIAN TEA CAKES

1 c. soft butter
½ c. powdered sugar
1 t. vanilla

2¼ c. flour (sifted Gold Medal)
¼ t. salt
¾ c. finely chopped nuts

Mix together butter, powdered sugar, and vanilla.
Add flour, salt and nuts. Chill dough.   Roll in 1 in. balls.
Place 2½ in. apart on ungreased cookie sheet.
Bake until set but not brown (10-12 min.) at 400°F.
While still warm roll in powdered sugar.
Cool and roll in powdered sugar again.

Katie Miller (Gift Shop)

SLICE O' SPICE OVERNIGHT COOKIES

3 c. sifted flour
1 t. soda

1 t. cream of tartar
½ t. salt

Sift together, and set aside.

½ c. butter
½ c. shortening
2 c. brown sugar, firmly packed

2 eggs, unbeaten
1 t. vanilla
1 c. quick-cooking oats

Cream butter, shortening and sugar. Blend in eggs and vanilla. Stir in dry ingredients. Add rolled oats, and mix well. Shape dough into rolls and chill. When ready to bake, roll each cookie in:

½ c. sugar
4 t. cinnamon

Elsie R. Miller (Grill Cook)

Three months after the first Katydid begins "hollerin'," the first killing frost will come.

SNICKERDOODLES

1 c. shortening
1½ c. sugar
2 eggs
2¾ c. flour
1 t. cream of tartar

1 t. salt
1 t. soda
2 t. cinnamon
2 T. sugar

Mix together shortening, sugar, egg, stir in flour, cream of tartar, soda and salt. Chill dough. Roll in balls the size of walnuts. Roll in mixture of cinnamon and sugar. Place 2 in. apart on ungreased cookie sheets. Bake 8-10 min. in 350° oven.

Joyce Bechtel (Waitress)

SOUR CREAM COOKIES

1 c. brown sugar	1 t. salt
1 c. white sugar	4 t. baking powder
1 c. shortening	4½ c. flour
2 or 3 eggs	2 t. vanilla or lemon
1 c. sour cream	1 c. nuts can be added
2 t. soda	

Mix ingredients together well, then drop by teaspoonfuls on cookie sheet and bake 10-12 min. at 375°.

Mrs. Harley Miller (Miller's Orchard)
Applebutter

SPICY SUGAR COOKIES

Cream together:

1½ c. shortening
2 c. sugar

Blend in:

2 eggs	4 T. milk
½ c. honey	2 t. vanilla

Sift together and add to creamed mixture:

5 c. sifted flour	1½ t. nutmeg
3 t. soda	2 t. cinnamon
1½ t. salt	

Beat and mix well, chill, then form dough into small balls. Dip one side in milk, then in sugar. Place on greased cookie sheet, sugar side up. Bake 375° 8-10 min. Let stand briefly before removing from cookie sheet. This is a good chewy cookie.

Mrs. Roseanna Chupp (Cook)

SPICY COOKIES

2 c. brown sugar
1 c. shortening
1 c. plus 4 T. milk
3 eggs, beaten
2 t. baking powder
2 t. soda

1 t. cinnamon
¼ t. cloves
1 t. vanilla
4 c. flour
1 c. chopped nuts

Mix in order given, drop by teaspoon on greased cookie sheet, and bake at 375° for 10 min. Ice while warm.

Icing

Brown 6 T. butter and add 3 T. hot water and 1 t. vanilla. Thicken with powdered sugar until thick enough to spread.

Betty A. Hershberger (Grill Cook)

SPICY COOKIES

2 c. brown sugar
1 c. shortening
1 c. plus 4 T. milk
3 eggs, beaten
2 t. baking powder
2 t. soda

1 t. cinnamon
¼ t. cloves
1 t. vanilla
4 c. flour
1 c. chopped nuts

Mix in order drop cookies. Bake 10 min. at 375°. Frost while still warm.

Frosting

1 stick butter
1 c. brown sugar
¼ c. sweet milk

Boil together 2 min. Cool and add powdered sugar and 1/8 t. cinnamon. Stir until smooth.

Amanda Troyer (Waitress)

SQUASH COOKIES

1 c. lard
2 c. squash or pumpkin, cooked
2 c. sugar
4¼ c. flour, sifted

2 t. soda
2 t. baking powder
2 t. cinnamon

Cream together lard, pumpkin or squash and sugar. Then sift in dry ingredients. Add 1 c. nuts, raisins or dates. Frost while still warm. Bake at 350°.

LaVerda Miller (Waitress)

SUGAR COOKIES

2 c. wesson oil
3 c. sugar
4 eggs
2 c. buttermilk

2 t. soda
6 c. flour (Robin Hood)
6 t. baking powder
3 t. vanilla

Mix oil, sugar, egg; add soda to buttermilk, add flour, baking powder, vanilla; drop on lightly greased cookie sheet. Sprinkle cookies with sugar (color or plain). Bake at 350° for 12 min.

Ida Miller (Cook)

SUGAR COOKIES

1½ c. sugar
1 c. shortening

1 c. milk
3 eggs

Sift together:

5 t. baking powder
1 t. soda

¼ t. salt
4 c. flour

Bake 350° 10-12 min.

Wilma Weaver (Waitress)

SUGAR COOKIES

5 c. sugar	6 t. baking powder
4 eggs	3 t. soda
3 c. milk	1 t. vanilla
3 c. lard	10-12 c. flour

Combine all ingredients but flour. Mix well, add flour. Can be cut or dropped by tsp., then flatten with bottom of glass, dipped in sugar. Bake at 375°. Do not over bake.

Mrs. Marie Miller

DELICIOUS SUGAR COOKIES

Mix ingredients in order:

8 c. sugar	2 c. melted margarine
2 t. vanilla	8 c. flour
8 eggs	8 t. baking powder
4 c. buttermilk	¾ c. sweet cream
4 t. soda	2 T. salt
2 c. melted lard	8 c. flour

Drop onto greased cookie sheets and bake at 375° or 400°F. Do not over bake. Cookie is done before the top is brown.

Dorothy Chupp (Hostess)

DROP SUGAR COOKIES (AMISH CHURCH COOKIES)

1 c. brown sugar	2 t. soda
½ c. white sugar	2 t. baking powder
1 c. shortening	2 t. vanilla
1 c. sweet milk	4 c. flour
1 t. salt	3 eggs, well beaten

Drop on a cookie sheet and flatten a little. Sprinkle sugar on top. Bake 375°.

Mrs. Harley Miller (Miller's Orchard)
Applebutter

OLDTIME BROWN SUGAR COOKIES

4 c. flour
1 t. baking powder
1 t. soda
2 c. brown sugar
3 eggs

1 c. shortening
½ t. vanilla
½ t. lemon flavoring
½ t. salt

Roll in balls and flatten. Bake at 375° 10-12 min.

Lydia Mae Troyer (Cook)

Why does everyone want to be in the front of the bus, the rear of the church, and the middle of the road?

VANILLA WAFERS

⅔ c. margarine
½ c. sugar
1 egg
2 T. milk

1 t. vanilla
1¼ c. flour
1 t. baking powder

Cream margarine, sugar, egg, milk, and vanilla. Beat in flour and baking powder. Blend well. Drop teaspoonfuls on well greased cookie sheet. Bake at 350° for 10 min.

Lizzie Ann Bontrager (Cook)

"God seldom speaks to a man — while man himself is talking."

WHOOPIE PIES

Sandwich cookies.

1 c. lard
2 eggs
1 t. salt
¾ c. cocoa

2 c. sugar
5 c. flour
1 c. sour milk

Last of all add:

1 c. hot water
2 t. soda

Mix lard, eggs, sugar, set aside. Mix flour, salt, cocoa together. add to lard mixture alternately with sour milk. Last add hot water and soda. Drop on cookie sheet and bake 375° 10-12 min. Frost when cool and stick 2 together.

Filling

Beat 2 egg whites
Add:

2 T. vanilla
4 T. milk
2 c. powdered sugar

Beat thoroughly.
Add 2 more c. powdered sugar and 1 c. crisco. Mix well.

Lydia Ann Miller (Cook)

The winter will be hard if hickory nuts have a heavy shell, or if pine cones open early.

WHOOPIE PIES

1½ c. lard	1½ c. cocoa
3 c. sugar	6 c. flour
1½ c. sour milk	3 t. salt
3 eggs	3 t. soda
3 t. vanilla	1½ c. water

Cream lard and sugar. Add well beaten eggs, sour milk, vanilla, flour, cocoa and salt. Dissolve soda in hot water, add to mixture. Drop by teaspoonfuls. Bake 375° 10-12 min.

Filling

3 egg whites	6 T. milk
3 t. vanilla	3 c. powdered sugar
1½ c. crisco	

Beat egg whites until stiff. Add vanilla, milk, crisco and powdered sugar. Mix well, put filling between 2 cookies.

Esther Nisley (Pie Baker)

WHOOPIE PIES

Beat together:

1 c. shortening	1 c. sour milk
2 c. sugar	2 t. soda *dissolved in*
2 eggs	1 c. hot water
5 c. flour	1½ t. salt
½ c. cocoa	

Mix together flour, salt and cocoa and alternate flour, milk and water when mixing to the first part. Drop by spoonfuls and bake 375° 10-12 min.

Frosting

2 egg whites, beaten	2 T. milk
2 t. vanilla	2 c. powdered sugar

Mix together.

1 c. oleo, softened
2 c. powdered sugar

Mix and add to first part. Frost cookies and make sandwiches.

Mrs. Ruth Elaine Miller (Waitress)

175

BRIDGE MIX BARS

3 T. oleo
½ pkg. white cake mix or 1 pkg. of the Jiffy Mix
1½ c. miniature marshmallows
1 - 6 oz. pkg. chocolate chips
1 c. flaked coconut
1 c. nuts, chopped
1 can Eagle Brand Milk

Heat oven to 350°. Melt butter in a 9x13 in. pan, spread evenly. Sprinkle dry cake mix over batter. Add: marshmallows, choc. chips, coconut and nuts. Pour Eagle Brand Milk evenly on top. Bake 30 min. or until golden brown.

Betty A. Hershberger (Grill Cook)

BROWNIES

4 oz. unsweetened chocolate	1¼ c. flour
⅔ c. shortening	1 t. baking powder
2 c. sugar	1 t. salt
4 eggs	1 c. nuts
1 t. vanilla	

Melt chocolate and shortening in large saucepan over low heat. Remove from heat. Mix in sugar, eggs and vanilla. Stir in remaining ingredients. Bake at 350° for 30 min. or until brownies start to pull away from sides of pan. Do not over bake. Cool slightly, cut into bars.

Karen Lehman (Waitress)

BROWNIES

2 c. white sugar	4 eggs, beaten
¾ c. butter and lard combined	1 t. vanilla
1 c. all purpose flour	½ c. cocoa
½ t. salt	½ c. chopped nuts
1 t. baking powder	

Cream sugar and shortening well. Add eggs, vanilla and nuts. Sift together flour, salt, cocoa and baking powder. Add to sugar mixture and stir well. Bake in greased and floured 8x14 in. pan at 350°. Sprinkle the top with powdered sugar.

Joyce Bechtel (Waitress)

BROWNIES

⅔ c. sifted flour	½ t. baking powder
¼ t. salt	⅓ c. shortening
2 sq. Bakers Unsweetened Choc.	2 eggs, well beaten
½ c. chopped walnuts	1 t. vanilla
1 c. sugar	

Sift flour once, measure, add baking powder and salt. Melt shortening and chocolate over hot water. Add sugar gradually to eggs, beating thoroughly. Add melted chocolate mixture, and stir to blend. Add flour and mix well, add nuts and vanilla. Bake in 8x8x2 in. square pan at 350° 20 min. or till done. Cut in squares and serve.

Lydia Ann Miller (Cook)

GRANDMA'S BROWNIES

18 graham crackers (rolled fine)	1 small bag choc. chips
1 can Eagle Brand milk	1 t. vanilla

Bake at 350°, for 30 min. Let cool and roll in powdered sugar. 12x8 inch pan.

Dawn Swihart (Waitress)

MARSHMALLOW BROWNIES

¾ c. shortening or oleo	2 T. cocoa
1⅓ c. sugar	⅓ t. salt
3 eggs	1½ t. vanilla
1⅓ c. flour	¾ c. chopped nuts
½ t. baking powder	

Mix in order given. Bake at 325°, for 20 min. Take out of oven and cover with miniature marshmallows. Put back in oven for 3 min.

Icing

¾ c. brown sugar	4 T. butter
⅓ c. water	1½ t. vanilla
3 T. cocoa	

Boil for 3 min. Let cool. Add 2 c. powdered sugar.

Patty Kauffman (Grill Cook)

CHINESE CHEWS

½ c. oleo
2 T. white sugar
1 c. flour
1½ c. brown sugar
1 t. vanilla

2 eggs
¼ c. coconut
¾ c. nuts
2 T. flour

Mix together the oleo, white sugar, 1 c. flour and press into 9x9 inch pan. Bake at 350° for 15 min.

Second part: Mix eggs, coconut, nuts, brown sugar, flour, vanilla and place over the above baked part. Bake again at 350° for 25 min.

Joyce Bechtel (Waitress)
Ida Miller (Cook)

"A little of the oil of Christlike love
will save a lot of friction."

CHURCH WINDOW COOKIES

½ c. butter or oleo
1 pkg. (12 oz.) chocolate bits
1 c. chopped nuts
1 pkg. (10 oz.) colored marshmallows
1 pkg. (14 oz.) flaked coconut

Melt butter and chocolate bits over low heat. Allow to cool slightly. Stir in nuts and marshmallows. Spread coconut on wax paper. Divide chocolate mixture into two rolls. Roll in coconut. Place in refrigerator for 24 hours. Cut in ½ inch slices.

DO NOT BAKE!

Makes about 4 doz. slices. (You could also put in mold and set in frig.)

Edna Mae Schmucker (Dishwasher)

 Flattery is soft-soap, and soft-soap is ninety percent lye!

COCOA DROP COOKIES (UNBAKED)

Boil together 5 minutes:

2 c. white sugar
½ c. cocoa
½ c. milk

½ c. butter
1 t. vanilla

Mix well with 3 c. quick oats. Drop by spoonfuls on waxed paper and cool.

Edna Mae Schmucker (Dishwasher)

DREAM BARS

First Part

1 c. flour
½ c. brown sugar
½ c. butter

Mix until crumbly. Press in bottom of a greased pan (8x10 in.). Bake in 250° oven for 10 min.

Second Part

1 c. brown sugar
2 T. flour
2 eggs, beaten
1 t. vanilla

½ t. baking powder
¼ t. salt
1 c. chopped nuts
1½ c. coconut

Mix all together and spread over first mixture and continue baking for 25-30 min. Cool and cut into squares.

Mrs. Harley Miller (Miller's Orchard)
Applebutter

179

GRAHAM CRACKERS

2 c. brown sugar
¼ c. butter
1 c. lard
2 c. flour
1 t. baking powder

1 t. salt
1 t. soda
1 c. milk
1 t. vanilla
4 c. graham flour

Mix well. Then roll out and cut into squares. Place on cookie sheet and bake at 350°.

Lizzie Ann Bontrager (Cook)

GRAHAM CRACKERS

7 c. graham flour
1 c. thick sweet cream (or butter)

1 pt. sweet milk
2 t. baking powder

Rub the baking powder into the flour, add the cream with a little salt, then the milk; mix well; roll as thin as soda crackers, and cut in any shape desired. Bake quickly 350° and leave near stove for a few hours to dry thoroughly.

Leora V. Kauffman (Purchasing)

LEMON SQUARES

Crust

½ c. margarine
¼ c. powdered sugar

1 c. flour
salt

Mix like pie dough. Put into 9 in. square pan or oblong pan. Bake 15 min. at 350°.

Filling

2 eggs, slightly beaten
1 c. sugar

2 T. flour
3-4 T. sour orange juice or lemon juice

Pour over baked crust and bake another 20 min. at 350°. Sprinkle with powdered sugar and cut into squares when cooled.

Mabel Hershberger (Pie Baker)

TOWNHOUSE PEANUT BUTTER COOKIES

In a double boiler melt:

12 oz. pkg. chocolate chips
½ stick of paraffin

Meanwhile in another saucepan melt:

½ c. oleo
2 T. peanut butter

To this stir in enough powdered sugar for a spreading consistency.
Spread between 2 townhouse crackers, and dip in melted chocolate.

Elsie R. Miller (Grill Cook)

"He gives food to all flesh, for His steadfast love endures forever."
Psalm 136:25

PUMPKIN BARS

2 c. flour
2 t. baking powder
½ t. salt
2 t. cinnamon
4 eggs

Bake at 350° 25-30 min.

1 c. walnuts
2 c. pumpkin
1 t. soda
2 c. sugar
1 c. oil

Icing

1 stick oleo
8 oz. cream cheese
Powdered sugar until thick.

Edna Nissley (Waitress)

PUMPKIN BARS

1 c. oil	2 c. sugar
4 eggs	2 t. cinnamon
2 c. pumpkin	1 t. vanilla
1 t. soda	2 c. flour
2 t. baking powder	½ t. salt

Bake at 350° for 25-30 min. (nuts may be added)

Frosting

¾ stick butter or oleo
3 oz. cream cheese
1¾ c. powdered sugar

Beat until right consistency to spread; add a little milk if needed.

Mary Esther Yoder (Pie Baker)

FROSTED PUMPKIN BARS

4 eggs	1 t. soda
1 c. salad oil	1 t. baking powder
2 c. sugar	2 c. flour
1 c. pumpkin	½ t. salt
2 t. cinnamon	

Combine all ingredients and pour into a greased and floured large cookie sheet. Bake at 350°.

Frosting

3 oz. cream cheese	1 t. vanilla
6 T. margarine	1 t. milk, if needed
¾ lb. powdered sugar	

OLD FASHIONED RAISIN BARS

1 c. raisins
1 c. water
½ c. shortening
1 slightly beaten egg
1¾ c. flour
1 c. sugar
¼ t. salt

1 t. soda
1 t. cinnamon
1 t. nutmeg
1 t. allspice
½ t. cloves
½ c. nuts

Combine raisins and water. Bring to boil, remove from heat. Stir in shortening, cool to lukewarm. Stir in sugar and egg. Sift together dry ingredients. Beat into raisin mixture. Stir in nuts, pour into greased 13x9x2 in. pan. Bake at 375° 20 min. or till done. Cut into bars. Dust with powdered sugar. Makes about 2 doz.

Patty Kauffman (Grill Cook)

"Any housewife, no matter how large her family, can always get some time to be alone — by doing the dishes."

ROCKY ROAD SQUARES

Line 9x12 in. pan with whole graham crackers.

½ c. oleo
1 egg, beaten

1 c. powdered sugar
6 oz. pkg. butterscotch chips

Melt these 4 ingredients over low heat, to boiling point. Cool slightly. Add 2 c. marshmallows. Pour over graham crackers. Cool in refrigerator and cut in squares.

Lavera Hooley (Waitress)

WAFFLE COOKIES

1 c. oleo
4 sq. choc.   (4 T. cocoa and 2 t. butter = one choc. square)
4 eggs
1½ c. sugar
2 c. flour
2 t. vanilla
⅓ t. salt

Heat waffle iron, but not too hot (med.). Melt oleo and choc. together. Stir in eggs, sugar, flour, salt, and vanilla. Drop by tsp. on waffle iron. Bakes in about 1 min.

Arlene Miller (Cook)

CARAMEL CORN

2 c. brown sugar (packed)   ¼ t. cream of tartar
½ c. light corn syrup   1 t. salt
½ lb. butter or oleo

Boil rapidly, stirring constantly until mixture reaches 260°. Remove from heat. Stir in: 1 t. soda; stir mixture thoroughly and pour immediately over 6 qts. popped corn. Stir until all of the corn is covered. Pour out in a large buttered roasting pan. Bake the caramel corn for 1 hr. at 200°, stirring 3 or 4 times to break apart. Remove from oven and cool completely, store in a tightly covered container.

Katie Cross (Waitress)

CARAMEL CRUNCH

4 c. sugar
1½ c. white karo
3 c. margarine

Boil slowly to 300°, stirring quite regularly.

Add:

1 T. vanilla and pour over 10-12 qts. popped corn.

Lydia Ann Miller (Cook)

CARAMEL POPCORN

2¼ c. brown sugar   pinch of salt
¾ c. white karo   2½ bars of butter

Melt butter, add sugar, karo and salt. Boil 5 min.

8 qt. popped corn

Pour over popped corn and mix. Put on cookie sheets or cake pan, and bake 1¼ hr. at 200°. Stir every ½ hr.

Ida Miller (Cook)

CRACKERJACK

½ lb. butter
1 c. karo syrup
2 c. sugar

Melt butter, add karo and sugar. Cook till it threads, then add ¼ t. soda and cook till it breaks up real fine in cold water. Pour this over a cherry can full of popped corn.

Polly Yoder (Cook)

CANDY

2½ c. rice krispies   2½ c. marshmallows
2½ c. captain crunch   2 lb. almond bark or white fudge
2½ c. peanuts

Melt fudge in double boiler and mix all together.

Lavera Hooley (Waitress)

The best way for a man to remember his
wife's birthday is to forget it just once.

CARAMEL CANDY

2 c. white sugar
1½ c. white karo
½ c. oleo

2 c. sweet cream
1 t. vanilla
a little paraffin - size of a walnut

Mix sugar, karo, oleo, ½ of cream together and cook till it forms a soft ball. Then add the other half of cream, and boil again till soft ball. Add vanilla and wax after taking off heat. Cool and cut, wrap. Nuts can also be added.

Sharon Boley (Waitress)

GRANDMOTHER'S CARAMEL

1 c. sugar
½ c. corn syrup
1½ c. cream

1 t. vanilla
nuts

Combine sugar, corn syrup and ½ c. cream. Cook until soft ball stage. Add ½ c. more cream. Cook again until soft ball stage. Add last ½ c. of cream. Cook until soft ball stage again. Remove from heat and add vanilla and nuts. Pour into buttered pan.

Esther Hershberger

NUT CARAMELS

2 c. brown sugar
½ c. white karo

1/8 t. salt
¼ c. cream

Cook together until it forms a fine thread when dripped from spoon. Then add another ¼ c. cream very slowly and 5 T. butter and cook until mixture forms a hard boil in cold water, stir almost constantly.

Take candy off heat, add 1 t. vanilla and pour into buttered pan. Let cool and mark into squares; press one walnut into each square.

Laura Miller (Grill Cook)

186

CARAMEL PECAN CANDY TURTLES

2 c. white sugar
½ c. light karo
¼ lb. butter

½ c. milk
1 t. vanilla

Cook all ingredients except vanilla to a stiff ball stage 250°. Remove from heat and add vanilla. Do not stir more than necessary. Have a pan 10x12 in. ready, buttered and covered with pecans. Cover with caramel mix. Cut in squares and dip in chocolate. Takes about 1 lb. chocolate.

Susie Bontreger (Grill Cook)

DATE BALLS

¾ c. brown sugar
1 stick oleo
1 lb. chopped dates

Cook brown sugar, oleo, dates on low heat, stirring constantly until soft and tasty. Add:
1 t. vanilla
1 c. nuts
3 c. rice krispies

Roll in balls the size of walnuts; then roll in white sugar.

Rosalie Bontrager (Waitress)

DIVINITY

2½ c. granulated sugar
½ c. light corn syrup

2 egg whites
1 t. vanilla

In 2 qt. saucepan, combine sugar, corn syrup, ¼ t. salt, ½ c. water. Cook to hard ball stage (260°) stirring only till sugar dissolves. Meanwhile beat egg whites to stiff peaks. Gradually pour syrup over egg whites at high speed with mixer. Add vanilla and beat till candy holds its shape (4-5 min.). Quickly drop by teasponfuls on waxed paper.

Mabel Hershberger (Pie Baker)

DIVINITY FUDGE

Boil together until it spins a thread.

2 c. sugar
½ c. water
⅓ c. white karo

Beat together until stiff, but not dry:

2 egg whites
½ t. cream of tartar
¼ t. salt

Then slowly add hot syrup, stirring all the time until mixture thickens. Nuts or fruits may be added. Put in greased pan and cut or drop by spoonfuls on waxed paper.

Laura Miller (Grill Cook)

BROWN SUGAR FUDGE CANDY

1 c. brown sugar
1 c. white sugar
¾ c. milk
a pinch of salt

Boil to soft ball stage. Remove from heat and add:

2 T. butter
¼ t. maple flavoring
1 t. vanilla

Cool to lukewarm. Stir and add ¾ c. nuts.

Lizzie Ann Bontrager (Cook)

"Charity begins anywhere, and should have no end!"

TWO FLAVORED FUDGE

2 c. brown sugar
1 c. evaporated milk

1 c. white sugar
½ c. oleo or butter

Bring to boil, boil 15 min. at med. heat, stirring occasionally. Remove from heat and add:

1 jar marshmallow creme (10 oz.) size
6 oz. pkg. butterscotch chips
1 c. walnuts

6 oz. pkg. chocolate chips
1 t. vanilla

Blend till dissolved. Pour in 9x9 in. pan, chill till firm. (app. 2½ lbs.)

Mrs. Enos R. Miller

PEANUT BRITTLE

2½ c. white sugar
1 c. white karo
½ c. cold water

Cook this till it threads from the spoon. Then put in 3 cups peanuts, let boil again till a light brown, then add 2 t. soda, stir it good, put on buttered pans to cool.

Vera Slabach (Dishwasher)

PEANUT BUTTER CANDY

3 lbs. powdered sugar
3 c. peanut butter
1 lb. oleo or butter

Mix together and shape into balls.

Melt:

2 lbs. sweet chocolate
½ block paraffin

Dip balls into chocolate.

Laura Miller (Grill Cook)

PEANUT BUTTER CUPS

Mix together:

1 lb. margarine
2 lb. crunchy peanut butter
3 c. powdered sugar

Shape into small balls. Chill. Dip in chocolate.

Esther Nisley (Pie Baker)

RED ROCK CANDY

2 c. sugar
1 c. light corn syrup
½ c. water

1 t. butter
½ c. cinnamon red hots

Combine sugar, corn syrup and water; cook over low heat, stirring until sugar dissolves. Cook to soft ball stage. Add red hots. Cook to hard crack stage, stirring often. Remove from heat and add butter, stir slightly. Pour into well greased 13x9 in. pan. Break into pieces when cold.

Katie Cross (Waitress)

SPICED PEANUTS

1½ lb. raw spanish peanuts
1 egg white
1 T. water

1 c. white sugar
1 t. salt
½ t. cinnamon

Beat egg white and water until foamy, not dry and stiff. Pour in peanuts and stir until coated well. Mix sugar, salt, cinnamon; mix in peanuts. Place in large pan, bake 45 min. at 300° and stir every 15 min. Very good.

Millie Whetstone (Cook)

 "Give us this day our daily bread."   Matthew 6:11

SUGARED NUTS

3 c. walnut halves
1½ c. pecan halves
2 c. sugar

1 c. water
¼ t. cinnamon

Mix ingredients in heavy skillet. Cook until water disappears and nuts have a sugary appearance. Remove from heat and pour nuts onto a baking sheet. Separate "quickly" with 2 forks.

Sharon Boley (Waitress)

TAFFY CANDY

4 c. sugar
2 c. karo
2 c. cream

Boil for 15 min., add 1 envelope plain gelatine, dissolved in ½ c. water. Boil to 250°. Pour in greased pans and let cool. As soon as cool enough to handle, pull taffy till white, then stretch out. Cut in pieces and wrap.

Lucy Eash (Cook)

MOM'S TAFFY CARAMEL CANDY

1 c. brown sugar
¾ c. white syrup
½ c. cream

Bring brown sugar, white syrup and ½ c. cream to a rolling boil, then add ½ c. cream, bring to a rolling boil again and add another ½ c. cream, boil till it is a "soft ball" on candy thermometer. Then take off stove and add 2 T. butter and 1 T. vanilla. Add nuts of your choice and pour into greased pan. When cool, cut in squares and dip in chocolate

Edna Nissley (Waitress)

"When God measures men He puts the tape around the heart and not the head."

VALLEY TAFFY

2 c. sugar (white)
2 c. canned milk or cream
¼ c. water

2 c. light karo syrup
1 pkg. knox gelatine
paraffin the size of a walnut

Put gelatine in cold water. Put all other ingredients in kettle and boil 15 min., then add gelatine and continue boiling until a hard ball forms when tested in cold water. Put in pie pans and cool enough to handle. Have two people pull it till it gets nice and light colored. Very good.

Lydia Ann Miller (Cook)

ENGLISH TOFFEE DELICIOUS

½ lb. oleo
½ lb. butter, room temp.   Mix with:

1 box powdered sugar
6 egg yolks

Whip egg whites, fold in 1 t. vanilla. Then add ½ c. pecan nuts. Add 3 squares melted unsweetened chocolate. Cool it before adding to rest of mixture, beat well. Crush 1 box vanilla wafers. Grease pan, put ½ crumbs in cake pan, add rest on top. Very good.

Mrs. Harley Miller (Miller's Orchard)
Applebutter

TURTLE CANDY

2 c. white sugar
¾ c. light corn syrup
¾ c. oleo

2 c. cream
1 T. vanilla

Put all of syrup, sugar and ½ of cream in pan and bring to a boil. Stir mixture constantly. Add rest of cream and oleo slowly so mixture does not stop boiling. Boil to soft ball on candy thermometer. Add vanilla and pour over pecans. Have pecans ready, single layer on pan.

Amanda Troyer (Waitress)

TURTLE CANDY

2 c. white sugar
½ c. butter

¾ c. white karo
1 c. cream

Cook and stir the above ingredients until it boils. Then add 1 more cup cream. Cook to soft ball stage or 238°. Pour over chopped pecans in buttered pan. When cold cut in squares and dip in chocolate. Melt chocolate in top of double boiler.

Lizzie Ann Bontrager (Cook)

Pies

SUNSHINE PIE

A lb. of patience, you must find.
Mixed well with loving words so kind.
Drop 2 lbs. of helpful deeds.
And thoughts of other people's needs.

A pack of smiles, to make the crust.
Then stir and bake it well you must.
And now, I ask that you may try
The recipe of this Sunshine Pie.

Katie Miller (Gift Shop)

COOKING HINTS

*Apricot pie is greatly improved by a few drops of vanilla.

*Raisin pie is improved by adding a T. of cider.

Pies

PIE CRUST

3 c. pastry flour
1 c. shortening

½ c. ice water
pinch of salt

Mix together flour, shortening and salt, to crumbs. Cut in water. Do not over mix.

Sue Miller (Manager)

CRISCO PIE CRUST CRUMBS

1 - 3 lb. can crisco
5 lbs. Gold Medal flour
1 T. salt

1 T. baking powder
½ c. sugar

When ready to use add a little water.

Laura Miller (Grill Cook)

"The present moment is divinely sent. Make good use of it that it may bear fruit to the end of time."

MY FAVORITE PIE CRUST

2 c. shortening
1 c. hot water

pinch of salt
6 c. flour (approx.)

Pour hot water over shortening and stir till smooth, add salt and flour till dough comes off hands easy. Makes 4 (2 crust pies)

Lydia Ann Miller (Cook)

SHORT CUT PASTRY

2 c. flour
2 t. sugar
1¼ t. salt

3 T. milk
⅔ c. cooking or salad oil (scant)

Combine flour, sugar and salt. Add oil and milk. Mix with fork until all flour is moistened. Save about ⅓ c. of dough to top pie. Press remaining dough evenly in pie pan covering bottom and sides. Crimp the edges. Add the fruit filling. Bake as fruit pie recipe directs. Can be used for pot pie dough too.

Katie Ann Lehman (Cook)

PIE PASTRY

6 c. flour
1 t. salt
2 c. shortening

2 eggs beaten
2 t. vinegar
⅔ c. cold water

Mix flour, salt, and shortening. Mix liquids together, and add to flour.

Esther Nisley (Pie Baker)

"A man of words and not of deeds, is like a garden full of weeds!"

ANGEL FOOD PIE

1¼ c. sugar
¼ c. cornstarch
2 c. boiling water
1 c. crushed pineapple, drained

2 egg whites, beaten
salt
vanilla

Sift sugar, cornstarch and salt. Add to hot water and boil till thick. Pour over beaten egg whites and beat well. Add pineapple and vanilla. Pour in baked pie shell and top with whipped cream.

Lydia Mae Troyer (Cook)
Martha Otto (Pie Baker)

APPLE PIE

3 c. sliced apples
1 c. sugar
1 T. flour

2 T. rich milk
2 T. butter
½ t. cinnamon

Mix apples, flour, sugar and spice together. Put in unbaked pie crust and add milk and butter. Put top crust on and bake at 375° for 40-45 min. Makes 1 pie.

Mabel Hershberger (Pie Baker)

APPLE PIE

5 c. sliced apples
1 c. water

Heat. Mix:

1 c. granulated sugar
1 c. brown sugar

3 T. cornstarch
2 T. grapefruit juice or lemon juice

Add a little rich milk to make a thickening. Add with apples and bring to boiling point. Remove from heat, add 2 T. butter. Put in 2 unbaked pie crusts. Sprinkle with cinnamon. Put top crusts on and bake at 375°.

Mabel Hershberger (Pie Baker)

199

APPLE PIE

3 c. thinly sliced apples
3 T. min. tapioca
¾ c. sugar

dash of cinnamon
¼ t. salt
3 T. water

Mix all together in a bowl and pour in unbaked pie shell. Dot with 1½ T. butter or oleo. Put on top crust. Bake at 375° till done.

Mrs. Ray E. (Susie) Miller (Cook)

DUTCH APPLE PIE

2 c. sliced apples
2⅔ c. water
1 c. sugar

2 T. Clear Jel
½ c. water

Add:
¼ t. cinnamon
¼ t. nutmeg

Cook apples in water and sugar. Thicken with Clear Jel and water and add spices. Pour in an unbaked pie shell, top with a mixture of 1 c. flour, ½ c. brown sugar and 3 T. butter. Bake at 450° until brown.

Sue Miller (Manager)

DUTCH APPLE PIE

3 c. diced apples
1 c. sugar
2 T. rich milk

½ t. cinnamon
1 T. flour
2 T. butter

Mix together and put in unbaked pie shell. Put crumbs on top and bake.

Crumbs

½ c. sugar
⅓ c. butter
¾ c. flour

Mix real good and put on pie to bake at 450°

Katie Cross (Waitress)

FRENCH APPLE PIE

7 c. sliced apples   ½ t. cinnamon
⅔ c. sugar   1½ T. butter

Mix together.

Topping
Combine:
1 c. flour   ½ c. butter
½ c. brown sugar   ¼ t. cinnamon

Bake 425° for 15 min. Reduce to 375° and bake 35 min.

Esther Nisley (Pie Baker)

SHOESTRING APPLE PIE

2½ c. white sugar   pinch of salt
2 T. flour   4 T. water
3 eggs, well beaten   4 c. shoestring apples

Mix all together and put in 2 unbaked pie shells. Sprinkle cinnamon
on top and bake 325° until done.

Martha Otto (Pie Baker)
Vera Slabach (Dishwasher)
Katie Miller (Gift Shop)

APRICOT PINEAPPLE PIE

1 qt. canned apricot
1 c. pineapple
1 qt. juice and water

Add 1 c. sugar. Take 3 T. cornstarch and mix with a little water to
make a thickening. Add to apricot mixture and bring to boil. Add 2
T. butter, and a pinch of salt. This will make 3 small 2 crust pies.
Bake at 425°.

Mabel Hershberger (Pie Baker)

Middle age is when you know all the answers and nobody asks you the questions.

BLUEBERRY PIE

Bring to a boil:

2 c. fresh blueberries
1½ c. water

Stir in a mixture of:

1 c. sugar   pinch of salt
2 T. clear-jel   a few drops of lemon juice

Cook until thick. Pour it warm or cold in unbaked pie shell. Put top on and glaze with milk, and sprinkle a little sugar on top of milk. Bake at 400° until brown.

Sue Miller (Manager)

BOB ANDY PIE

1 c. brown sugar   ½ t. cloves
1 c. white sugar   1 T. butter (heaping)
3 T. flour, large   3 eggs
1 t. cinnamon   3 c. milk

Mix together dry ingredients, add butter, beaten egg yolks and milk. Then fold in beaten egg whites and pour into 2 unbaked pie shells. Bake at 450° for 10 min. Reduce to 350° till done (approx. 35 min.).

Katie Miller (Gift Shop)

BUTTERSCOTCH PIE

1 c. brown sugar
1 c. boiling water
2 T. flour

2 eggs
2 T. butter

Boil water and butter. Beat eggs, add flour and sugar, dissolved in a small amount of cold water. Pour this mixture into hot water. Cook until thickened. Pour into baked pie shell.

Anne Yoder (Waitress)

BUTTERSCOTCH PIE

3 c. brown sugar
3 T. butter
10 T. cream

Boil the above together for 5 minutes. Cream together the following and add to first mixture.

4 c. milk
4 T. flour

2 T. cornstarch
3 eggs, beaten

Cook until thickened. Makes 3 pies. Pour in baked pie shells. Top with whipped cream.

Sue Miller (Manager)

FRENCH CHERRY PIE

1 - 3 oz. Philadelphia cream cheese
½ c. powdered sugar
1 c. whipping cream (whipped)

½ t. vanilla
1 can prepared cherry pie filling

Cream the cheese, sugar and vanilla. Fold in whipped cream. Pour into baked pie shell. Spread evenly over the bottom of pie shell, then spread cherry pie mix over the top of cheese mixture. Chill and serve.

Edna Nissley (Waitress)

CHERRY PIE

Bring to a boil:

2 c. fresh or canned cherries
1½ c. water or fruit juice

Stir in a mixture of:

1 c. sugar
½ c. water
2 T. clear-jel
¼ t. each lemon juice and almond flavor
pinch of salt

Boil 2 mins. longer, and add a few drops of red food color. Pour warm or cold in unbaked pie shell. Put a lid on and glaze it with milk. Sprinkle with sugar. Bake at 450° until golden brown.

Sue Miller (Manager)

GEORGE'S CHERRY PIE

2 c. fresh cherries
¾ c. water
2 t. almond extract

1 c. sugar
2 level T. minute tapioca

Mix, and let stand while making pie dough.

Mary Troyer (Dishwasher)

SOUR CHERRY PIE

1 pt. canned cherries
1 c. sugar

pinch of salt
4 T. flour

Red food color may be added to brighten them up. Mix together. Put in unbaked pie shell. Put on top crust and bake in 425° oven until done. (9 in. pie)

Lydia Ann Miller (Cook)

CHOCOLATE PIE

1 c. sugar	butter size of a walnut
1 t. cocoa	½ c. cream
2 T. flour, heaping	1½ c. hot water
pinch of salt	1 t. vanilla

Mix flour, cocoa, sugar, salt, vanilla and cream; pour in hot water; stir constantly until thick. Remove from heat and let cool, then pour into a baked pie crust. Put whipped topping on top and serve.

Mattie J. Yoder (Grill Cook)

CHOCOLATE CHIFFON PIE

1½ c. sugar	2½ c. milk
4 T. cocoa	pinch of salt

Bring to a boil. While soaking 2 T. gelatin in ½ c. water, add to above while hot. Cool till it starts to get thick, then add 5 c. of whipped topping. Pour into baked pie shell. Makes 2 pies.

Betty A. Hershberger (Grill Cook)

 Hurry is the mother of most mistakes!

GERMAN CHOCOLATE PIE

1 pkg. baker's chocolate	3 eggs, slightly beaten
¼ c. butter or margarine	½ c. sugar
1⅓ c. coconut	1 unbaked 9 in. pie shell
1 can (13 oz.) evaporated milk	

Melt chocolate and butter over low heat in a medium saucepan. Add milk, coconut, eggs and sugar and stir until blended. Pour into pie shell. Bake at 400° for 30 min. Cool or serve warm with whipped cream, or ice cream, if desired. Store in refrigerator.

Sue Miller (Manager)

COCONUT MACAROON PIE

1½ c. sugar
2 eggs
½ c. soft butter
½ t. salt

¼ c. flour
½ c. milk
½ c. shredded coconut
½ t. vanilla

Beat eggs, sugar, and salt till mixture is lemon colored. Add butter and flavor and blend well. Add milk, fold in ½ c. coconut. Pour in pie shell and sprinkle a little coconut on top. Bake in slow oven (325°).

Esther Yoder (Cook)

IMPOSSIBLE PIE (COCONUT)

1 egg
1 c. sugar
1 c. milk
¼ c. flour
½ t. vanilla

pinch of salt
¼ t. baking powder
¼ c. oleo, melted
1 c. coconut

Beat all together. Bake at 350° 30-35 min. Needs no crust - check with knife blade for doneness, or when golden brown.

Mrs. Enos R. Miller

COLLAGE PIE

1 c. sugar
1 egg

1 c. water
½ t. vanilla

Put this in unbaked crust.

2 c. sugar
1 egg
½ c. lard

1 c. buttermilk
3 c. flour
1 t. soda

Put this on top. Bake at 350° for 45 min.

Lucy Eash (Cook)

MOM'S COLLAGE PIE

1 egg	1 c. maple syrup
1 c. sugar	1 t. flavoring
1 pt. cold water	

Mix all ingredients and pour in 4 unbaked pie crusts. Then mix:

2 c. sugar	1 t. soda
1 c. sour milk	1 egg
½ c. lard	3 c. flour

Drop on top with spoon. Makes 4 pies. Bake at 350° for 45 min.

Lydia Ann Miller (Cook)

"Man may whitewash himself, but only God can wash him white."

COLLAGE PIE

First part

2 c. white sugar	2½ c. flour
½ c. shortening	2 eggs
1 c. sour milk	vanilla
1 t. soda	salt

Mix together and divide into 4 unbaked pie shells.

Second part

2 eggs	2 T. flour
1 c. molasses	2 c. brown sugar
4 c. water	vanilla

Mix and pour over first part and bake 350° for 45 min.

Martha Otto (Pie Baker)

OLD-FASHIONED CREAM PIE

⅓ c. all-purpose flour
½ c. melted butter
1 c. brown sugar

2 c. whipping cream,
  unwhipped
1 unbaked 9-inch pie shell

Blend flour into melted butter. Add brown sugar. Mix thoroughly. Add cream and stir until well blended. Pour into unbaked pie shell. Bake in a 375° oven 50 to 55 minutes. Cool. Serves 6 to 8.

Sue Miller (Manager)

OLD FASHIONED CREAM PIE

1 c. cream
1 c. hot water
1 c. white sugar

⅔ c. brown sugar
½ c. flour
vanilla and nutmeg

Pour into an unbaked pie crust. Bake in 325° to 350° oven.

Mrs. Andrew Miller

CRUMB PIE

Boil together:

1 c. brown sugar
2 T. flour
1 c. light corn syrup

1 pt. hot water
1 t. vanilla

Pour into 2 unbaked pie shells and cover with crumbs.

Crumbs

2 c. flour
1 t. soda
1 t. cream of tartar

1 c. brown sugar
½ c. butter

Bake in slow oven 350° for 45-60 min.

Polly Hershberger (Cook)

CUSTARD PIE

4 eggs, slightly beaten
1 c. sugar
pinch of salt

1 t. vanilla
2 c. milk (hot)

Add hot milk with top mixture and pour in unbaked pie shell. Bake at 400° for 10 min., then at 350° till done. Sprinkle with nutmeg.

Ida Miller (Cook)

Nothing annoys a woman more than to have friends drop in unexpectedly and find the house looking as it usually does.

CUSTARD PIE

Beat together:

4 eggs
½ c. sugar

Add:

2½ c. scalded milk
¼ t. salt
1 t. vanilla

Pour in unbaked pie shell. Bake in 400° oven, 25-30 min. Just before serving, mix together:

¼ c. brown sugar
2 T. soft butter
½ c. flaked coconut

Sprinkle on pie and broil 3-4 inches from heat, 2-4 min.

Anne Yoder (Waitress)

CUSTARD PIE

4 eggs   2½ c. milk
½ t. salt   ½ c. sugar
1 t. vanilla

Heat milk to scalding point. Beat eggs, sugar, salt, vanilla; add milk.
Bake 425° for 10 min. Reduce heat to 325° until set.

Esther Nisley (Pie Baker)

VELVET CUSTARD PIE

4 eggs   ½ t. vanilla
¾ c. sugar   pinch of salt
2½ c. scalded milk

Beat eggs, sugar, vanilla and salt together. Pour the hot milk in,
and beat again. Pour in unbaked pie shell. Sprinkle nutmeg on top.
Bake at 425° for 10 min. Reduce heat to 325° till done.

Sue Miller (Manager)

VELVETY CUSTARD PIE

4 slightly beaten eggs   1 t. vanilla
½ c. sugar   2½ c. milk, scalded
¼ t. salt   1 - 9 in. unbaked pie shell

Thoroughly mix eggs, sugar, salt, and vanilla. Slowly stir in hot
milk. At once pour into unbaked pastry shell. Sprinkle with nutmeg,
and cinnamon if desired. Bake in a very hot oven, 475° for 5 min.
Reduce heat to 425° and bake 10 min. Cool on rack.

Sharon Boley (Waitress)
Mrs. Levi R. Miller

"Go often to the house of your friends,
for weeds choke up the unused path."

DATE PIE

2 c. sugar	⅔ c. butter
3 egg yolks	4 T. cornstarch
3 c. chopped dates	4 c. milk
1 c. chopped nuts	3 egg whites whipped and folded in last.

Pour into unbaked pie shells, and bake until set. Makes 3 pies. Bake at 400° for 10 min. and then at 375°.

Leora V. Kauffman (Purchasing)

DELUXE PEANUT PIE

2 eggs	¾ to 1 c. white sugar
1 c. Karo or maple syrup	2 T. butter, melted
1/8 t. salt	½ c. roasted peanuts

Beat eggs, add syrup and remaining ingredients. Bake 45 min. 350°-375°. Makes 1 pie.

Other kinds of nuts may be used.

Lizzie Ann Bontrager (Cook)
Mattie Yoder (Grill Cook)

FRUIT PIE

May use cherries or raspberries.
1 qt. fruit-4 c. juice and water or if fresh fruit, 4 c. water, and 2 c. sugar.

Make a thickening with 3 rounding T. cornstarch and water.

Cook until nice and clear, put in pie crusts when still hot. Dot with butter. Put top crust on and bake at 375° oven until nice golden brown. Makes 3 pies.

Polly Hershberger

If we could see ourselves as others do,
we would often deny ourselves.

GRAPE NUTS PIE

½ c. grape nuts
½ c. warm water

Soak for 10 min.

¾ c. sugar
1 c. dark corn syrup
3 eggs

1/8 t. salt
3 T. butter
1 t. vanilla

Mix together and place in unbaked pastry shell. Bake at 375° for 10 min.; then at 350° for 25 min.

Sharon Boley (Waitress)

GRAPE NUTS PIE

½ c. grape nuts
½ c. lukewarm water
1 c. brown sugar
1 c. dark corn syrup

¼ c. butter
1/8 t. salt
3 eggs, beaten
1 T. vanilla flavor

Soak grape nuts in lukewarm water till water is absorbed. Combine sugar, dark corn syrup, butter, and salt in saucepan. Bring quickly to a boil, stirring until sugar is dissolved, remove from heat. Beat eggs till foamy. Add small amount at a time of hot syrup to eggs, beating well. Stir in softened grape nuts and vanilla. Pour into unbaked pie shell. Bake at 375° 40-45 min. Serve with whipped cream.

Esther Yoder (Cook)

By the time a man gets old enough to watch his step, he is too old to go anywhere.

LEMON PIE FILLING

1 egg
2 c. white sugar
4 T. flour

butter, size of an egg
2 pts. water
lemon flavor

Mix flour with sugar and add to water. Stir in egg and bring to boil. Add lemon and butter. Pour into 2 baked pie shells.

Makes 2 pies.

Amanda Troyer (Waitress)

MOCK MINCE PIE

1 c. dark karo
2 c. sugar
1 c. vinegar
1 c. water
1 c. bread crumbs

1 egg
2 c. raisins
2 t. cinnamon
1 t. cloves
1 t. allspice

Take a whole box of raisins and add 1 c. water and 1 c. vinegar to cook them. It calls for 1 c. of crumbs but I usually put more in. Add everything of the above and cook with the raisins after raisins are tender. Pour in unbaked pie shells and bake at 375° for 40-50 min.

Lucy Eash (Cook)

OATMEAL PIE

2 eggs
¾ c. quick oatmeal
½ c. sugar
¼ c. milk
¾ c. dark corn syrup

¼ c. melted butter or margarine
1 t. vanilla
1 t. cinnamon
½ c. nut meats (walnuts or pecans)

Combine all ingredients and mix well. Pour into an 8 in. unbaked pie shell and bake 15 min. at 350°. Reduce heat to 325° and bake for 30 min.

Dorothy Chupp (Hostess)

OATMEAL PIE

4 eggs
1 c. sugar
1 c. white corn syrup
2 T. flour

1 T. butter
1 t. cinnamon
1 c. oatmeal

Beat eggs, sugar, corn syrup, flour, butter and cinnamon together. Stir in oatmeal and pour in an unbaked pie shell. Bake at 350° till done (approximately 1 hr.).

Sue Miller (Manager)

OATMEAL PIE

3 eggs
¼ c. butter
½ c. white sugar

1 c. white karo
½ c. rolled oats
1½ t. vanilla

Pour in unbaked pie shell and bake 1 hr. at 350°.

Lizzie Ann Bontrager (Cook)

Don't pray for rain if you are going
to complain about the mud.

PEACH PIE

Mix 1 beaten egg, 2 T. flour, 1 c. sugar, with 2 c. fresh sliced peaches. Pour in unbaked pie shell and cover with crumbs, made of 2 T. butter, ½ c. brown sugar, 2 T. flour. Bake 15 min. at 425°, then reduce heat to 350° and bake ½ hr. longer.

Mabel Hershberger (Pie Baker)

Your neighbors' windows look a great deal better when you first wash your own.

PEANUT BUTTER PIE

Mix together:

1 c. powdered sugar
⅓ c. peanut butter

Form small crumbs. Line baked pie shell with crumbs and add vanilla pudding. Top with whipped cream and sprinkle a few crumbs on top.

Either scratch vanilla filling or mix may be used.

Sharman Miller (Buss Girl)

VANILLA PIE FILLING

3 c. milk, scalded
½ c. cornstarch
1⅓ c. sugar
pinch salt
1 t. vanilla
3 egg yolks
1 c. cold milk

Mix cornstarch, sugar, eggs, salt, vanilla and cold milk. Pour in scalded milk. Stir constantly until thick. Remove from heat and let cool, then pour into a baked pie shell. Serve with whipped topping on top. For coconut pie, add ¾ c. coconut. For raisin pie, add ¾ c. raisins. For banana pie, slice 1 banana and add to pudding.

Sue Miller (Manager)

PEANUT BUTTER PIE

1 c. corn syrup
½ c. sugar
⅓ c. plain or chunky peanut butter

3 eggs slightly beaten
½ t. vanilla
1 unbaked pie crust

Mix together corn syrup, sugar, eggs, vanilla and peanut butter. Pour into pie crust, bake at 400° 5 min. Reduce heat to 350° and bake 30-45 min.

Esther Nisley (Pie Baker)

PEANUT BUTTER ICE CREAM PIE

1½ c. graham cracker crumbs
⅓ c. butter, melted
¼ c. sugar
1 qt. vanilla ice cream, softened

1 c. peanut butter
½ pt. whipping cream, whipped
graham cracker crumbs
roasted peanuts for garnish

Combine crumbs, butter, and sugar. Press into 9 in. pie plate. Chill. Soften ice cream so it can be stirred with spoon. Stir in peanut butter. Fold in whipped cream, until well blended. Pour into shell. If desired, sprinkle with more graham cracker crumbs and peanuts. Place in freezer to harden. (To store in freezer for more than a few hours, cover with freezer wrap.)

Sharon Nofziger (Waitress)

PECAN PIE

3 eggs
1 c. light karo
1 c. brown sugar

1 T. butter
1 t. vanilla
1 c. pecans

Pour in unbaked pie shell. Bake at 400° for 10 min. then at 325° till set.

Katie Miller (Gift Shop)

 It's a big job to build a sunny future on a shady past.

PECAN PIE

3 beaten eggs
1¼ c. karo
3 T. butter

1 t. vanilla
⅓ t. salt
1 c. pecans

Beat eggs. Add syrup and remaining ingredients. Bake 45 min. in moderate oven.

Mrs. Levi R. Miller

PECAN PIE

4 eggs
1 c. sugar, white
1 c. white karo

2 T. flour, level
1 T. butter
pinch of salt

Beat together, and add 1 c. pecans. Pour in unbaked pie shell, and bake at 450° for 10 min. Then reduce heat to 350° till done.

Sue Miller (Manager)

HARRY'S PECAN PIE

3 eggs
1 c. dark molasses
1 c. sugar

Mix well. Pour in unbaked crust. Cover the top with pecans (use plenty). Bake slow 250°-325° 40-50 min.

Mary Troyer (Dishwasher)

MOCK PECAN PIE

¼ c. butter or oleo
½ c. white sugar
1 c. dark karo
¼ t. salt

3 eggs
½ c. coconut
½ c. oatmeal

Bake in 350° oven for 50 min.

Katie Miller (Gift Shop)

NOT SO RICH PECAN PIE

¾ c. sugar
¾ c. karo, light
2 eggs
2 T. cream

1 T. flour
½ t. salt
1 c. water
1 c. nuts or more if you wish.

Bake 350-375°.

Lydia Ann Miller (Cook)

PUMPKIN CUSTARD PIE

1 c. cooked pumpkin
3 eggs
1 T. flour
¼ c. brown sugar
½ c. white sugar

½ t. salt
⅓ t. nutmeg
½ t. cinnamon
1 pt. fresh milk

Mix ingredients in order listed. Pour in unbaked pie shell and bake. Bake 350-375°.

Mrs. Enos R. Miller

The only sure way to reduce is to set the bathroom scales in front of the refrigerator.

RAISIN PIE

Cook 1 c. raisins and 1 c. water together. Add 1 c. sugar and 1 T. butter. Take 1 T. cornstarch and mix with a small amount of water to make a thickening. Stir in to sugar and raisin mixture and bring to boiling point. Remove and put in a 2 crust pie and bake at 375°.

Mabel Hershberger (Pie Baker)

RAISIN PIE

Cook 1 to 1½ c. raisins with 1 c. water. Add 1 T. butter. Make a thickening of 1 c. sugar, 2 T. clear-jel, ½ t. lemon juice, and a little water. Pour it into raisin and water mixture. Cook a few minutes until thick. Then pour it warm or cold in a 2 crust pie shell. Bake at 400° till golden brown.

Sue Miller (Manager)

RAISIN PIE

1½ c. milk	1 c. stewed raisins
1 T. cornstarch	1 T. butter
2 eggs	1 t. vanilla
1 c. sugar	

Cook this together and put in an unbaked 2 crust pie shell. Bake at 400° till golden brown.

Martha Otto (Pie Baker)

RAISIN CREAM PIE

½ c. sugar	butter (size of an egg)
1 c. milk	½ c. cooked raisins
2 egg yolks	1 t. vanilla
1 T. flour, large	¼ t. salt

Mix sugar, flour and salt, add eggs and enough milk to form a smooth mixture. Then add to milk which was heated in saucepan. Stir constantly. Cook until thick. Remove from heat, and add vanilla, butter and raisins. Pour in baked pie shell. Top with whipped cream.

Katie Miller (Gift Shop)

219

RAISIN CREAM PIE

1 c. sweet cream or whole milk
1 c. raisins
1 c. nuts

1 c. sugar
yolk of 1 egg
1 T. flour

Mix some milk with it and cook to a custard. Pour in baked pie shell. Makes 1 big pie. White of egg may be whipped and put on top or whipped cream. All whole milk may be used instead of cream, unless you want a very rich pie.

Martha Otto (Pie Baker)

RITZ CRACKER PIE

Beat 3 egg whites until stiff adding 1 c. sugar gradually.
Fold in 1 t. baking powder
1 c. pecans
24 Ritz cracker crumbs
1 t. vanilla

Bake in buttered dish pan at 350° for 25 min. Top with whipping cream.

Bertha Viola Bontrager

RHUBARB PIE

2 eggs, beaten
1½ c. sugar

1 T. flour
pinch of salt

Then add 2 c. rhubarb and 5 T. water. Dot with butter, put in unbaked pie shell and sprinkle with cinnamon. Makes 1 pie.

Mrs. Robert W. Miller

Keep thy eyes wide open before marriage and half shut afterwards.

RHUBARB PIE

3 eggs
1 c. sugar
2 T. flour

1 c. water
pinch of salt

Beat this together and pour over 2 c. cut up rhubarb, which has been put in an unbaked pie shell. Dot with butter and sprinkle with cinnamon. Bake at 350° for about 45 min.

Sue Miller (Manager)

RHUBARB CRUMB PIE

2 c. finely cut rhubarb
1 egg, beaten
1 T. flour

1 c. white sugar
½ t. vanilla
pinch of salt

Mix altogether and pour into unbaked pie crust, then top with the following crumbs.

¾ c. oatmeal
½ c. brown sugar
⅓ c. butter

Bake 15 min. at 425° then at 350° for 30 min.

Barbara Bontrager (Cashier)

RHUBARB CUSTARD PIE

2 c. rhubarb, cut
1¼ c. white sugar
1 T. flour, rounded

½ c. cream
2 eggs
½ c. water

Cut rhubarb in small pieces, put in pie shell. Mix rest of ingredients and pour over rhubarb. Sprinkle top with nutmeg. Bake at 400° for 10 min. then at 325° till set.

Katie Miller (Gift Shop)

Bibles that are coming apart usually belong to people who are not.

He's on a garlic diet. He hasn't lost any weight, but quite a few friends.

RHUBARB CUSTARD PIE

2 c. diced rhubarb
1 c. milk
2 egg yolks
¾ c. sugar

2 T. flour
¼ t. salt
2 T. butter

Add sugar, salt, flour to the slightly beaten egg yolks. Scald the milk and add butter. When butter is melted pour the milk to the egg mixture. Line an 8 in. pan with pastry, and spread rhubarb in pastry shell. Cover with egg and milk mixture. Bake at 425° for 20 min. Reduce heat to 325° and bake 25 min. longer. Top with meringue of 2 egg whites, pinch of salt, and 2 T. powdered sugar. Then put back in oven till nice and brown.

Martha Otto (Pie Baker)

RHUBARB CUSTARD PIE

Mix 1½ c. sugar, ¼ c. all purpose flour, ¼ t. ground nutmeg, and a dash of salt. Add to 3 beaten eggs; beat smooth. Stir in 4 c. sliced rhubarb.

Prepare pastry for 9 in. lattice-top pie. Line 9 in. pie plate with pastry. Fill with rhubarb mixture. Dot with 2 T. butter. Adjust lattice top; seal. Bake at 400° for 50 min.

Kathryn Hershberger

"If God is a reality, and the soul a reality, and you are an immortal being, what are you doing with your Bible shut?"

FRENCH RHUBARB PIE

1 egg, beaten   2 c. diced rhubarb
1 c. sugar   2 T. flour
1 t. vanilla

Mix the above together and put in unbaked pie shell.

Topping:

¾ c. flour
⅓ c. butter
½ c. brown sugar

Mix till crumbly and put on top of rhubarb mixture. Bake at 400°
for 10 min, then at 350° for 30 min.

Sharon Boley (Waitress)

SHOOFLY PIE

2 c. flour
1½ c. brown sugar
¼ t. salt
4 T. oleo
Mix together till crumbly. Take out 2 c. of crumbs for top of pies.
To remainder of crumbs add:

2 beaten eggs
2 c. molasses
1½ c. hot water (not boiling)

Mix well. Dissolve 2 t. soda in ½ c. hot water and add to mixture.
Pour in 2 unbaked pie shells and top with reserved crumbs. Bake at
450° for 10 min. Reduce heat to 375° and bake for 30 min. or until
top is dry and done. Instead of molasses you can use: 1½ c. dark
karo, ½ c. light karo, 2 t. vanilla and ¼ t. maple flavoring.

SOUR CREAM PIE

3 c. sour cream
3 c. sweet milk
3 c. white sugar

2 eggs
4 T. flour, rounded
½ t. soda

Sprinkle nutmeg on top. Bake at 400° for 50 min. Don't make crusts too full or you will have a messy oven to clean. Makes 3 pies.

Susie Bontreger (Cook)

STRAWBERRY PIE

Whip 2 egg whites till stiff, then add 1½ c. fresh strawberries and whip till very creamy, then add 1 c. sugar.

Whip 1 c. cream; fold into strawberry mixture. Pour into graham cracker pie crust. Freeze.

LaVerda Miller (Waitress)

STRAWBERRY PIE

Pie Crust

1 c. flour
1 stick margarine
3 T. powdered sugar

Pat into pie pan, crimping over the edge slightly. Bake about 10 min. at 350°, cool.

Filling

1 c. sugar
1 c. water
3 T. cornstarch

Cook until thick and clear. Add 3 T. strawberry jello; stir till dissolved. Pour over halved berries (approx. 1 qt.) and refrigerate till firm.

Mildred Two (Cake Decorator)

FRESH STRAWBERRY PIE

4 pkg. knox gelatin   5 c. water
1⅓ c. sugar   ½ t. salt

Soften gelatin in 1 c. cold water, heat the other 4 c. water and add gelatin mixture. Add sugar and salt. Cool. Mash 4 qts. strawberries and sweeten with 2 c. sugar as for sauce. Add gelatin mixture and let set. When set put in baked pie crusts and top with whipped cream or whipped topping. Makes 4 pies.

Variation: Strawberries can also be mashed and thickened with instant clear-jel and sugar instead of knox gelatin. Then put in pie crusts and top with topping.

Lydia ann Miller (Cook)

FROZEN STRAWBERRY PIE

Beat 2 egg whites until stiff.
Add 1 c. sugar and beat until sugar is dissolved.
Add 2 c. strawberries (frozen or fresh) and beat.
Whip 2 c. cream and fold into strawberry mixture.
Pour into a graham cracker crust and freeze.
Makes 2 pies.

Susie Bontrager (Grill Cook)

STRAWBERRY PIE

1¼ c. water   1 pkg. strawberry jello
2 T. cornstarch   1 c. mashed strawberries
¾ c. sugar

Cook together sugar, cornstarch and water until clear. Then add the jello. Cool. Add strawberries. Top with whipped cream.

Variations: Also peaches and peach jello.

Fannie Yoder (Cook)

STRAWBERRY PIE

1 c. sugar
2 T. white karo
3 T. cornstarch

1 c. water
pinch of salt

Cook until thick, then add 3 T. strawberry jello, mix and cool. Then mix in fresh strawberries (approx. 1 qt.). Pour in baked pie shell. Top with whipped topping.

Lizzie Ann Bontrager (Cook)
Karen Lehman (Waitress)

UNION PIE

2 c. sour cream
2 c. sweet milk
4 T. flour
2 c. white sugar

2 eggs
½ t. cinnamon
a little soda

Bake in unbaked pie shell 350°. Makes 4 pies.

Lucy Eash (Cook)

VANILLA CRUMB PIE

1½ c. sugar (either brown or white or half and half)
2 c. light karo
3 T. flour, heaping
2 pts. cold water
2 eggs, well beaten

Boil together. Add 3 t. vanilla, pour into 3 unbaked pie shells. Then cover with crumbs made of the following:

2 c. flour
½ c. sugar
1 t. soda

1 t. cream of tartar
½ c. butter

Bake at 400° for approx. 35 min.

Katie Miller (Gift Shop)

VANILLA CRUMB PIE

1 c. sugar
1 c. molasses
1 pt. water

1 T. flour, heaping
1 egg, well beaten

Boil all together, set aside to cool. Then before you put it in the pan add 1 t. vanilla.

Crumbs

2 c. flour
½ c. sugar
½ c. lard

1 t. soda
1 t. cream of tartar

Bake at 350° for 45 min.

Ida Miller (Cook)

Desserts, Ice Cream & Beverages

Before heating milk in saucepan, rinse pan in water and it will not scorch so quickly.

Add a little salt to applesauce, takes less sugar and brings out a richer flavor.

If a level t. of baking powder is added to each quart of fruit when making apple or cranberry sauce, it will take half as much sugar.

Leora Kauffman (Purchasing)

Desserts, Ice Cream & Beverages

ALMOND CHOCOLATE PUDDING

1 c. milk
30 marshmallows
½ pt. cream

Melt marshmallows in hot milk over low heat. Cool and add ½ pt. whipped cream. Then melt ¼ c. butter. Add ¼ c. sugar to 10 crushed graham crackers. Line dish with this mixture and pour above pudding into lined dish in layers, putting 1 large almond chocolate bar (grated) between layers and on top.

Mary Esther Miller (Waitress)

APPLE CRUNCH

4 c. apples (put through Saladmaster Shoestringer)
½ c. sugar
1 T. flour

Put in baking dish. Top with the following:

¾ c. quick oats   ¼ c. white sugar
¼ c. flour   ¼ c. butter
¼ c. brown sugar

Bake at 375° until apples are done. Serve with ice cream or milk.

Katie Miller (Gift Shop)

APPLE CRUNCH OR DELIGHT

1 qt. sliced apples
1 c. sugar
1 T. flour

1/8 t. salt
1 t. cinnamon

Topping:

¾ c. oatmeal
¾ c. brown sugar

¼ c. melted butter
¼ t. soda

Pare and slice apples, combine sugar, salt, cinnamon, and flour and sprinkle over apples in bottom of greased pan. Combine oatmeal, brown sugar, and soda. Add melted butter and rub into oatmeal mixture, to make crumbs. Place crumbs on top of apples, patting them down evenly. Bake at 375° for approximately 40 min. Serve with rich milk or cream, as desired.

Ida Miller (Cook)

CLEANING CUPBOARDS

Today while cleaning cupboards
With neat, housewifly art
I suddenly decided
To clean the cupboards of my heart.

I threw out criticism
To the trashpile — to the fire!
I put in appreciation
And worthwhile thoughts that will inspire.

I threw out condemnation
Which says, you're wrong, I'm right!
I put in consideration
For all folks, brown, black and white.

Yes, out went complaining
Grumbling about trivial things
I put in smiles and laughter,
To ease the tensions each day brings.

Friends, let's all clean our cupboards,
With help from God above
Throw out pride and hatred, too.
Put in humility and love.

OLD FASHIONED APPLE DUMPLINGS

6 medium-sized baking apples   ½ t. salt
2 c. flour   ⅔ c. shortening
2½ t. baking powder   ½ c. milk

Sauce:

2 c. brown sugar
2 c. water
¼ c. butter
¼ t. cinnamon or nutmeg (optional)

Pare and core apples. Leave in halves. To make pastry, sift flour, baking powder and salt together. Cut in shortening until particles are about the size of small peas. Sprinkle milk over mixture and press together lightly, working dough only enough to hold together. Roll dough as for pastry and cut into 12 squares and place half an apple on each. Fill cavity in apple with sugar and cinnamon. Pat dough around apple to cover it completely. Fasten edges securely on top of apple. Place dumplings 1 inch apart in a greased baking pan. Pour over them the sauce made as follows:

Combine brown sugar, water and spices. Cook for 5 minutes, remove from heat and add butter. Bake at 375° for 35-40 min. Baste occasionally during baking. Serve hot with rich milk or ice cream.

Sue Miller (Manager)

BAKED APPLES

Boil together until thickened:

1 c. sugar (granulated)   1 c. brown sugar
½ c. flour   1 c. water
1 t. cinnamon   2 t. butter

Pour mixture over apples that have been peeled and cut in half and placed in a 13x9 inch baking dish. Bake 30-45 min. in 350° oven. (Till apples are soft.) 8-10 apples.

Lydia Ann Miller (Cook)

APPLE PUDDING

2 c. diced apples
1 c. sugar
1 egg well beaten
1 c. flour
½ t. salt

1 t. soda
1½ t. cinnamon
1 t. vanilla
½ c. nuts

Mix together apples and sugar, then add egg. Sift together dry ingredients; add to apple mixture and mix well. Stir in vanilla and nuts. Pour into ungreased 8x8 inch baking pan. Bake at 350° for 35 min.

Sauce:

½ c. sugar
½ c. brown sugar
¼ c. oleo

2 T. flour
1 c. water

Cook sauce until thick and pour over pudding as soon as it comes out of the oven. Serve warm with whipped cream or ice cream.

Esther Nisley (Pie Baker)
Esther Hershberger

BLACK CHERRY TAPIOCA

Heat 2 qts. water to boiling, and add 1 c. fine pearl tapioca. Boil about 2 min., remove from heat, cover and let stand until tapioca looks clear.

Add:

1-1½ c. sugar
1 - 3 oz. box black cherry jello
1 pkg. black cherry kool-aid

Before serving add 1 qt. frozen or canned black cherries and whipped Riches topping. I use 2 c. of topping mix.

Mary Ann Schlabach (Waitress)

BLUEBERRY CHEESECAKE (no bake)

12 graham crackers, rolled fine
2 T. sugar, melted in ½ stick butter or oleo

Put in bottom of oblong pan.

1 - 8 oz. pkg. Philadelphia cream cheese, softened
1-1½ c. powdered sugar
2 T. milk

Mix and beat these ingredients real well, then add to whipped "Riches Topping." I use 2 c. of the topping mix. Beat everything together real well and pour on the cracker crust. Top with blueberry filling or other fruit can be used.

Mary Ann Schlabach (Waitress)

OLD FASHIONED BREAD PUDDING

2 c. milk, heat to scalding
pour over 4 c. coarse bread crumbs
cool and add:

½ c. melted butter   ¼ t. salt
½ c. sugar   1 c. seeded raisins
2 slightly beaten eggs   1 t. cinnamon or nutmeg

Pour into 1½ qt. buttered casserole pan. Bake at 350° 40-45 min., or until knife inserted comes out clean. Serve warm - 6 servings.

Meda Bontrager (Waitress)

After dinner, members of a lot of families suffer from dish-temper.

BUTTERSCOTCH PUDDING

¼ c. butter browned in heavy saucepan
Add 3 c. milk, bring to boiling

Mix together:

2 c. brown sugar	vanilla
⅔ c. flour	1 c. milk
2 eggs	

Add this to boiling milk. Cool. Serve with nuts, bananas and graham cracker crumbs.

Katie Miller (Hostess)

BUTTERSCOTCH CARAMEL PUDDING (or pie filling)

Brown 2 T. butter
Add 1½ c. brown sugar

Stir until sugar is mostly melted. Add 1 qt. water and boil for 10 min. Add 1 qt. milk, and before it comes to a boil, add the following:

Stir together:

½ c. white sugar	2 c. milk
⅔ c. cornstarch	½ t. salt
⅔ c. flour	vanilla to taste
4 eggs	

Stir in hot mixture and cook till thick.

Katie Miller (Hostess)

The best helping hand you can find is at the end of your arm.

BUTTERSCOTCH TAPIOCA

6 c. boiling water
1 t. salt
1½ c. small pearl tapioca

Cook 15 min. Add 2 c. brown sugar. Cook till done (Stir often).

Mix together and add:

2 beaten eggs
1 c. milk
½ c. white sugar

Cook until bubbles. Brown 1 stick butter and add 1 t. vanilla. Cool and add whipped cream, bananas, and diced candy bar if desired.

Amanda Troyer (Waitress)

CARAMEL PUDDING

½ c. sweet milk
¼ c. white sugar

1 T. butter
2 t. baking powder

Add enough flour to make a stiff dough. Drop by spoonfuls into this sauce.

Sauce

1½ c. brown sugar
1½ c. boiling water

1 T. butter
1 t. vanilla

Boil to a syrup. Bake in a hot oven till brown over top. Serve with whipped cream.

Amanda Troyer (Waitress)

CHEESECAKE

1 (3 oz.) lemon or orange jello	1 T. lemon juice
1 c. boiling water	1 (13 oz.) can milnot (whipped)
1 c. sugar	3 c. graham cracker crumbs
1 (8 oz.) pks. cream cheese	½ c. butter (melted)

Dissolve jello in hot water and chill until slightly thickened. Cream together cream cheese, sugar and lemon juice, then blend into jello. Fold in stiffly beaten milnot. Mix graham cracker crumbs and butter. Pack ⅔ of crumbs in 9x13 pan. Fill with cheese mixture and put remaining crumbs on top.

Mrs. John R. Miller

CHERRY O CREAM CHEESE PUDDING

Graham cracker crust
1 pkg. cream cheese (8 oz.)
1⅓ c. Bordens Eagle Brand Milk (14 oz. can)
⅓ c. lemon juice
1 t. vanilla extract
1 can prepared cherry pie filling (1 lb. 6 oz.)

Soften cream cheese. Whip till fluffy. Add milk, continue to beat until blended. Add lemon juice and vanilla. Pour into 9x13 pan. Chill 2-3 hrs. Garnish top with cherry pie filling.

Fannie Yoder (Cook)
Katie Ann Lehman (Cook)

CHERRY TORTE

6 egg whites	¾ c. nutmeats chopped
1 T. cream of tartar	2 t. vanilla
2 c. sugar	2 boxes dream whip prepared
2 c. soda crackers	1 can cherry pie filling
broken into small pieces	

Beat egg whites until frothy. Add cream of tartar beat until stiff. Add sugar gradually; beat until whites stand in peaks. Fold in soda crackers; add nut meats and vanilla. Bake in 9x13 inch greased pan for 20-25 min. at 350°. Let cool. Top with cherry pie filling. Let stand overnight or at least 2 hrs. Yield 12-16 servings.

Olive Bontrager (Cashier)

CHERRY CHEESECAKE

Mix:

16 graham crackers, crushed
¾ c. white sugar
½ stick butter or oleo

Press in 9x13 inch cake pan.

Mix:

2 eggs, beaten
2 - 8 oz. pkg. cream cheese

1 c. white sugar
1 t. vanilla

Spread over graham cracker mixture. Bake at 375° for 15 min. When cool, pour cherry pie filling over it. Then chill. Serve with whipped cream on top. Other fruits may be used instead of cherries.

Katie Miller (Gift Shop)

COCONUT CREAM DESSERT

1 c. margarine melted
2 c. flour
⅔ c. nuts (chopped)
1 pkg. (8 oz.) cream cheese
1 c. powdered sugar
a carton (9 oz.) whipped topping
2 pkg. (3 oz. each) instant coconut cream pudding mix
2½ c. cold milk

Mix margarine, flour and nuts. Put in 9x13 inch pan and bake in 350° oven for 15-20 min. Blend cream cheese and powdered sugar. Add 1 c. whipped topping to cheese mixture. Spread over cooled crust. Combine both packages pudding mix with milk. Spread over top of cheese mixture. Top this with remaining whipped topping.

Patty Kauffman (Grill Cook)

CROW NEST PUDDING

1 c. sugar
1 egg
1 t. baking powder
½ c. milk
1 t. vanilla
butter, size of a walnut
flour to make a little stiffer than cake batter and bake in 9x13 in. pan 375° 20-30 min.
When cool cut in little squares.

Chocolate pudding

3 c. milk and water, half of each
2 T. cornstarch
1 T. flour

sugar to suit your taste
(approx. ½ c.)
2 T. cocoa
1 t. vanilla

Mix sugar, flour, cornstarch and cocoa, add to milk and water and bring to boil, add vanilla. Put this on the squares and serve while hot.

Lucy Eash (Cook)

CROW NEST PUDDING

1 c. sugar
1 egg
pinch of salt
butter, size of a walnut
1 c. milk

1 t. vanilla
1 t. baking powder
flour, enough to make a stiff dough
(about 2 cups)

Place in 9x13 in. pan and bake 375° 20-30 min. Let cool, then add filling.

Filling

Brown - butter, size of a walnut
1 pt. milk and water
½ c. sugar

flour enough to thicken
flavor with vanilla

Cook as for pudding and add to cooled cake. Cut into squares and serve warm.

Mrs. Henry A. Yoder

240

CINNAMON PUDDING

1 c. brown sugar
¾ c. cold water
1 T. butter
2 c. flour
1 c. sugar

2 t. baking powder
2 t. cinnamon
2 T. butter
1 c. milk
1 c. pecans

Combine brown sugar, water, butter, and boil. Pour into baking pan. Sift flour, sugar, baking powder, and cinnamon. Add butter and milk, beat well. Pour over first mixture. Add pecans. Bake at 350° about 45 min. in 9x13 pan.

Karen Lehman (Waitress)
Mrs. Betty Graber (Waitress)

CINNAMON PUDDING

Syrup

2 c. packed brown sugar
1½ c. water
2 or 3 T. butter

Bring to boil, remove from heat.

Pudding

1 c. white sugar
2 T. butter or oleo creamed
2 t. cinnamon
2 t. baking powder (rounded)
½ c. walnuts

2 c. flour (scant)
1 c. milk
1 t. vanilla
pinch of salt

Beat together until batter is light. Pour in a greased 9x9x2 pan.

Sprinkle chopped nuts over batter and pour on warm syrup. Bake at 350° 35-40 min. Serve with whipped cream or ice cream.

Esther Nisley (Pie Baker)

COCOA FUDGE PUDDING

2 c. flour
4 T. shortening
1¼ c. sugar

4 t. baking powder
1 t. salt
milk (approx. 1 c.)

Put in milk to make a dough, about like a cake batter. Put in cake pan. Then mix 2 c. brown sugar and 8 T. cocoa, sprinkle over top of cake batter. Then pour 3 to 3½ c. hot water over it and bake 350° 45 min.

Lydia Mae Troyer (Cook)

BAKED CHOCOLATE PUDDING

1 c. flour
¼ t. salt
2 t. baking powder
1½ T. cocoa
¾ c. sugar

½ c. milk
2 T. butter, melted
½ c. nuts, chopped
1 t. vanilla

Sift first 5 ingredients. Add milk and vanilla, stir to a smooth batter. Add melted butter and nuts, and blend well into mixture. Pour into greased cake pan. Bake at 350° for 45 min.

Cambridge Sauce

⅓ c. butter
1 c. powdered sugar
2 t. flour

1½ T. cold water
½ c. boiling water

Cream butter and sugar together. Make a paste of flour and cold water. Add hot water gradually and cook 5 min. Then pour hot mixture over creamed butter and sugar. Stir till smooth. Yield: 1 cup. Pour over pudding when ready to serve.

Betty A. Hershberger (Grill Cook)

"As empty vessels make the loudest sound, so they that have least wisdom are the greatest babblers."

CREAM PUFFS

1 c. water	1 c. sifted gold medal flour
½ c. butter	4 eggs

Heat oven to 400°. Heat water and butter to a rolling boil in saucepan. Stir in all the flour at once. Stir vigorously over low heat until mixture leaves the pan and forms a ball (about 1 min.). Remove from heat. Beat in eggs thoroughly, 1 at a time. Beat mixture until smooth and velvety. Drop onto ungreased baking sheet forming 8 mounds, 3 inches apart. Bake 45-50 min. or until puffed, golden brown and dry. Allow to cool slowly, and away from drafts. Cut off top with sharp knife. Scoop out any filaments of soft dough. Fill with custard. Serve immediately or refrigerate.

Rich Custard Filling

½ c. sugar	2 c. milk
⅓ c. gold medal flour	4 egg yolks, or 2 eggs beaten
½ t. salt	2 t. vanilla

Mix sugar, flour, and salt in saucepan. Stir in milk, cook over medium heat, stirring until it boils. Boil 1 min. Remove from heat, stir a little over half of mixture into egg yolks. Blend into hot mixture in saucepan. Bring just to boil. Cool and blend in vanilla.

Mrs. Harley Miller (Miller's Orchard)
Applebutter

"He who relates the faults of others to you, designs to relate yours to others. Scandal always runs best in the gutter of evil minds."

CRUNCH PUDDING

1 c. flour
½ c. pecans
½ c. butter

Mix the above ingredients together till crumble fine. Spread in cake pan and bake 15 min. at 375°. Cool a little. Mix the following well.

1 c. powdered sugar
1 c. whipped cream
1 - 8 oz. pkg. cream cheese

Spread on baked crust before it is quite cold. Mix 2 pkg. butter pecan instant pudding with 3 c. cold milk. Put on top and chill.

Lizzie Ann Bontrager (Cook)

Often those of whom we speak least on earth are best known in heaven.

DATE PUDDING

½ lb. dried dates, chopped
1 t. soda
1 c. boiling water
2 eggs
1 c. sugar
2 T. shortening

½ t. salt
2 c. flour
1 t. baking powder
1 c. chopped nuts

Add soda to ½ lb. dates; pour boiling water over mixture. Beat eggs, add 1 c. sugar and melted shortening. Combine this mixture with hot dates. Add flour, salt and baking powder that have been sifted together. Fold chopped nuts into mixture. Pour in a greased baking dish and bake 40-45 min. at 325°. Cut into small cubes after cool and serve with whipped cream and bananas. Serves 6 to 8.

Sue Miller (Manager)

DATE PUDDING

2 c. brown sugar
1 T. butter
3 c. hot water
Boil this 3 minutes and put in a pan. Drop batter in and bake.

Batter

1 c. brown sugar   4 t. baking powder
3 T. butter   1 c. dates
1 c. sweet milk   ½ c. nuts
2 c. flour

When cool serve with whipped cream.

Lucy Eash (Cook)

DELICIOUS DESSERT

Crust
1 c. flour
½ c. chopped nuts
½ c. margarine

Blend and press in 9x13 inch pan. Bake in oven at 350° for 15 min.
Cool.

Next Layer
¾ c. powdered sugar
8 oz. cream cheese
1 c. cool whip

Cream powdered sugar and cheese; fold in cool whip; pour over crust.

Next Layer
2 pkg. vanilla pudding
3 c. milk

Mix, cook, and cool pudding. Pour over cream cheese mixture.
Top with remaining Cool Whip of a large container.
Toast ½ c. coconut and garnish.

Mrs. Harley Miller (Miller's Orchard)
Applebutter

FROZEN DESSERT

1 can Eagle Brand Milk	1 can crushed pineapple
1 can cherry pie filling	1 lg. Cool Whip

Mix together and freeze.

Marilyn Joan Mast (Waitress)

FRUIT SALAD DESSERT

2 (3 oz.) pkg. orange jello dissolved in 1 c. boiling water.
Add 1 pt. orange sherbert and mix well.
When partially set, add 1 can (11 oz.) mandarin oranges.
Fold in 1 c. heavy cream (whipped).

Idella Yoder (Pie Girl)

DREAM WHIP DESSERT

Press graham cracker crumbs in bottom of pan.

Whip Dream Whip (2 pkgs.) as directed on box. Add 3 oz. melted cream cheese and ½ c. powdered sugar. Put pie filling on top. (any kind)

Polly Yoder (Cook)

"When you have to swallow your own medicine the spoon always seems about three times as big!"

GRAHAM CRACKER FLUFF

2 egg yolks
½ c. sugar
⅔ c. milk
1 pkg. gelatin (1 T.)
½ c. cold water
2 egg whites

1 c. whipping cream
1 t. vanilla
3 T. melted butter
3 T. sugar
12 graham crackers

Beat egg yolks and add sugar and milk. Cook in top of double boiler until slightly thickened. Soak gelatin in the cold water. Pour hot mixture over softened gelatin and stir until smooth. Chill until slightly thickened. Add stiffly beaten egg whites, vanilla and whipped cream to chilled mixture. Combine melted butter, cracker crumbs and sugar to make crumbs. Sprinkle half of crumbs in bottom of serving dish. Add mixture and top with remaining crumbs. Let chill in refrigerator until set. Makes 6 to 8 servings.

Sue Miller (Manager)

GRAHAM CRACKER PUDDING

18 graham crackers
¼ c. sugar
½ c. butter
Break or roll crackers. Add butter and sugar. Line a dish with these crumbs saving a few to put on top.

Custard Filling

¾ c. milk
3 egg yolks

1 pkg. lemon or orange jello
½ c. sugar

Bring milk to a boil. Add eggs and sugar. Remove from heat and add jello. Allow to cool and partly set, then fold in 3 egg whites beaten stiff, and ½ to ¾ c. cream (whipped). Pour in dish lined with crumbs. Sprinkle with remaining crumbs and chill.

Mrs. Tobias Hochetetler

HEATH BAR DELIGHT

1 pkg. Lorna Doon Cookies, crumbled
1 stick melted butter or oleo

Mix and press in bottom of dish

2 pkgs. Instant Vanilla Pudding
2 c. milk
1 qt. softened Heath Bar Ice Cream or any other

Mix pudding, milk, and ice cream and pour over crumb mixture. Refrigerate 6 hours or overnight. Top with 1 small carton of Cool Whip. Crush 6 Heath Bars and sprinkle over top.

Edna Mae Schmucker (Dishwasher)

JELLO SUPREME

½ c. lemon jello or 1 box
½ c. orange jello or 1 box

Dissolve in 2 c. boiling water. Add 1½ c. cold water. Let cool and add 1 med. size can of drained pineapple, and 2 dozen small marshmallows.

Topping
Cook:

1 c. pineapple juice
½ c. sugar
1 egg

2 T. flour
1 t. butter

When cool add 1 c. dream whip. Put on top of jello mixture. Then sprinkle ½ c. of grated cheese on top.

Patty Kauffman (Grill Cook)

A suffering Christian is one whom God has under treatment.

JELLO TAPIOCA

6 c. boiling water
⅔ c. tapioca
pinch salt

When cooked add:

1 c. sugar
1 small box of jello or ½ c. Do not stir while cooling.

Mrs. Roseanna Chupp (Cook)

OLD FASHIONED JELLY ROLL

¾ c. cake flour
¼ t. salt
¾ c. sugar
1 c. tart red jelly

¾ t. baking powder
4 eggs
1 t. vanilla

Sift flour then measure. Combine baking powder, salt and eggs in bowl. Beat with egg beater adding sugar gradually until mixture becomes thick and light colored. Gradually fold in flour, then vanilla. Turn into 15x10 inch pan, which has been lined with paper then greased. Bake in hot oven 400° 13 min. or till done. Turn cake out on cloth or towel, dusted with powdered sugar. Quickly remove paper and cut off crisp edges of cake. Let cool about 10 min., unroll, spread cake with jelly and roll again. Wrap in cloth; place on cake rack to finish cooling.

Lydia Ann Miller (Cook)

Remember, you are not only the salt of the earth, but the sugar.

LAYERED FRUIT FLUFF

Melt:

½ lb. (32-34) marshmallows or 4 miniature marshmallows with 1 c. milk in top of double boiler over boiling water. Chill until completely cold and slightly thickened.

Combine:

1¼ c. Pillsbury's Best all-purpose flour
½ c. firmly packed brown sugar
¼ t. salt

Cut in:

½ c. butter or margarine until particles are fine. Place mixture in a 12x8 or 13x9 in. pan. Bake at 400° for 10-12 min., stirring occasionally until golden brown. Cool. Remove ½ c. of mixture, press remainder into bottom of pan.

Beat:

1 c. whipping cream with
¼ t. vanilla until thick. Fold cooled marshmallow mixture into whipped cream. Turn ⅔ of mixture into pan; spread to cover crumb layer. Spoon 1 can (lb. 6 oz.) cherry, blueberry, or other pie filling over marshmallow mixture. Sprinkle reserved crumbs over top. Chill at least 6 hours or overnight before serving. Serves 12.

Mrs. Tobias Hochstetler

Teacher: "Really, Tommy, your handwriting is terrible! You must learn to write better."

Tommy: "Well if I did, you'd be finding fault with my spelling."

LEMON CHEESECAKE

1 lg. pkg. (8 oz.) cream cheese
2 c. whole milk
1 pkg. lemon instant pudding
1 - 8 inch graham cracker crust

Stir cream cheese until very soft. Blend in ½ c. milk. Add remaining milk and the pudding mix. Beat slowly with mixer until well mixed, about 1 min. Pour in crust, sprinkle some crumbs on top. Chill 1 hr.

Betty Schrock (Angel Food Cakes)

LEMON CREAM CHEESE CAKE

First Layer:

½ c. oleo   ½ c. nuts
1 c. flour   1 t. sugar

Mix ingredients, bake 15 min. at 350°; cool.

Second Layer:

8 oz. pkg. cream cheese
1 c. powdered sugar
1 c. whipped topping

Mix powdered sugar and cream cheese, add whipped topping, and beat until smooth. Spread on first layer.

Third Layer:

2 boxes instant lemon pudding
3 c. milk

Mix and add to second layer. Last of all, spread whipped cream on top, if desired.

Betty A. Hershberger (Grill Cook)
Sharon Boley (Waitress)
Mildred Two (Cake Decorator)

LEMON PUDDING

1 c. flour
1 stick oleo
½ c. pecans (crushed)

Mix and press in greased pan. Bake 15 min. at 375°.

1 - 8 oz. cream cheese
1 c. powdered sugar
1 c. whipped topping

Mix and pour over cooled flour mixture, chill: 2 pkg. lemon instant pudding and 3 c. milk. Whip till thick and pour on cream cheese. Top with whipped cream if you wish.

Amanda Troyer (Waitress)

LIME JELLO DESSERT

2 boxes lime jello dissolved in 3 c. hot water
add 1 c. drained crushed pineapple

Set in flat dish

1 large pkg. cream cheese (soften and add a little milk). Stir well. Whip 1 c. cream stiff. Add the cheese, whip again until light and fluffy. Spread on set jello mixture. Top with topping.

Topping

1 c. sugar
2 beaten eggs

3 T. flour (level)
1 c. pineapple juice

Mix all together and bring to boil. Cook until thick and spread on cheese mixture. If you do not have enough pineapple juice, add water to make 1 c.

Mary W. Miller

MARASCHINO CHERRIES

5 c. cherries (yellow)
5 c. sugar
1 c. water

1 t. almond
1 oz. red food color

First put the following over cherries overnight:

1 qt. hot water
2 t. salt
1 t. alum

Drain the cherries the next day and put clear water on a while. Seed and put in above syrup and bring to a boil. Do this 2 or 3 mornings till cherries are nice and red. Can as other fruit.

Lydia Ann Miller (Cook)

PEACH-A-BERRY COBBLER

1 T. cornstarch
¼ c. brown sugar
½ c. cold water
2 c. fresh sugared sliced peaches

1 c. fresh blueberries
1 T. butter or margarine
1 T. lemon juice

Cobbler Crust

1 c. flour
½ c. sugar
1½ t. baking powder

½ t. salt
½ c. milk
¼ c. margarine

Nutmeg Topper

¼ t. nutmeg
2 T. sugar

Mix first 3 ingredients with fruit. Cook and stir till thick. Add butter and lemon juice. Pour in baking dish. Sift dry ingredients, add milk and butter at once. Beat till smooth. Spread over fruit. Sprinkle with nutmeg topping. Bake at 350° for 30 min. Serve with milk.

LaVerda Miller (Waitress)

PEANUT BUTTER CREAM CHEESE DESSERT

1 c. graham cracker crumbs
¼ c. brown sugar
2 T. oleo melted
¼ c. peanut butter
Mix together, put ⅔ of the mixture in a 6x10 in. pan.

Beat together:
1 pkg. (3 oz.) cream cheese
6 T. sugar
1 c. cream (whipped)
Spoon ½ of the cheese mixture over crumbs. Spoon 1 can apple pie filling over cheese mixture. Sprinkle ¼ t. cinnamon over apples.

Mix together:
½ c. powdered sugar
3 T. peanut butter
Put ⅔ of this mixture over apples. Top with remaining cheese, remaining cracker crumbs, and remaining powdered sugar crumbs.

Betty A. Hershberger (Grill Cook)

PHILADELPHIA CREAM CHEESE PUDDING

⅓ box graham crackers (rolled fine)
1 T. sugar
¼ lb. oleo

Mix together and put ½ in bottom of baking dish, set the rest aside.

Dissolve 1 pkg. (3 oz.) lemon jello in ¾ c. boiling pineapple juice. Add 1 pkg. Philadelphia Cream Cheese (8 oz.). Beat together and cool.

Beat one can Milnot until very stiff. Add ¾ c. sugar, slowly beat one minute. Add into jello mixture and mix well. Stir 1 can drained crushed pineapple. Pour into lined dish. Sprinkle remaining crumbs on top and chill until firm.

Katie Ann Lehman (Cook)

PUFF PUDDING

1 c. of sour cream, 2 t. baking powder and ½ t. salt as for biscuits; stir in 2 c. flour until very stiff. Spread in a 2 qt. pudding pan and bake until brown. Take 3 nice tart apples, stewed smooth; add 1 T. butter, ½ c. sugar, yolk of 1 egg. Pour mixture over pudding in pan and return to oven. When done, beat the white of an egg, 2 T. sugar, season to taste. Spoon over pudding, apple mixture in pan and return to oven again and brown the meringue. Bake 425°-450° 15-20 min.

Leora V. Kauffman (Purchasing)

A DELICIOUS SMOOTH PUDDING

4 pkg. instant pudding mix (3 vanilla - 1 butterscotch or lemon)
3 c. milk

Mix and add:
1 qt. of ice cream
1 lg. container Cool Whip

Line pan with graham cracker crust:

24 graham crackers, crushed
½ c. powdered sugar
½ stick oleo

Add pudding to top of crust.

Mrs. Harley Miller (Miller's Orchard)
Applebutter

PUMPKIN ROLL

3 eggs beaten   1 t. baking powder
add gradually 1 c. sugar   2 t. cinnamon
⅔ c. pumpkin   1 t. ginger
1 t. lemon juice   ½ t. nutmeg
fold in ¾ c. flour

Bake at 375° for 15 min., in a greased and floured cookie sheet. While warm roll up in towel sprinkled with powdered sugar. Unroll when cool and add this filling:

1 c. powdered sugar   4 T. oleo
8 oz. cream cheese   1 t. vanilla

Mix until smooth. Add nuts if desired. Freeze or keep in refrigerator.

Mary Esther Miller (Waitress)

RHUBARB BUTTER CRUNCH

Combine:

3 c. fresh rhubarb
1 c. sugar
3 T. flour

Place in greased 6x10 inch baking dish.

Combine:

1 c. brown sugar
1 c. raw rolled oats
1½ c. flour
Cut in ½ c. butter & ½ c. other shortening

Sprinkle over rhubarb mixture. Bake at 375° mod. oven 40 min.
Serve warm with cream.

Ann Yoder (Waitress)

RHUBARB COBBLER

1 c. sugar	¾ c. milk
1 c. flour	1 t. vanilla
2 t. baking powder	Dash of salt
2 T. shortening	3 c. rhubarb (cut into pieces)

Combine all ingredients and pour into 8x8x2 inch pan. Pour over
this batter:

1 c. sugar
1 c. hot water

Mixed together. Bake at 375° for 30-35 min.

Edna Nisley (Waitress)

RICE DIVINE

Use 2 c. of cooked rice. Chill.

Add:

¼ c. sugar
1 t. vanilla
1 c. whipping cream

Put in mixing bowl and whip. Refrigerate. Serve with chocolate sauce or fresh fruit sauce.

Meda Bontrager (Waitress)

RICE PUDDING

2 c. cooked rice   4 eggs
2 c. sugar   a little salt

Beat together well. Add:

4 level T. flour   1 t. vanilla
1 c. raisins   4 c. milk

Mix all together and pour in a pan. Bake in moderate oven. 325° 20-30 min.

Lucy Eash (Cook)

RITZ CRACKER TORTE

1 t. vanilla
whites of 4 eggs beaten to soft peaks
¼ t. cream of tartar

Next add: 1 c. sugar
Last add: ½ c. nut meats and 18 Ritz crackers crumbled

Bake in greased pie tin at 350° till brown.
Serves 5 or 6 with whipped cream and cherry on top.

Mildred Two (Cake Decorator)

STRAWBERRY LONG CAKE

2 c. flour
6 T. sugar
4 t. baking powder
⅔ c. milk

¾ t. salt
⅓ c. shortening
1 egg beaten

Sift together flour, sugar, baking powder and salt. Mix in ⅓ c. shortening, then add egg and milk. Spread in a greased 8x10 in. baking dish.
Cream together:

¼ c. butter
¼ c. brown sugar
3 T. flour

Drop this on top of first mixture. Bake at 400° approximately 30 min. Serve with fresh strawberries and cream while still warm.

Ida Miller (Cook)

STRAWBERRY SHORTCAKE

2½ c. flour
2 t. baking powder
½ t. salt
2 eggs

1 c. sugar
1 c. milk
2 T. butter, melted
1 t. vanilla

Sift flour; measure and add baking powder and salt. Sift again.
Sift dry ingredients together.
Beat eggs and add sugar, milk and flavoring.
Combine egg mixture with dry ingredients.
Add melted butter and beat until thoroughly blended.
Pour into greased cake pan.
Bake at 375° for 25-30 min.
Serve warm with crushed, frozen or fresh strawberries and milk or ice cream.

Sue Miller (Manager)

STRAWBERRY YUM-YUM

1 c. flour
½ c. butter

¼ c. brown sugar
½ c. chopped nuts

2 egg whites
1 c. sugar
2 t. lemon juice

1 - 10 oz. frozen strawberries
1 pkg. Dream Whip

Mix until crumbly the first four ingredients and press into an 8x8 in. pan. Bake at 350° for 20-25 min. Cool and break into crumbs. Place crumbs in a 9x13 pan. Set aside. Combine the egg whites, lemon juice, sugar, and strawberries and beat at medium speed for 15-20 min. Spread strawberry mixture over crumbs and freeze. Serve frozen.

Esther Hershberger
Betty A. Hershberger (Grill Cook)

VANILLA TARTS

Dough

2 c. sugar (scant)
1 egg
½ c. lard

1 c. sour milk or buttermilk
1 t. soda
2 c. flour

Juice

1 egg
1 c. sugar
1 c. syrup (karo)

1 pt. cold water
1 t. vanilla

Put dough in unbaked pie shell and pour juice over it. (4 tart size pies) Bake 425° about 20 min.

Mrs. Robert W. Miller

WHOLE WHEAT PUDDING

1½ c. graham flour
¾ c. white flour
¾ c. sugar
1 c. sour milk
1 c. raisins

2 T. shortening
1 egg
½ t. salt
1 t. baking powder
1 t. nutmeg

Pour in greased pan. Bake at 350° for 35-40 min. Serve hot with milk or whipped cream.

Laura Miller (Grill Cook)
Susie W. Miller (Cleaning)

ICE CREAM

Cook together:
1 qt. milk
2 c. sugar
½ t. salt

2 T. flour
4 eggs

Add 1 T. vanilla
2 c. cream (whipped)
Enough milk to fill up can and freeze
Makes 1 gal.

Mabel Hershberger (Pie Baker)

BUTTERSCOTCH ICE CREAM

2½ qts. milk
12 T. cornstarch

3 eggs
½ t. salt

Mix thoroughly and cook until thickened taking care that mixture doesn't scorch.
Remove from heat and add:
3 c. brown sugar
1 c. white sugar

3 T. vanilla
2 cans of evaporated milk

Cool and freeze. More milk may be added to mixture for less rich ice cream. Make in 1 gal freezer.

Dorothy Chupp (Hostess)

COFFEE ICE CREAM

Boil together:

6 t. instant coffee powder	3 T. flour
3¾ c. sugar	⅓ t. salt
7½ c. milk	

9 egg yolks, beaten	3 T. vanilla
1 qt. cream	1 c. chopped nuts

Combine first 5 ingredients in large kettle. Gradually stir in milk and cook, stir constantly, until mixture is slightly thickened. Pour some of the hot mixture over the eggs, blending well. Slowly stir egg mixture into hot mixture. Cook 1 min. Strain, chill well. Stir in cream, vanilla and nuts. Pour into 1½ gal. freezer filling ¾ full.

Katie Cross (Waitress)

DAIRY QUEEN ICE CREAM

2 qts. scalded milk	1 pt. cream
4 pkgs. Knox gelatine	3 t. vanilla
softened in cold water	1¼ t. salt
2½ c. sugar	1 can Carnation milk

Mix and put in freezer can and add milk to ¾ full and freeze. 1½ gal.

Lydia Ann Miller (Cook)

DAIRY QUEEN ICE CREAM

1½ gallon freezer

2 qts. scalded milk	1 pt. (Burger's) cream
4 pkgs. gelatin (Knox)	1 can Carnation milk
4 c. sugar	3 T. vanilla
1¼ t. salt	

Bring milk almost to a boil. Then soften gelatin in water (2 T. for each pkg.). Add this to hot milk. Also add the sugar and salt to the hot milk. Cool. Add cream and vanilla last and freeze.

Betty A. Hershberger (Grill Cook)

ICE CREAM

Come to boil:

2 qt. milk
1 c. sugar

Combine:

3 heaping T. flour	1 c. sugar
3 T. cornstarch	5 or 6 beaten egg yolks

Add to the milk and cook till thickened, stirring constantly. Beat the egg whites, add 1 c. sugar, ½ c. karo and ½ c. brown sugar. Beat. Pour cooked mixture into can, then add egg white mixture. Stir altogether. Add half and half, milk, or whipping cream. For chocolate ice cream add 1 box of instant chocolate pudding to cooked mixture. Makes 1 gal.

LaVerda Miller (Waitress)

DAIRY QUEEN ICE CREAM

For 1½ gallon.

2 qt. scalded milk	1¼ t. salt
4 pkg. gelatin - 4 pkgs. in one box	2 qt. cream
4 c. sugar	3 T. vanilla

Bring milk almost to a boil, then soften gelatin in water (2 T. water to 1 pkg. gelatin). Add this to hot milk. Then also add sugar to hot milk and salt. Cool then add cream and vanilla.

Elnora Yoder (Pie Baker)

Q. "If a rooster laid an egg on the top of a hill, which side would the egg roll down?"

A. "Neither side . . . a rooster can't lay eggs."

ORANGE JELLO ICE CREAM

Beat together:
2 c. sugar
5 eggs
Dissolve 2 boxes jello in 1 c. boiling water
Add this to above mixture.
Stir well, then add enough milk to fill 1 gal. freezer.

Katie Cross (Waitress)

VANILLA ICE CREAM

Heat: 5 qt. milk (rich)
Mix together:

6 to 8 eggs   ½ c. flour
3 c. white sugar   ½ c. cornstarch

Mix this with 1 qt. milk and stir in heated milk, cook until it thickens.
Take off heat and add:

1 c. brown sugar
4 t. vanilla

Makes enough for 2 gal. freezer.

Laura Miller (Grill Cook)

VANILLA ICE CREAM

Prepare 3 boxes of instant pudding (2 vanilla, 1 butterscotch).
Set aside for 5 min.

Mix 5 or 6 well beaten eggs   1½ to 2 c. cream
1½ c. white sugar   pudding

Put these in freezer can after they are mixed and add enough milk
to have ¾ full. Freeze.

Various flavored puddings may be used.

Makes 1½ gal.

Edma Mae Schmucker (Dishwasher)
Mrs. Levi R. Miller

VANILLA ICE CREAM (uncooked base)

4 c. milk	½ t. salt
2 T. plain gelatin	2 c. whipping cream
1 c. cold water	2 t. vanilla
2 c. sugar	

Scald milk in top of double boiler. Add sugar and salt and stir until dissolved. Soak gelatin in cold water. Add gelatin to milk and blend together. Cool. Add vanilla and pour into freezer container. For maple flavored ice cream, use brown sugar and maple flavoring. Enough mix for ½ gal. freezer.

Sue Miller (Manager)

HOT FUDGE SAUCE FOR ICE CREAM

6 T. margarine	1 (13 oz.) can evaporated milk
1 c. sugar	1 t. vanilla
6 T. cocoa	

Mix together margarine, sugar and cocoa in a saucepan. Cook over medium heat until butter is completely melted. Slowly add evaporated milk. Bring to boil and boil 1 min. stirring constantly. Remove from heat and add vanilla. Serve hot or cold. Makes about 2 cups.

LaVerda Miller (Waitress)

STRAWBERRY TOPPING FOR ICE CREAM

1 c. cold water
1 box Sure-Jell

Boil one minute and stir into the following mixture:

4 c. crushed strawberries
5 c. sugar

Mix until the sugar is well dissolved, approximately 5 minutes. Also makes good milk shakes.

Denise Henke (Waitress)

BEST-EVER GRAPE JUICE

10 lbs. grapes, picked from stems
2 qts. water
2 lbs. white sugar

Wash the grapes, then add water and boil for 10 minutes. Drain but do not squeeze. Add sugar, then bring to the boiling point again. Squeeze through clean cloth to remove seeds and skins. Can. Makes 1 gallon.

Esther Nisley (Pie Baker)

GREEN PUNCH

1 pkg. lemon-lime Kool-Aid®   2½ c. pineapple juice
4 c. water   ¼ c. lime juice
¾ c. sugar   1½ qt. 7-Up® or ginger ale

Combine all ingredients and chill. Makes 14 cups.

Betty Graber (Waitress)

HOT CHOCOLATE MIX

1 lb. powdered sugar   6 oz. non-dairy coffee creamer
2 lb. Nestles Quik™   1 box powdered milk (8-qt. size)

Mix all ingredients together. For each serving, put ½ c. of mix in a cup and fill with boiling water. Makes about 1 gallon of mix.

Martha Otto (Pie Baker)

O taste and see that the Lord is good: blessed is the man that trusteth in him.

O fear the Lord, ye his saints: for there is no want to them that fear him.

The young lions do lack, and suffer hunger: but they that seek the Lord shall not want any good thing.

Psa. 34:8-10

HOT CHOCOLATE MIXTURE

1 lb. dry milk   1 lb. Nestles Quick
3 oz. Coffee Mate   3 c. powdered sugar

Mix together. Enough to mix to 7 or 8 qts. hot water. Ready to use.

Katie Cross (Waitress)

INSTANT COCOA MIX

32 oz. dry milk
8 oz. Pream (coffee cream substitute)
2 lbs. powdered sugar
1 - 2 lb. can Nestles Quick

Mix all together. Fix by putting ⅓ c. mix in a cup and filling with hot water. This keeps a long time if put in tight containers.

Katie Ann Lehman (Cook)
Alma W. Miller

HOT OR COLD PERKY PUNCH

1 - 46 oz. can pineapple juice   2 T. whole cloves
1 - 1 qt. bottle cranberry juice   1 T. whole allspice
3 c. water   ½ t. salt
6 cinnamon sticks   1 c. brown sugar

Pour fruit juice and water into 30-36 c. automatic coffee maker. Place remaining ingredients in basket.

Plug in coffee maker and perk. Makes 25 - 4 oz. servings. May be served hot or cold.

Betty Graber (Waitress)

RED PUNCH

1 pkg. cherry Kool-Aid®
1 pkg. strawberry Kool-Aid®
2 c. sugar
3 qt. water

1 can frozen orange juice (6 oz.
1 can frozen lemonade (6 oz.)
1 qt. 7-Up® or ginger ale

Combine all ingredients and chill. Makes 1½ gallons.

Sharon Boley (Waitress)
Esther Hershberger

PUNCH

1 can frozen lemonade (12 oz.)
1 lg. can pineapple juice (liquid)
2 lg. bananas, mashed

1 can frozen orange juice (12 oz.)
4 c. water
4 qt. 7-Up® or lemon-lime soda

Combine all ingredients except soda pop and freeze until ready to serve. Then add soda pop.

Betty A. Hershberger
(Grill Cook)

QUICK ROOT BEER

2 c. white sugar
3-4 t. root beer extract

1 t. yeast
½ c. warm water

Dissolve yeast in ½ c. warm water for 15 minutes. Dissolve sugar and extract in 3½ qt. water while yeast sets. Mix together in 1-gal. jug. Cap jug and let set in a warm place for one day, then refrigerate.

Debbie Oesch (Waitress)

Go thy way, eat thy bread with joy, and drink thy wine with a merry heart; for God now accepteth thy works. Let thy garments be always white; and let thy head lack no ointment.

Eccl. 9:7-8

RHUBARB DRINK

In 4 qt. kettle, put half full of rhubarb and fill up with water. Bring to a boil, let stand ½ hr., and drain. This can be canned.

Drink

2 qt. rhubarb juice
1 small can frozen lemon juice
1 small can frozen orange juice

3½ qts. water
1 pkg. raspberry Kool-Aid
2 c. sugar

May add ice cubes.

Mrs. John R. Miller

RUSSIAN TEA

2 c. tang
1¼ c. sugar
½ c. instant tea
1 t. cinnamon
2 pkgs. (10 cent) lemonade mix
½ t. cloves

Mix and store in a dry place. 2½ t. per cup boiling water.

Joyce Bechtel (Waitress)

SPICED CIDER

6 c. sweet cider
20 whole cloves
3 sticks cinnamon

½ t. grated lemon rind
½ t. grated orange rind

Combine spices and 3 c. cider and place over low heat. Bring to boiling point and simmer 5 minutes. Remove from heat and let stand 30 minutes. Add remaining cider, orange and lemon rind. Chill. When ready to serve, pour over ice cubes. Garnish with orange or lemon slices. Makes 8-10 servings.

Sue Miller (Manager)

Soups, Pickles & Relishes

Use spices and herbs sparingly, they are best when you have to guess which ones are really used.

Pour the hot water from your cold packer along the sidewalk to kill weeds.

When canning use rain water in cookers, it will keep cans and cooker cleaner.

To prevent milk or cream from curdling when used with tomatoes, add a bit of soda to tomatoes before adding milk.

Soups, Pickles & Relishes

BEAN SOUP

1 pkg. (1 lb.) navy beans
2½ qt. water

¼ t. soda
1 t. salt

Boil together for 2 min. Let set 1 hr.
Add:

Ham
2 stalks celery
3 carrots

2 onions
pepper
2 whole bay leaves

Simmer for 2 hrs. Remove leaves and bones. Store or freeze. When serving add ½ can stewed tomatoes, catsup or juice.

LaVerda Miller (Waitress)

OLD FASHIONED BEAN SOUP (Amish Church Soup)

½ stick butter
1 med. onion (chopped)
3 c. cooked navy beans

salt to taste
4 qts. milk
bread (cut in bite size)

Brown onions in butter. Add beans and milk. Bring to a boiling point. Add bread cubes. Serves approximately 15 people.

Sue Miller (Manager)

CELERY NERVE-TONIC SOUP

3 c. chopped celery
    (some leaves also)
½ c. chopped onion
2 T. butter
2 c. chicken stock

1 c. water
2 c. cream or top milk
2 T. flour
2 c. milk
salt and pepper

Sauté celery and onion in butter until tender. Put through sieve if you want smooth soup. Add chicken stock and water. Mix cream, flour, and milk; add to soup and cook till thick. Salt and pepper to taste.

These proportions serve 8.

Esther Nisley (Pie Baker)

CHICKEN AND NOODLE SOUP

4 old hens, skinned and cut up
8 qt. water
2 qt. celery, diced
2 qt. carrots, sliced

1 onion
1 gal. noodles
2 qt. potatoes, diced
sprigs of parsley

Stew chickens in water until tender. Remove bones. Cook noodles in broth for 10 minutes. Combine all ingredients, put in canning jars, and cook in pressure cooker for 30 minutes at 10 lbs. pressure.

Mattie J. Yoder (Cook)

CHILI SOUP

2 lb. ground beef
3 medium onions
1 qt. kidney beans

2 qt. water
1 qt. tomato juice
1 level t. chili powder

Fry the ground beef with salt, pepper, and onions. Drain grease. Add other ingredients, heat, and serve.

Lydia Ann Miller (Cook)

CHILI SOUP

1½ gal. tomato juice
½ gal. tomato soup
1 - #2 cans (approx. 1½ qt.)
   tomato puree

2 qts. water
⅔ c. brown sugar
3 rounded T. chili powder

Heat all above ingredients together and add 5 lbs. hamburger which has been fried with salt, pepper and onions. Add to hot broth. Add 1 gal. red kidney beans. Makes 3½ to 4 gal. Very good to can and use later.

Sue Miller (Manager)

COLD MILK SOUP

2 qts. cold milk
¾ c. brown sugar

1 t. vanilla
Bread cut to bite size

Mix milk, brown sugar and vanilla. Pour over bread cubes. Serve with strawberries, peaches or bananas or any other fruit. Serves 6-8 people.

Sue Miller (Manager)

POTATO SOUP

3 potatoes
1 qt. milk
2 slices onion
3 T. butter
2 T. flour

1½ t. salt
¼ t. celery salt
1/8 t. pepper
dash of cayenne
1 t. chopped parsley

Cook the potatoes in salted water; when soft rub through sieve. Scald the milk with the onion, remove the onion and add the milk slowly to the potatoes. Melt half the butter, add the dry ingredients, stir until well mixed, then stir into boiling hot soup, cook 1 min., add remaining butter and sprinkle with parsley.

Leora V. Kauffman (Purchasing)

COUNTRY POTATO SOUP

3 c. potatoes, peeled and diced	½ t. salt
½ c. celery, diced	2 c. milk
½ c. onion, diced	1 c. sour cream
1½ c. water	2 T. flour
2 chicken bouillon cubes	1 t. chives, chopped

Combine potatoes, celery, onion, water, bouillon cubes, and salt in a large saucepan. Cover and cook for about 20 minutes or until potatoes are tender (not mushy). Add 1 c. milk and heat. Mix the sour cream, flour, chives, and remaining milk in a medium bowl. Stir this sour cream mixture into the soup base gradually. Cover and simmer over low heat, stirring constantly until thickened. Yields 6 cups.

Esther Hershberger

Be kindly affectioned one to another with brotherly love; in honour preferring one another; Not slothful in business; fervent in spirit; serving the Lord; Rejoicing in hope; patient in tribulation; continuing instant in prayer; Distributing to the necessity of saints; given to hospitality.

Rom. 12:10-13

RIVEL SOUP

Soup:	*Rivels:*
2 T. butter	¾ c. flour
2 qt. milk or beef broth	1 egg, medium
	1 t. salt

Brown butter in saucepan, add milk, and bring to boiling point.

To make rivels, mix the flour, egg, and salt until crumbly. Scatter the rivels into soup slowly, stirring constantly, then bring to a boil. Serves 6.

Sue Miller (Manager)

SALMON SOUP

⅓ can salmon
1 qt. scalded milk
2 T. butter

4 T. flour (Optional)
1½ t. salt
sprinkle of pepper

Drain the oil from salmon, remove skin and bones, crumble the salmon and add gradually to seasoned hot milk. If thickening preferred, make a thin paste with the flour and add.

Leora V. Kauffman (Purchasing)

TOMATO SOUP

14 qts. sliced tomatoes (not peeled) cook with 5 qts. water.

Add:

7 med. onions, chopped
14 stems celery
14 sprays parsley

Cook this mixture until it can be put through a ricer.

Add:

14 T. flour
16 T. sugar
pepper to taste

8 T. salt
14 T. melted butter

Mix with cold water to make a thick batter. Then add to the boiling tomato pulp and cook 30 min. Seal at once. Add an equal amount of milk to serve.

Esther Nisley (Pie Baker)

VEGETABLE SOUP

1½ gal. tomato juice
½ gal. tomato soup
2 #2 cans (approx. 1½ qts.)
    tomato puree

2 qts. water
1 gal. beef broth
⅔ c. brown sugar

Heat and add:

1 to 1½ qts. beef chunks (cooked)
1 to 1½ gal. mixed vegetables, or any vegetable, like corn, peas, green beans.

Makes 6 to 7 gal., depending on the amount of vegetables you put in. Very good to can and use later.

Sue Miller (Manager)

BREAD AND BUTTER PICKLES

30 medium-sized cucumbers
    (1 gal. sliced)
8 medium-sized onions
2 large red or green peppers
½ c. salt

5 c. sugar
5 c. vinegar
2 T. mustard seed
1 t. tumeric
1 t. whole cloves

Slice cucumbers in thin rings. Do not pare. Slice onions in thin rings. Cut peppers in fine strips. Dissolve salt in ice water and pour over sliced vegetables. Let stand 3 hours and drain. Combine vinegar, sugar and spices and bring to a boil. Add drained vegetables and heat to boiling point. Do not boil. Pack into sterilized jars and seal.

Denise Henke (Waitress)

DILL PICKLES

Pickles may be left whole or larger ones sliced. Put loosely in jars, with 2 or 3 garlic buds, 1/8 t. alum, and 1 or 2 dill heads in each can.

Heat:
5 qts. water
2 qts. vinegar
1¾ c. salt

Pour boiling hot over pickles and seal. (Makes 15 qts.)

Mrs. Leroy J. Yoder

GARLIC DILL PICKLES

Put 2 heads of dill in a qt. can. Slice full of dill size pickles. Put 3 or 4 garlic buds on top.

Heat:
2 c. vinegar   2 T. salt
2 c. water   3 c. sugar - heat to boil

Pour over pickles. Cold pack till boiling point. Do not let boil. Remove cans right away. Good in two weeks. Makes 4 qts.

Lydia Mae Troyer (Cook)
Esther Nisley (Pie Baker)
Lucy Eash (Cook)
Sarah Bontrager

KOSHER DILL PICKLES

20-25 4 inch cucumbers   3 qts. water
fresh dill   1 qt. vinegar
garlic cloves   1 c. salt
powdered alum   grape leaves

Wash cucumbers. Let stand in cold water overnight. Pack in hot sterilized jars. To each qt. add 2 heads dill, 1 clove garlic, and 1/8 t. alum. Combine salt, water, vinegar; heat to boiling, fill jars. Put grape leaf on top of each jar, seal. Makes 6 to 8 qts.

Esther Nisley (Pie Baker)

ICICLE PICKLES

2 c. salt
1 gal. boiling water
2 gal. small cucumbers (quartered lengthwise)
1½ T. alum

Juice:

2 qt. white vinegar
1 gal. white sugar

2 oz. pickling spice
2 sticks cinnamon bark

Add salt to boiling water and pour over pickles. Let stand 1 week. Stir once every day. Drain, then cover with boiling water. Let stand 24 hours. Then drain and cover with fresh boiling water to which alum has been added. Let stand 24 hours and drain.

Juice—Mix juice ingredients, bring to boil and pour over pickles. For 3 mornings, drain juice, reheat to boiling and pour over pickles. The 4th morning, heat juice and pickles to simmering (do not boil). Pack loosely in jars and seal.

Sue Miller (Manager)

SWEET DILL PICKLES

2 c. vinegar
3 c. sugar
2 c. water

2 T. salt
Dill and garlic

Wash pickles and slice. Put in jars with 2 garlic buds and 2 heads of dill. Heat vinegar mixture and pour over pickles. Cold pack for 5 min. and remove from heat. Enough liquid for 6 pts.

Mary Esther Miller (Waitress)

MIXED PICKLE

⅔ c. sugar
1 t. salt, heaping
4 T. vinegar

Mix and put in cans filled with raw vegetables. Then fill up with water. This is for 1 qt. Cold pack for 2 hrs.

Lucy Eash (Cook)

RELISH

4 pecks peeled ripe tomatoes
24 lg. onions
16 bunches celery
20 green peppers
1 lb. salt

¼ lb. celery seed
¼ lb. mustard seed
1¼ gal. vinegar
8 lbs. brown sugar

Chop the vegetables and sprinkle with salt and let set overnight. Drain. Dissolve the sugar in the vinegar and mix in the celery and mustard seed. Mix very well and seal in airtight containers or process for 15 min. Keep the key to the pickle cellar hidden or you will be tempting your neighbors to sneak in.

Leora V. Kauffman (Purchasing)

CORN RELISH

2 qts. cut corn
1 qt. chopped cabbage
1 c. chopped sweet red peppers
1 c. chopped sweet green peppers
1 c. chopped onions
1 T. celery seed
1 T. salt

1 T. tumeric
2 T. dry mustard
1 T. mustard seed
1 c. water
1 qt. vinegar
2 c. sugar

To prepare corn boil 5 min. Cut off from cobs. Combine with remaining ingredients and simmer 20 min. Bring to boiling, pack boiling hot into jars. Process 15 min. Yield about 6 pt.

Lucy Eash (Cook)

PICKLE RELISH

1 gal. ground pickles
1 pt. ground onions
Put a handful of salt on for 2 hrs., then drain off juice and add:

6 c. sugar
2 t. tumeric
3 t. mustard seed

3 t. celery seed
3 c. vinegar

Heat all together. Put in cans and seal.

Lydia Ann Miller (Cook)

HOT DOG RELISH

1 gal. ground pickles
1 pt. onions

2 peppers
Add celery if you wish

Mix this with some salt and let stand a few hours.

Mix and heat:

6 c. sugar
1 T. flour
3 t. mustard seed
1 qt. vinegar

2 T. cornstarch
3 t. celery seed
3 t. tumeric
2 glasses of water

Heat juice and then add to ground pickle mixture and bring to boil. Seal in small jars.

Mary Troyer (Dishwasher)

PICKLE RELISH

1 gal. chopped (fine) cucumbers
1 pt. chopped onions

Add ¼ c. salt, and let set 2 hrs., then drain.

Add:
6 c. sugar
3 t. mustard seed
2 t. tumeric

3 t. celery seed
2 c. vinegar

Heat altogether and put in jars and seal.

Katie Cross (Waitress)

PICKLED CORN

4 qts. corn
2 qts. cabbage
1 c. sugar
1 T. salt

2 T. mustard seed
2 T. celery seed
Enough vinegar and water to cover.

Boil and put in cans. Make it sour to suit your taste.

Lucy Eash (Cook)

GREEN TOMATO MINCE

1 peck green tomatoes, chopped
   fine — drain off juice
Add boiling water (2-3 qts.)
Add ½ peck apples, chopped
5 lb. brown sugar
2 t. salt

1 t. nutmeg
1 c. vinegar
2 lbs. raisins
1 t. cloves
2 t. cinnamon

Boil 1 hr. slowly and can while hot.

Katie Cross (Waitress)

SANDWICH SPREAD

6 large onions
6 large cucumbers
6 large green peppers
12 green tomatoes
1 pt. vinegar

1 pt. water
5 c. white sugar
3 T. salt
1 pt. prepared mustard

Grind the vegetables fine. Let stand 1 hour, then drain. Boil vegetables, sugar, salt, and vinegar for 15 minutes. Add water to 5 T. flour to make a thick paste. Add mustard and 1 T. tumeric, and 2 T. celery seed. Put this mixture in the vegetable mixture and boil a little longer. Put in jars and seal hot.

Debbie Oesch (Waitress)

CATSUP

2 gal. tomato juice
8 T. salt
2 c. vinegar

¼ c. cinnamon oil
¼ t. clove oil
1 or 2 onions (Chopped Fine)

Cook down ⅓ from where you started. Add 8 c. sugar, boil real good. Add 8 or 10 T. cornstarch or clear-jell dissolved in water. Put in jars or bottles and seal.

Katie Cross (Waitress)

CATSUP — BEST

2 gal. thick tomato juice (drained) 2 large onions (cup up)
2½ c. vinegar 1 T. mixed pickling spice

Boil together until onions are soft. Put thru sieve. Put back on to boil (about 1 hr.). Then add the following:

8 c. sugar ½ t. cinnamon
8 heaping T. clear-jell 7 T. salt
½ t. cloves

Mix these together dry and stir in. Then boil 10-15 min. more. Put in hot bottles and seal.

Mrs. Clara Miller

TEN MINUTE CATSUP

1 peck tomatoes
4 large onions

Put onions in cloth to cook, cook till tender. Put through sieve. Drain tomato juice in sack 1 hr. or overnight (I usually drain overnight as I think it's thicker.) Take pulp and add:

2 c. vinegar 1 T. salt
2 c. sugar spice to suit taste

Put in catsup spice after you remove from stove. When mixture starts to boil, boil 10 min., stirring constantly. I make my own catsup spice.

Catsup Spice

2 T. ground cinnamon ½ t. ground cayenne pepper
1 T. ground cloves (red pepper)
2 t. ground allspice 3 T. paprika
1 t. ground nutmeg

Usually more than needed for 1 recipe. I add all spices in small bowl and mix.

Mrs. Robert W. Miller

RED CATSUP

2 gal. tomato juice
¼ t. red pepper
2 large onions (tied in bag)
3 c. vinegar
6 c. sugar

8 t. salt
20 drops oil of cinnamon
20 drops oil of cloves
6 rounded T. cornstarch
red food coloring (optional)

Bring to boil, juice, onions, salt, vinegar, red pepper and the oils. Add only ½ of sugar to juice. Let boil down ⅓. Make paste with ½ of sugar and cornstarch adding to juice almost last. Can and seal.

Mary Ann Schlabach (Waitress)

Add a small amount of ammonia to washing water to make glassware sparkle. Also is good for washing windows, then polish with crumpled newspapers.

Hardening of the heart is worse than hardening of the arteries.

Use 1 T. salt to 4 of alcohol to remove grease spots from clothing, by sponging.

Paint spots on clothing will come out with several applications of equal parts of ammonia and turpentine, then wash in soap suds.

Use baking soda equal to 1 t. to a pint of water to remove stains from plastic kitchen ware.

Salt or baking soda sprinkled on small fires usually, will put it out by smothering it. Never use flour.

To soften brown sugar lumps, put in a jar with a piece of moist paper towel under the lid, or heat in oven for several minutes.

A t. of vinegar added to homemade syrup will keep it from candying after it stands.

A doctor recommended 1 t. of soda, 1 t. salt and 1 t. vinegar in ½ c. of warm water, to be used as a (poor man's) gargle or mouthwash. Just as effective as the high priced sweet tasting ones.

It is a good idea to keep your words soft and sweet, you never know when you may have to eat them.

Laura Miller (Grill Cook)

BEDBUG KILLER

Hydrag Bichlor Carros	4 drams
Wool alcohol	8 oz.

Mix - apply to crevices and beds with a feather. Be sure and try this remedy if you are troubled with bedbugs. Nothing better can be compounded.

TOOTHACHE

Creosote	1 dram
Chloroform	1 dram
Oil of cloves	1 dram

Saturate a small piece of cotton and put in the tooth. Repeat often until relieved. This soul-harrowing trouble can be stopped suddenly by using the above. This remedy does the work, as hundreds can testify.

COCKROACH POWDER

Napthalin	1⅓ drams
Powdered angelicia root	8 oz.
Oil of Eucalyptus	1/5 oz.

Distribute this mixture around the infested places, and every roach will be driven away.

SWEATING FEET

Thymol	20 grains
Boric acid	3 drams
Alcohol	2 oz.
Dist. Ext. witch hazel	6 oz.

Apply night and morning, rubbing well. This liquid will be found excellent for the ladies who perspire too freely under the arms.

Jellies, Jams & Misc.

CORNS

Saliclylic acid	30 grains
Collodion	1 oz.
Ext. cannobis Indiea	10 grams

Mix - apply with camel's hair brush for four nights. Then soak the foot in very hot water for twenty minutes, and the corn can be lifted entirely out. This remedy may be relied upon.

CHAPPED LIPS

Take 6 T. of boiling hot mutton suet. Stir in 6 T. glycerine, 1 T. olive oil. Remove from heat and stir in 1 T. powdered camphor. Stir until cold. "1887" cookbook.

TO REMOVE DANDRUFF

Wash the head every two days with a strong solution of salt water. Where sea salt is not available use a small handful in a basin of water. This has removed dandruff where every other means had failed.

COMPUTING DOSE OF MEDICINE FOR CHILDREN

A teaspoon is sixty drops. In computing a dose of medicine for children, take a child's age plus one and divide by twelve. For example, if adult dose is one teaspoonful of sixty drops, and child's age is three years. Three plus one is four: Divide four by twelve, which is one-third: one-third of sixty drops is twenty drops — the correct dose in this instance.

These remedies were taken from an old "Farm Accounting" Record Book.

Edna Nissley (Waitress)

Jellies, Jams & Misc.

APPLE BUTTER

2 gal. apples
5 lbs. white sugar

Mix and let stand overnight. Next morning, boil 3 hours (covered). Strain if you have to. Then add cinnamon to add taste.

Marilyn Bontrager (Waitress)

CIDER JELLY

4 c. cider
⅔ c. red hots candy

1 box Sure-Jell
5 c. sugar

Heat cider and red hots with Sure-Jell until dissolved. Bring to boil and add sugar. Bring to rolling boil. Boil 1 min.

Esther Hershberger

ELDERBERRY JELLY

3 c. elderberry juice
¼ c. lime flavor

1 box Sure-Jell
4½ c. sugar

Mix juice, flavor and Sure-Jell. Bring to a hard boil, add sugar at once and bring to a full rolling boil. Boil hard for 1 min. Skim off foam with a metal spoon. Pour into glasses, leaving ½ in. from top; seal with melted paraffin.

Denise Henke (Waitress)

RHUBARB JELLY

2 c. rhubarb, cut up
2 c. sugar
8 oz. can crushed pineapple

Combine all ingredients and bring to boil. Simmer 15 min. Stir in 1
3 oz. pkg. of strawberry jello. Refrigerate to set.

Elsie Rebecca Miller (Grill Cook)

RHUBARB JELLY

4 c. rhubarb
3 c. sugar
1 small box jello (any flavor)

Cut rhubarb in small cubes and put enough water in to cook tender.
When tender, stir in jello and sugar, and let cool.

Amanda Troyer (Waitress)

JAM

1 qt. fruit juice
1 qt. light syrup
6 lbs. white sugar

Put all together and boil. It is about thick enough when it boils right.
Makes almost 1 gal.

Amanda Troyer (Waitress)

GRAPE JAM

6 c. grapes   1 orange (cut up)
6 c. white sugar   1 t. Sure-Jell to each c.

Cook the pulp of the grapes and put them through a strainer. Mix
all the ingredients together and cook at least 10 min. Can be tested
on a small dish. Pour into sterilized glasses and seal.

Ruth Miller (Waitress)

RHUBARB JAM

5 c. rhubarb
5 c. sugar

Let stand overnight. Cook 3 min. Add 1 large box raspberry jello. Put in jars.

Esther Nisley (Pie Baker)

RHUBARB JAM

4 c. rhubarb
4 c. sugar

Stir and put on stove, let come to boil 4 or 5 min. Take off and stir in 1 box jello (any flavor).

Mrs. Freddie S. Bontrager

RHUBARB JAM

5 c. rhubarb
1 c. pineapple

4 c. sugar
1 pkg. strawberry jello

Put in jars and seal.

Mrs. Robert W. Miller

OLD FASHIONED PEACH PRESERVE

2 qts. sliced, peeled ripe peaches (about 10 large peaches)
6 c. sugar

Combine fruit and sugar. Let stand 12-18 hrs. in a cool place. Bring slowly to a boil, stirring frequently. Boil gently until fruit becomes clear and syrup thick, about 40 min. Stir frequently to prevent sticking. Skim if necessary. Pour boiling hot in jars. Adjust lids. Process 15 min. Yield about 7 half-pint jars.

Lucy Eash (Cook)

NO COOK STRAWBERRY JAM

2 c. fully ripe, completely crushed, strawberries
1 box Sure-Jell
4 c. sugar

Mix sugar into berries, let stand 10 min., stir to dissolve sugar. Mix ¾ c. water and Sure-Jell in saucepan. Bring to a boil and boil 1 min., stirring constantly. Stir into berries, continue stirring 3 min. Ladel into containers, cover with lids and let set 24 hrs. at room temperature. Store in freezer.

Sue Mullet (Bread Baker)

IMITATION HONEY

5 lbs. granulated sugar
1½ pts. water

Boil a few minutes till clear and add 1 t. alum. Boil 2 min. more. Remove from heat and add 40 red and white clover blossoms and cover, let set 10 min. and strain. You may add extra blossoms if you like.

Mrs. Levi R. Miller

PEAR HONEY SPREAD

4 lbs. ground pears
5 lbs. sugar
1 medium sized can crushed pineapple

Cook 20 min. Put in jars and seal.

Mrs. Leroy J. Yoder

AMISH CHURCH PEANUT BUTTER SPREAD

3 lbs. crunchy or smooth peanut butter
2 qt. light karo
2 qt. marshmallow topping

Mix until smooth. Add more karo if too thick.

Lydia Ann Miller (Cook)

ANDERSON SAUCE

2 c. brown sugar
1 c. cream

Boil till soft ball stage. Take off stove and slowly stir in ½ gal. karo. If you use white sugar, use dark karo. Very good to spread on bread instead of honey, etc.

Mrs. Edna Miller

CHEESE BALL

1 - 8 oz. cream cheese
½ tube soft smoked cheese
pinch of garlic salt
1 t. onion flakes

1 t. worcestershire sauce
½ t. Lawry's seasoned salt
½ pkg. dried beef (ground)

Mix all together and chill. Form into ball. Garnish ball with ¼ c. ground nuts and 1 T. parsley flakes. Serve with crackers.

Sharon Boley (Waitress)

CHEESE BALL

2 - 8 oz. cream cheese
1 tube of soft smoked
    Hickory cheese
garlic salt (to taste)
Lawry's salt (to taste)

2 t. minced onion
2 t. worcestershire sauce
2 t. parsley flakes
1 pkg. dried beef
 (chopped in blender)

Mix all together, chill 1 hr., then roll in ½ c. ground nuts. Put parsley on top.

Patty Kauffman (Grill Cook)

CHEESE BALL

1 large pkg. cream cheese
1 smoked cheese
  (small round tube)
½ pkg. dried beef (cut up)

1 t. onion flakes
1 t. worcestershire sauce
¼ t. garlic salt
chopped onions, if desired

Mix together and shape into a ball. Sprinkle with nuts if desired.

Mary Esther Miller (Waitress)
Katie Miller (Hostess)

BACON CHEESE BALL

8 oz. cream cheese
6 oz. bacon flavored cheese
garlic, onion, and celery salt
or ¼ T. seasoning salt

2 T. worcestershire sauce
¼ T. minced onion
1 pkg. dried beef, cut up

Roll in crushed nuts.

Lydia Mae Troyer (Cook)

CHEESE ROLL

6 oz. blue cheese
4 - 3 oz. pkgs. cream cheese
6 oz. cheddar cheese (processed cheese roll)
2 T. grated onion
1/8 t. monosodium glutamate
1 t. worcestershire sauce
1 c. ground pecans (use ½ c. in roll)
½ c. parsley (use ¼ c. in roll)

Chill. Roll in remaining parsley and pecans.

Idella Yoder (Dessert Girl)

BLACKBERRY CORDIAL

Boil together for 15 min. a quart of blackberry juice, a pint of sugar, a T. each of cloves, allspice, cinnamon, and nutmeg. Pour boiling hot into jars and seal.

Leora V. Kauffman (Purchasing)

HONEY VINEGAR

Mix together in a crock, one quart of strained honey and eight quarts of warm water. Allow the mixture to stand in a warm place until fermentation ceases. The resulting vinegar is white and of excellent quality. Put in jars and seal.

Leora V. Kauffman (Purchasing)

STRAWBERRY VINEGAR

Put 4 qts. strawberries into a bowl, add 2 qts. vinegar. Cover bowl and set in a cool place for 2 days.

Strain through cheesecloth. Put 4 qts. fresh strawberries in the bowl and pour over them the vinegar strained from the first lot. Cover and set in a cool place for 2 days, then strain the vinegar as before. Put the strained juice in a large kettle and add 3 qts. of sugar, heat the mixture slowly; when it boils, skim it carefully. Continue boiling for 20 min., then pour into jars and seal.

2T. in a glass of cold water makes a refreshing drink.

Note: Other fruit may be used instead of strawberries.

Leora V. Kauffman (Purchasing)

PANCAKE SYRUP

2¼ c. white sugar	1 t. Mapeline
¼ c. brown sugar	1½ c. hot water

Mix until sugar is dissolved. Makes approximately 1½ pt.

Sue E. Miller (Manager)

SYRUP TABLE FOR FRUITS

Thin syrup - 1 part sugar, 3 parts water
Medium syrup - 1 part sugar, 2 parts water
Thick syrup - 1 part sugar, 1 part water

Katie Miller (Gift Shop)

AMAZING CLEANSER

1 c. ammonia
½ c. vinegar

¼ c. soda
1 gal. water

This is for cleaning walls and taking wax off floors.

Laura Miller (Grill Cook)

COLD SOAP RECIPE

5 pts. cold water
2 cans lye
4 T. white sugar
4 T. ammonia
½ c. Sal Soda

½ c. borax
2 oz. glycerine
1 oz. oil of sassafras
1 box Tide

Combine all the above ingredients. Let come to right temp. (lukewarm). Then pour this mixture into 10 lbs. of melted lard (Never pour the lard into lye). Stir until it is creamy. Let harden but cut into pieces before it gets too hard. Use granite or iron kettle to mix it in.

Mrs. Urias V. Miller

MAGIC GARDEN

6 T. liquid blueing
6 T. water

6 T. salt
6 T. ammonia

Mix this and pour over small chunks of soft coal in a deep dish or fish bowl. Add food coloring by drops and watch it grow.

Alma W. Miller

PLAY DOUGH FOR CHILDREN

| 2 c. flour | 1 T. alum |
| 1/2 c. salt | 1 T. liquid shortening |

Mix together then bring 2 c. water to a boil. Add food color then pour over flour mixture and stir. It will be lumpy. Knead thoroughly as soon as it is cool enough to handle. Keep in airtight container when not in use. Stays nice for a long time.

Mrs. Marie Miller

FRECKLES

Sweet almonds (blanched)	1 oz.
Bitter almonds (blanched)	1/2 oz.
Hydrarg Vichlor Carros	16 grains
Alcohol	4 drams
Acqua Pura, q. s. to make	16 oz.

Make an emulsion of the almonds with the water and strain, then add the corrosine sublimate dissolved in the alcohol. Do not apply to raw or blistered surface. This is a most valuable remedy for freckles. and is splendid for the skin.

Index

299

300

301